Time-Life Book of
Home Design Techniques

Time-Life Book of Home Design Techniques

Consulting Editors

NICHOLAS SPRINGMAN

JANE CHAPMAN

Step-by-step Authors

JULIAN CASSELL

PETER PARHAM

ANN CLOTHIER

TIME
LIFE
BOOKS

ALEXANDRIA, VIRGINIA

Time-Life Books is a division of Time Life Inc.
Time-Life is a trademark of Time Warner Inc. and
affiliated companies.

TIME LIFE INC.
Chairman and Chief Executive Officer: Jim Nelson
President and Chief Operating Officer: Steven Janas
Senior Executive Vice President and Chief Operations
Officer: Mary Davis Holt
Senior Vice President and Chief Financial Officer:
Christopher Hearing

TIME-LIFE BOOKS
President: Larry Jellen
Senior Vice President, New Markets: Bridget Boel
Vice President, Home and Hearth Markets:
Nicholas M. DiMarco
Vice President, Content Development: Jennifer L. Pearce

TIME-LIFE TRADE PUBLISHING
Vice President and Publisher: Neil S. Levin
Senior Sales Director: Richard J. Vreeland
Director, Marketing and Publicity: Inger Forland
Director of Trade Sales: Dana Hobson
Director of Custom Publishing: John Lalor
Director of Rights and Licensing: Olga Vezeris

TIME-LIFE BOOK OF HOME DESIGN
TECHNIQUES
Director of New Product Development:
Carolyn M. Clark
New Product Development Manager: Lori A. Woehrle
Senior Editor: Linda Bellamy
Director of Design: Kate L. McConnell
Project Editor: Jennie Halfant
Technical Specialist: Monika Lynde

A Marshall Edition
Conceived, edited, and designed by
Marshall Editions Ltd, The Orangery,
161 New Bond Street, London W1S 2UF

First published in Great Britain in 2001
by Marshall Editions Ltd

Originated in Singapore by PICA
Printed and bound in Germany by Möhndruck
10 9 8 7 6 5 4 3 2 1

School and library distribution by Time-Life Education,
P.O. Box 85026, Richmond, Virginia 23285-5026.

CIP data available upon request:
Librarian, Time-Life Books
2000 Duke Street
Alexandria, Virginia 22314

ISBN 0-7370-0321-9

Note Every effort has been taken to ensure that all
information in this book is correct and compatible with
normal standards generally accepted at the time of
publication. This book is not intended to replace
manufacturers' instructions in the use of their tools or
materials—always follow their safety guidelines. The
authors and publisher disclaim any liability for loss,
injury, or damage incurred as a consequence, directly or
indirectly, of the use and application of the contents of
this book.

FOREWORD

The stylish interiors featured in glossy magazines can fire us with enthusiasm to make changes to our own homes, but knowing where to start can seem overwhelming. Whether you are decorating one room or need to replan your entire living space, this invaluable sourcebook will provide you with all the ideas and practical know-how you will need.

Divided into four interrelated chapters, *Home Design Techniques* opens by looking at the many style options available to you. Covering a wide range of design styles, from the traditional to the contemporary, and featuring stunning interiors from around the world, you will be able to build a clearer picture of the look that will work best for you, your home, and your lifestyle.

The next two chapters will help you turn these ideas into reality. All the important aspects of design are covered, from using color to planning your storage needs. Expert advice, tried-and-true decorating solutions, photographs showing an eclectic mix of styles, and useful diagrams will help you plan each room so that it fulfills your needs and reflects your tastes exactly. You will also learn how elements such as texture, pattern, lighting, proportion, and scale can be manipulated to your advantage.

The final section focuses on various practical techniques, including painting, wallpapering, flooring, working with wood, and soft furnishings. Directory spreads tell you which tools you will need, how long each project is likely to take, and the level of expertise required.

By offering a wealth of design inspiration and building up your practical knowledge, *Home Design Techniques* will guide you through the decorating maze and give you the confidence you need to create a home that is a pleasure to be in.

CONTENTS

CHOOSING YOUR STYLE

CHOOSING YOUR STYLE is an exciting but time-consuming process. Think hard about your needs, the effect that you would like to create, and, more importantly, what you would feel most comfortable with. Then think about how you can achieve this with fabrics, color, and furniture. Packed with inspirational photographs of interiors from around the world and featuring an eclectic mix of different design styles, this chapter will give you a flavor of some of the many options available and invite you to think about what would most complement your lifestyle, your personality, and the type of house you live in.

Although some people will want to replicate a particular look down to the last detail, others might want to integrate just one or two elements—the cool blue walls of a Swedish interior, perhaps, or the jewel-like textiles of an Eastern-inspired room. You don't have to adhere slavishly to one particular style. Sometimes the traditional and the modern, the ethnic and the minimalist can be successfully combined to create a home that is both stylish and full of originality.

TRADITIONAL STYLE

From the charming simplicity of a Shaker farmhouse to the formal gentility of a brownstone, living with traditional style allows us to connect with the past and form a link with previous generations. Vernacular building materials and paints, exposed beams and whitewashed walls, furniture with a patina of age, faded embroidered fabrics, open fires, and copper pans gleaming in the kitchen—these are just some of the things that conjure up a bygone age. But adopting this style is not about indulging in sentimental nostalgia. Many decorative elements from the past—the pale, chalky colors of Scandinavian interiors or the rustic quarry tiles found in country kitchens worldwide—have a timeless, unpretentious beauty that makes them completely in tune with modern living.

▲ The emerald green walls in this 18th-century dining room complement the dark oak table and chairs. The window, with its original lintel, is left uncurtained to draw the eye to the view. At night, the candles on the table and in the Venetian glass holder will be reflected in the window to provide twice the light.

◄ Terra-cotta floor tiles, a scrubbed table and chairs, exposed beams, and the knotty pine door leading to the pantry beyond create a pleasing combination of texture and color in this farmhouse kitchen. An English Gothic wall cupboard, stripped of its old paint, houses a collection of blue-and-white Cornish ware and white French porcelain. Note the end-grain butcher's block that can be moved around.

◀ Offset by the deep-pink walls, the heavily patterned antique fabrics create a mood of warmth and intimacy in this attic bedroom. The plain headboard has been loosely covered with an embroidered quilt. An old ladder-back rocking chair takes advantage of the natural light, while leather suitcases provide useful storage and are a decorative reminder of a bygone age.

▲ An enormous fireplace provides the main focal point in this light, airy Provençal room with its pale wood, stone floor and rugs, tall windows, and traditional armoire.

LIVING ROOMS

Whether you favor a simple, rustic style or a more elegant urban look, traditional living rooms offer a wealth of inspiration. Federal style married mellow wood flooring with such shades as pink, blue or midgreen, or light terra cotta on the walls. Furniture was carefully arranged around the room to give a sense of balance. Fabrics, such as brocade, cotton damask, or toile de Jouy, completed the look. In country-style rooms, low beams, an open fireplace, white or softly colored walls, painted or stained floors covered with rugs or kilims, and carved or painted furniture were among some of the defining decorative features.

▲ Though symmetry appears to be important in this double living room, the second fireplace is used to store wood, instead of having a second grate. Pale rugs accentuate the contrast between the dark wood and the light walls and chair cover. Huge dark-framed mirrors echo the wide arch between the two rooms and increase the sense of space.

◄ The beamed ceiling, large flagstones, comfortable seating, and simple pieces of country furniture give this room a relaxed charm. Note the old-fashioned knife sharpener and the oil lamp.

KITCHENS

The main focal point of the traditional kitchen was the fire or stove, where water was boiled, food cooked, and plates—and hands—warmed. Copper pans and other utensils were kept close by, and herbs would be hung up to dry. A scrubbed pine table would do double duty as a working and eating surface. Many of the elements that we associate with traditional kitchens are still popular today. An old-fashioned ceramic sink has an inherent charm and is deeper than many modern versions. Traditional materials such as terra cotta, marble, and granite are still appreciated for their aesthetic and practical qualities.

◄ In a country-style kitchen, such period details as a ceramic sink with hardwood draining boards, plate rack, and breadbox are left proudly on display, while modern appliances are tucked away. Note the airing rack above the stove and the conveniently positioned pan drawers to the side.

▲ An authentic bread oven is the main focal point in this rustic Greek kitchen. Typical of Mediterranean style, the small, shuttered windows and thick, whitewashed walls and white tiles are designed to keep the room cool in summer. Unglazed terra-cotta pots complement the blue paintwork.

DISPLAY

● Stand plates, dishes, and decorative pottery on a mellow-colored pine hutch.

● Old-fashioned utensils, such as copper pots, pans, jelly molds, colanders, spoons, or even a set of kitchen scales make decorative additions to a traditional kitchen.

● Prettily patterned cups, pitchers, and mugs can be hung on cuphooks screwed into shelves.

BATHROOMS

Many of the materials that have traditionally been associated with bathroom design, such as terra-cotta floor tiles or white or patterned ceramic tiles, are still popular today. In countries such as the United States and Australia, tongue-and-groove paneling on the walls is a feature, used either from floor to ceiling or at chair rail height, with the upper wall either painted or wallpapered.

An elegant rolltop enameled bathtub with claw feet has an enduring appeal that fits either a rustic or urban setting. Other options include a tub enclosed in wood or Masonite panels or an antique copper or zinc tub.

◄ Occupying what was once a bedroom, the pink-and-white scheme in this attractive bathroom was inspired by the hand-painted, marble-topped washstand. The original cabinets, which can be seen in the reflection in the grand, gilded mirror, are used for storing warm towels.

◄ Taking center stage in a country bathroom, an elegant rolltop bathtub has been positioned to take advantage of the view through the window. The undersides of the bathtub have been painted the same mallard green as the paneling, while the brass faucets pick out the sunny yellow on the walls. The bath mat is made from oilcloth, and the old wall-mounted cabinet once belonged in a church.

BEDROOMS

A beautiful old bedstead forms the centerpiece of the traditional bedroom, with styles ranging from fourposters, elegant Empire beds, or American arched tester beds to simpler designs in brass or painted iron. In farmhouses in such countries as France, beds were commonly built into alcoves, often close to the fire and usually enclosed with a curtain.

Bed linen could include antique lace, linen, or an appliqué quilt or heirloom patchwork. Decorative headboards—either handpainted, carved, or simply consisting of a piece of fabric draped over a pole—were another quintessential feature for the bedroom.

▲ In period homes, the size of the windows indicated the original owner's wealth and standing in the community. In this country bedroom, the original ceiling has been removed to accommodate the stately four-poster bed, which would have been built for a much larger, grander residence. The exposed beams have been painted white to increase the feeling of space.

◄ Converted from an old Quaker school, the wall between two rooms has been removed to create an airy bedroom. An attractive Florentine headboard and mosquito net grace the bed, and an old-fashioned teacher's desk is a reminder of the room's previous function.

CONTEMPORARY STYLE

The absence of clutter and overelaborate furniture in favor of clean lines, simple shapes, and subtle use of color in the contemporary home points to a desire to bring calm and order into our surroundings. Space is a key element. Furniture is not massed together, but given room to breathe, allowing us to appreciate the beauty of its shape and form. Materials, such as wood, wicker, seagrass, and unbleached linen, are chosen for their aesthetic qualities and textural contrasts, and window treatments are kept deliberately low key. However, this simple approach does not mean that the contemporary home is devoid of decoration. Rugs or jazzy cushions bring color to an otherwise monochromatic scheme, while neutral walls provide a perfect canvas for modern pictures.

▲ Gradations of blue on the walls and finishing touches combine with strong, geometric shapes to create a look that is dramatic without being overpowering. The sensuous curves of the sofa are a foil for the angular shapes of the marble fireplace and panels on the walls.

▼ A fireplace can be as important an architectural feature in modern interiors as in traditional homes. This contemporary version makes a pleasing focal point in a neutral room. Further decorative flourishes are provided by the pale blue daybed and exotic blooms.

▶ Although there is space in abundance, the hangarlike proportions of a loft space pose their own design challenges. Here, exposed brick walls and the overhead wooden beams provide texture and warmth. The couches, rugs, and textiles all, too, suggest an easy informality.

▶ It is the contrast between hard and soft textures—not color—that gives depth and warmth to this modestly sized, box-shaped room. The floor-to-ceiling window bathes the room in light and enhances the feeling of space and airiness. A sinuously shaped coffee table picks up the gentle curves of the sofa and terra-cotta pot.

▼ The impressive scale of the beech-wood dining table is entirely appropriate for the proportions of the high-ceilinged room and means guests will not feel dwarfed by the space as they dine at the table. The simple blinds are in keeping with the pared-down industrial look and filter daylight to create a flattering dappled effect.

LIVING ROOMS

Easy on the eye and relaxing to be in, the contemporary living room is a direct reaction to the highly decorated and heavily furnished style of previous decades. Linear and curvaceous shapes combine with hard finishes, and tactile fabrics are added to soften the look and also help to absorb sound.

Floor surfaces in wood, stone, or even painted concrete are appreciated for their clean lines. They also make a good background for an eye-catching rug with a bold geometric design. For a slightly softer floorcovering, such natural fibers as sisal, seagrass, and coir have an inherently tactile quality, their mellow tones complementing neutral walls and furnishings. Wool carpet is a warm, quiet option, but choose a muted sandy or biscuit shade instead of a loud pattern.

Lighting also plays an important role in the contemporary living room, where it is used to create interesting focal points and variations of mood.

▶ Two jazzy hues have been cleverly combined to create a look that is bold and modern without being jarring. The lime green used on the curtains and walls provides a dramatic backdrop for the purple sofa and chairs. Note how the same fruity shades are picked out in the cushions, rug, and ornaments.

▼ Simple block shapes and a neutral palette help define the classical proportions of this French apartment. The tall windows have been left unadorned, except for an unobtrusive shade, allowing the view to become an extension of the room. Paintings and flowers add further visual interest.

▲ A warm, harmonious color scheme of terra cotta, beige, and yellow is tempered by splashes of complementary blue in this unusual-shaped room. The small square windows that have been cut into the curved wall help to make the space feel lighter and less enclosed.

WINDOW TREATMENTS

● For an uncluttered look, choose floor-length curtains in natural materials such as unbleached muslin, voile, or sackcloth.

● You can hang curtains from an unobtrusive pole made of wood, wrought iron, steel, or bamboo (see p.88).

● Blinds, shades, and shutters have spare, clean lines that work well in a contemporary setting. Hanging two or three separate blinds can work well at a large window and also helps you to regulate the amount of light coming into the room more easily.

KITCHENS

Today's kitchen is no longer the exclusive domain of the cook. As the cohesive heart of the home, it is where families congregate, guests are entertained, and other tasks carried out. To fulfill this multifunctional role, the modern kitchen needs to be streamlined yet still welcoming. Adaptable, hardwearing work surfaces and storage that makes use of every inch of space need to be incorporated. Good ergonomic planning is necessary to make sure the main elements—stove, sink, and refrigerator—are safe and efficient to use. Sleek task lighting illuminates different areas of activity. Movable furniture, such as a trolley or butcher's block, is another worthwhile addition.

Taking inspiration from a professional caterer's kitchen, hard, shiny materials often predominate, with stainless steel units and mirror-finish appliances, glass shelving, smooth ceramic tiles, slate flooring, and chrome accessories.

▲ The cool blue, gray, and shiny metallics in this kitchen are warmed by the blondwood seats and work surfaces. The island table is used for food preparation and informal meals. Pots and pans are conveniently stored in the deep drawers under the stove.

◄ Removing the partition wall between two smaller rooms has created a spacious open-plan room. The central peninsula, with cabinets that open on both sides, is convenient for setting and clearing the table, and helps to mark off the kitchen from the dining area without isolating the cook. The round table is conducive to relaxed, informal entertaining and softens the angularity of the rest of the space. Discreet ceiling spotlights distribute light evenly.

BEDROOMS

The modern bedroom should project an atmosphere of calm and comfort. Furniture, appreciated for its clean lines and functionality, doesn't overcrowd the space. Fabrics are chosen for their reassuring tactile qualities—crisp linen sheets, soft velvet pillows, tweedy blankets, faux fur throws, and dreamy voile curtains. A neutral palette of white, cream, taupe, or biscuit, or such pastels as lilac or soft green, are conducive to a restful, soothing environment. Strong primary colors should play only a supporting role as accents on rugs or pictures.

▲ In the past beds were built high to avoid drafts at ground level, but modern beds can be nearer the floor. In a basement bedroom of almost monastic simplicity, this simple low bed enhances the Zen-like atmosphere of the space. Splashes of black help to counterbalance the purity of the white walls and bedding.

◀ Subtle injections of color and texture bring warmth and intimacy to this high-ceilinged room. The two bedside tables, although not a matching pair, help to create a sense of balance and symmetry, and the pictures have been deliberately arranged on the lower half of the walls to make the room feel cozier.

BATHROOMS

Although still usually the smallest room in the house, the bathroom now has more stringent demands placed on it than ever before. The contemporary bathroom should be clean and functional, suggesting clinical hygiene, but also warm and inviting, a place where we go to pamper ourselves and recharge our batteries. We want powerful showers that drench us with water, bathtubs that are long and deep enough to spread out in, sinks that are the right height, good task lighting that illuminates the angles of our faces, and plenty of storage space for our lotions and potions.

Today's fixtures combine sleek good looks with practical efficiency. Neat ceramic, glass, or aluminum washbasins with simple mixer faucets are less obtrusive than more traditional pedestal units. Wall-mounted toilets and bidets continue the streamlined look—and also make for easier cleaning. Chrome towel holders and accessories, mirrors, and glass shelving are chosen for their light-enhancing properties. Once-popular colored fixtures have been replaced by more pristine white versions. For walls, ceramic tiles complement the pared-down look.

▲ Ceramic tiles are a decorative and practical choice for a bathroom. Here a checkerboard of tiles creates a strikingly geometric look that is fresh and contemporary. The tiles on the floor are not as highly glazed as those on the walls, making them less slippery when wet. A wooden bath mat is an additional safety precaution.

◄ Geometric shapes, cool, glossy surfaces, and unbroken lines predominate in this serene, pared-down bathroom, where all extraneous clutter is kept out of sight. Decorative detail is provided by the sculptural washbasin and simple vase of flowers. The ceiling spotlights and mirrored wall add to the sense of glamour, which is echoed by the dramatic nighttime cityscape outside.

ETHNIC STYLE

Whether they are witnessed firsthand on travels abroad or glimpsed in books or magazines, the colors, patterns, furniture, textiles, and ornaments found in other parts of the world offer a wealth of design inspiration. Ethnic style is not about recreating a particular look, but involves interpreting and adapting elements from cultures distinct from our own that appeal to us or evoke strong memories. One or two well-chosen pieces—simple unglazed pots or a tribal stool from Africa, perhaps, or hand-carved Indonesian masks—can form the starting point of an eye-catching and original scheme. Draw on a rich palette of exotic color: from the hot salsa hues of Mexico to the spice shades, such as burnt umber, cinnamon, or terra cotta, widely used in North Africa.

▶ Although this bathroom is actually set in the English countryside, the arched window, painted floor tiles, and pretty wall motif all conjure up a distinctly serene Moorish style.

◀ In a restful entrance hall, the combination of cool green walls and mellow wood helps to make a transition between the interior and the exterior. Catching the gentle breeze, the foliage rustles and delights the hearing of those passing through, and it also provides a further link with the natural world outside.

▶ In hot climates, earthy tones are widely used on walls. Here, warm terra-cotta plaster is inlaid with attractive majolica tiles in blue and yellow on white to create a decorative surround for a fireplace.

DYEING METHODS

Plant and vegetable dyes have long been used on fabrics to produce interesting variations of pattern and color.

● Tie-dyeing involves knotting or tying areas of fabric so that they resist the dye.

● Batik, originating from Indonesia, is another form of resist-dyeing, where the areas of the cloth not to be colored are covered in removable wax.

● The distinctive patterns produced in Malaysian ikat printing are created by dyeing either the warp or the weft threads of a fabric before weaving.

▲ The earthy tones of the walls and floor tiles throw the brightly painted chairs into vivid relief in this Mediterranean courtyard. In cooler countries of the Northern Hemisphere, earthy shades, such as yellow ocher, peachy pink, or faded terra cotta, are much easier on the eye than brilliant whites, which can easily look dull and gray.

◄ A stone seat and table have been installed in a shady corner of a terrace intended for informal alfresco dining. The blue color-washed plaster helps to enforce the feeling of cool tranquillity.

LIVING ROOMS

Ethnic style has an inherent charm and informality that translates well to rooms meant for relaxation. Choose natural materials, such as stone, terra cotta, or dark wood, to bring warmth and layers of texture to a neutral scheme. Lay coir, sisal, or rush matting on the floor and hang gauzy voile, jewel-colored sari material, or cane blinds or shutters at the window. Scatter brightly colored ikat pillows over a plain sofa or wicker chair, and throw richly patterned dhurries or kilim rugs on the floor. For a touch of exotic opulence, add splashes of gold—with mirrors, light fixtures, or bowls—or pick out details on doors, walls, or furniture with gold leaf. Arrange bamboo, dried grasses, or tropical palms in large hand-thrown earthenware pots or Cretan urns. Be inspired by the colors, shape, or texture of ethnic pottery—a beautiful African pot or raku vase could become a focal point that will link the rest of the scheme.

◄ Eastern and Western influences mingle in this living room where an ottoman footstool contrasts with a more formal 18th-century French chair. The alcove shelving houses an eclectic collection of treasured souvenirs brought back from trips abroad.

▶ Wooden blinds that filter out the sun's glare and cast alluring shadows, cool whitewashed walls, and a towering tropical palm all combine to give this room a distinctly British colonial feeling. A lovely old palanquin—an Oriental litter that would originally have been carried on the shoulders of four men—has been commandeered into service as a table.

◀ Simple batik pillows inject subtle accents of color and pattern, and help to link the terra-cotta floor with the wooden frame of the old Javanese bed. An intricate candleholder hangs in place of a central light, and a huge chimney provides a strong architectural focus for the room.

▼ Echoing the shape of an adobe hut, this corner fireplace is raised on several steps, which means that it throws heat out more effectively.

BEDROOMS

Create a luxurious haven with sensual fabrics from different parts of the world. Drape soft Peruvian blankets over the bed or add a richly patterned Indian throw or an exotic Chinese silk bedspread. Re-create the calm minimalism of a Japanese bedroom with cool white cotton bed linen and a low-slung wooden bed, futon, or even a simple mattress. A bamboo screen and a tatami mat complete the look. For a more opulent look, hang brightly colored fabrics over a four-poster bed. A gauze canopy or mosquito net will bring a touch of tropical glamour, while a pretty Chinese lantern makes a decorative lampshade.

▲ In hot countries, simple window treatments are more appropriate than opulent, heavily patterned fabrics, which would fade in the sun. Here voile curtains are teamed with a limed, or pickled, floor (a process that gives floorboards a white look) and white bed linen to create an atmosphere of Eastern serenity in the bedroom of a Victorian house.

◄ A huge piece of African printed fabric has been hung from a pole to make an imposing headboard. Other tribal references are seen in the rugs, pots, and hand-carved statues.

BATHROOMS

The electric blues and sun-bleached whites of the Mediterranean or North Africa can bring a freshness and vitality to even the smallest, gloomiest bathroom. Be bold and use large amounts of eye-catching indigo or cerulean blue on the walls, or use them as accents on towels or a painted chair. For a cool Moroccan look, create a decorative backsplash with mosaic tiles in different shades of blue, or use them in swathes on the walls and floor and around the bathtub. White ceramic tiles or rough plaster painted white or soft dusky pink are further options for walls; and terra-cotta, stone, or slate floors complete the look.

◀ The mosaic tiles used on the floor have been continued on the side of the curvaceous bathtub. The same blue and white tiles have been used to frame the large wall mirror, however, the more muted tone of the wall tiles means that the scheme doesn't become overbearing. Ethnic influences are continued with the carved wooden table, low chair, and potted plant.

FLOORS AND WALLS

• For floorcoverings, choose materials such as brick, stone, rough flagstones, or old, unpolished wood, which all have charming natural irregularities. For a smoother finish, you could lay quarry tiles, ceramic or encaustic tiles, marble, or terrazzo.

• Traditional water-base paints, such as distemper or limewash, can be applied to bare plaster to create a flat textured finish. These paints will allow walls to breathe, and they can be mixed with colored pigments to create a rich, chalky finish that makes a good backdrop for ethnic-style furniture and textiles.

◀ Stone makes an aesthetically pleasing choice of material for this charming rustic bathroom. While in keeping with the room's style, the two lanterns suspended from the beamed ceiling are also correctly positioned on each side of the Moorish mirror.

COMBINING STYLES

Adhering too rigidly to one particular style of interior design can often result in a space that more closely resembles a museum or stage set than a warm, welcoming home. Finding the right balance between the old and the new, the ethnic and the minimalist can be the key to creating a look that most closely reflects your tastes and lifestyle. While cramming an ultramodern apartment with heavy period furniture would undoubtedly look anachronistic, and a sleek industrial-style kitchen is out of place in a low-beamed farmhouse, introducing one or two elements from a different design idiom can work extremely well. The high white walls of a modern loft space can, for example, provide the perfect backdrop for one or two pieces of antique furniture or a collection of ethnic ornaments.

◀ An eclectic mix of period furniture, modern paintings, and Oriental rugs fuses harmoniously in this traditional living room with whitewashed walls and exposed beams. High-ceilinged rooms require one or two tall pieces to give a sense of proportion, which is provided here by the grandfather clock, the stove flue, and the long curtains that are hung well above the window.

▲ Introducing one or two well-chosen pieces can be enough to conjure up a particular style. In a sparsely decorated room, with the bed as its centerpiece, a wall-hung rug and a statue help to evoke the serene atmosphere typical of an Eastern-inspired room.

◄ An inspired choice of modern and ethnic finishing touches helps to compensate for the lack of architectural detail in this box-shaped room in a modestly proportioned modern house. The glass table does not dominate the room the way that one made of a solid material would.

▲ Wooden siding is used internally—instead of its more typical external application—on the wall between the living room and the kitchen. Evocative of Scandinavian paneling or a log cabin, it gives a traditional twist to a contemporary apartment. The classic color combination of soft green and sunny yellow enhances the relaxed, rustic feel of the room.

MIX AND MATCH

Combining different styles—old and new furniture; shiny, pristine surfaces with rough, weather-beaten materials; antique pieces with artifacts from travels abroad—helps to define and personalize a room.

● In a traditional kitchen with a predominance of wood, shiny metallic surfaces such as chrome, aluminum, or punched tin bring textural variation and help to diffuse any heaviness. A modern sink complements the dark wood of an old cabinet (right).

● A neutral scheme in a contemporary living room makes a good background for brightly colored ethnic textiles such as ikat pillows or a kilim rug. Cover an old-fashioned couch with suede or cotton instead of fabrics such as brocade or damask. The timeless beauty of a colonial or Lloyd Loom chair complements even the most pared-down of modern living spaces.

● For a relaxed dining room, team modern seating, such as sleek aluminum Landi chairs with their distinctive punched holes (see p.17), with a traditional refectory table. Alternatively, simple pine chairs, perhaps in an assortment of designs or painted different colors, can make informal partners to a contemporary glass table. For tableware, mix fine white porcelain and country-style earthenware, cut glass, and chunky tumblers.

● In the bathroom, period bathtubs and washbasins can be revamped with the latest high-tech fixtures.

◀ Carved wooden artifacts and framed ethnic prints add detail to a plain modern bedroom. The antique chest of drawers, leather chair, and faux fur throw on the bed add tonal and textural variation.

▶ Although this compact kitchen is well designed and equipped with modern appliances, including a six-ring stove, finishing touches such as the old chair, wicker basket, and framed prints help give it a feeling of relaxed informality. The tall storage units make good use of space in a small area. Notice how the lampshades echo the shape of the exhaust hood.

◀ Instead of opting for traditional furniture and furnishings, the owners of this upstairs Victorian living room have chosen a cool contemporary scheme that complements the proportions and architectural features of the room. Traditional button-backed armchairs have been covered in fresh white cotton and sit side by side with a modern sculpture, a set of Arne Jacobsen dining chairs, and a strikingly geometric zigzag chair. The absence of curtains at the windows enhances the feeling of light and space.

▲ Traditional furniture fuses with contemporary art in this spacious living room, where a stunning wall of glass bricks filters light into the hall beyond. The large pots of cacti give the space a distinctly hacienda style.

HOME DESIGN PRINCIPLES

TRENDS IN INTERIOR DESIGN come and go at an alarming rate, and the array of colors, paint effects, and soft furnishings on the market is so vast that making an informed choice can be bewildering. You might be inspired by the zingy limes featured in a magazine or the coffee-and-cream shades seen in a restaurant, but be afraid to use them because you are not sure how they will look in your home. The aim of this part of the book is to bolster your decorating confidence by showing you how such key elements as light, color, texture, and pattern work and interrelate with each other, and the effect they have on the senses.

Makeovers of the same living room in four different color schemes will show you how profound an impact color—be it a bright, vibrant shade or a subtle neutral—can have. There are ideas to help you create the illusion of light and space, and tips for dealing with problem areas such as awkward corners or low ceilings. You will also see how you can introduce finishing touches to bring subtle accents of color, texture, or pattern that will cheer up the overall scheme and bring visual unity to the room.

COLOR THEORY

COLOR TERMINOLOGY

- **Primary colors:** Red, blue, and yellow at their maximum purity are the primary colors from which all other colors are made, and are the only colors that cannot be made by mixing together other colors.
- **Secondary colors:** Two primary colors mixed together in equal quantities to make green (blue and yellow), orange (yellow and red), or violet (red and blue).
- **Tertiary colors:** An equal mix of a primary color and its neighboring secondary color. These include flame (red orange), apricot (orange yellow), lime (yellow green), turquoise (green blue), indigo (blue purple), and maroon (red violet).
- **Neutral colors:** Black, white, gray, and brown are neutral colors that are added to other colors to reduce their intensity, or they can be used individually to provide a neutral background in a color scheme.
- **Complex colors:** The millions of other colors that are created by mixing adjacent colors together.
- **Hue:** The property of a color that differentiates it from another color. For example, crimson has a bluer hue than scarlet.
- **Tone:** The tonal value measures how light or dark a color is and affects how reflective or luminous a hue appears.
- **Tint:** A color that has white added to it. This lightens the color, making it more milky or pastel.
- **Shade:** A color that has black added to it. This darkens the color.
- **Pure color:** A color that has neither white, black, nor another neutral color added to it and displays its pure intensity.
- **Saturation:** Sometimes called chroma, this is a measure of the intensity of a color in terms of how vivid or how dull it is.

Color is the cheapest and most effective way to transform a room. If you understand it, you can use it to create a feeling of more or less space, as well as to create the kind of atmosphere and feeling that you are looking for. Under good light, the human eye can distinguish between 10 million different colors, all of which have a precise relationship with each other. In order to make your best choice of colors, you need to understand the relationship between them all and how they affect each other. All color is made up from three colors—red, blue, and yellow—which are called the primary colors. The tone of these colors is modified by adding black to create a darker version, called a shade, or by adding white to create a lighter version, called a tint.

THE BASIC COLOR WHEEL

Made up of 12 different pure colors, this wheel contains all of the primary, secondary, and tertiary colors. The colors are arranged to show their interrelationship, with the three primary colors spaced at equal distances apart around the wheel. Each of the three secondary colors is located midpoint between the two primary colors from which it is derived. Between each primary and secondary color is a tertiary color.

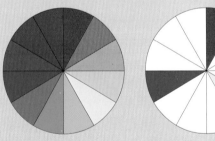

The basic color wheel
This color wheel contains a total of 12 colors. It includes all of the primary, secondary, and tertiary colors.

Primary colors
Red, blue, and yellow are the only three colors that cannot be made by mixing together other colors.

Secondary colors
Violet, green, and orange are the three secondary colors made by mixing two primary colors together evenly.

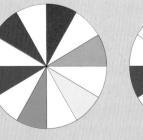

Tertiary colors
These are the six colors made from evenly mixing a primary color with a neighboring secondary color.

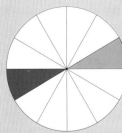

Complementary colors
Colors that lie directly opposite each other on the color wheel are known as complementary colors.

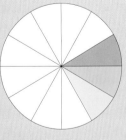

Harmonious colors
Colors that lie alongside each other on the wheel share hues in common and are known as harmonious colors.

HUES, TONES, AND SATURATION

When selecting color, three major characteristics need to be considered. Hue defines the spectrum of colors in terms of the different proportions of base color that are mixed together to make a color. Tone defines a color in terms of how light or dark it is. Saturation measures colors in terms of their intensity. Every time a color is mixed, it looses intensity; for example, gray is produced when the three primary colors are mixed together in equal proportions. A color sphere reveals how these three characteristics work in combination.

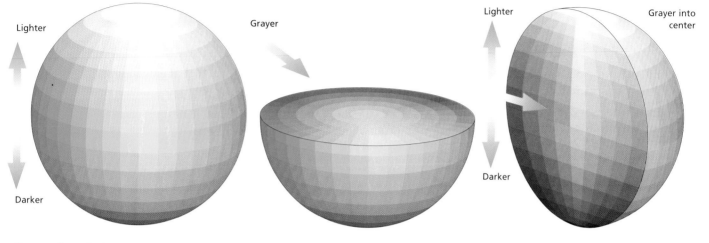

Outer surface of color sphere
The outer surface shows colors arranged by hue around the circumference and the tonal range of these colors along the meridian.

Horizontal section through color sphere
This cross section shows how the intense hues at the edge of the sphere become increasingly dull toward the center, which is gray.

Vertical section through color sphere
This cross section shows the tints and shades as they become more muted toward the center of the sphere.

USING A COLOR WHEEL

Most color wheels have numerous complex colors in addition to the 12 primary, secondary, and tertiary colors, providing users with an extensive range of hues to choose from. The main advantage of using a color wheel is that it shows at a glance which colors are mutually harmonious, which are complementary, and whether a color is warm or cool. The warm colors, such as red and orange, are located on the right side of the wheel and have a long wavelength, which makes them appear as if they are closer or advancing. The cool colors, such as blue and green, are located on the left side of the wheel and have short wavelengths, which make them appear as if they are farther away or receding. This structured layout enables users to visually assess the relationship of all the hues in the wheel, and to quickly select colors with the desired characteristics for the mood and effect they want to create.

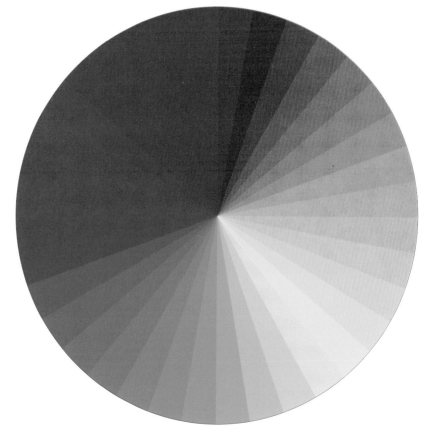

CONTRAST AND TONALITY

COMBINING COLOR

Each color has its own individual characteristics, but the impact a color has varies, depending on the other colors that surround it.

The full intensity of red is seen when set against white.

Red becomes more dramatic when seen with black.

Red and yellow are both vibrant primary colors.

The heat of red is counterbalanced by the cool of blue.

Red and green are complementary colors.

Red and maroon are harmonious colors.

Gray is neutral and does not compete with red.

Light blue is a soft color that is dominated by red.

Both red and orange are warm vibrant colors.

The combination of pale violet and red is challenging.

Decorating and furnishing a room in a single tint or shade of a color is invariably a mistake because the characteristics of that color will be overpowering. The monotony is overcome by using two or more colors to provide contrasting hues, or by employing the tints and shades of a color to give tonal relief. Some of the different ways of using colors in combination are shown here.

COLOR AND PROPORTION

TRIADIC COLOR SCHEMES

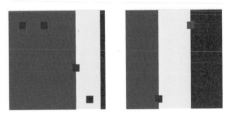

Triadic color schemes use three colors spaced at equal intervals on the color wheel in order to create bold contrasts. As a rule, colors with a high level of contrast compete for attention if used in equal proportions, which can be unsettling. To achieve a more balanced effect, it is advisable to allow one color to dominate, and to use the other two colors to offset it. Here, red, yellow, and blue are combined in various proportions.

COMPLEMENTARY COLOR SCHEMES

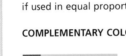

To achieve variety without producing a clash, complementary color schemes employ two colors that are directly opposite each other on the color wheel. Because the two colors share no base elements in common, they compete for attention if they are used equally. Soften the colors with gray or white; allow one color to dominate and use small amounts of the other two colors to offset it. Here, red, yellow and blue are combined in various proportions.

HARMONIOUS COLOR SCHEMES

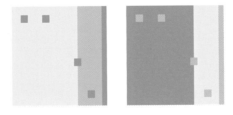

Harmonious color schemes, also known as analogous color schemes, use colors that lie alongside one another on the color wheel to provide subtle variations in hue. Since the colors used share base elements in common, the level of contrast is low. As a result, harmonious colors do not compete if used in equal proportions, but if used as an accent they can get lost. Here, yellow, lime, and green are combined in various proportions.

NATURAL LIGHTING

Highly effective color schemes can be created by using the tonal spectrum of just one color. In these monochromatic schemes, relief is provided by the contrast of light tints, dark shades, and middle tones. Tone also plays an important role in multicolored schemes, because white or black can be used to soften the intensity of aggressive colors that normally clash in their pure form, allowing them to work well with a wide range of other hues. As a general rule, if you are using strong, contrasting colors in even quantities, a narrow band of tones should be used. However, if the color scheme is monochromatic, or the colors used are harmonious or neutral, a broader range of tones should be put together to provide variety.

► All colors have a tonal spectrum that extends between white and black. Any pure color can be modified by adding white to create a range of tints, or by adding black to create a range of shades. As more white or black is added, the contrast between different colors diminishes.

◄ This connecting bathroom and bedroom has a monochromatic color scheme that employs a range of blue tones on the walls, floor, and ceiling, creating a restful, coordinated effect. The consistency of color cleverly unites the two spaces. Accents are provided by the yellow curtains around the bed, a wooden chest of drawers, and the white bathtub, basin, and mirror frame.

◄ Swatches of the blue tones used in this monochromatic scheme are set alongside the yellow accent color.

CHOOSING COLOR

W hen you decide to decorate a room, you should think in terms of the function and design of the space, and the effect that you want to achieve, instead of simply picking a color that you like. The room's size and proportions, the amount of daylight it receives, and the location of prominent features will all affect your choice. Once you have established an overall plan, select a color that will provide the main effect you want, whether you are creating a cool, spacious feel or a warm, intimate one. Key in all the other colors you select with this dominant color to give the room tonal variety and balance. Before you begin, it is advisable to use a mood board to assess and refine your color choice (see opposite page).

◀ ▼ Differences in tone are easier to see in black-and-white photographs than they are in color photographs. In this kitchen, the lime-green cabinets are lighter in tone than the walls, floors, and countertops. The contrast can be seen in the black-and-white photograph, where the cabinets are seen as a light shade of gray, and the walls, floors, and countertops appear as a darker shade of gray. The chrome, the white lampshade, and the stainless-steel oven provide lighter-tone accents.

USING A MOOD BOARD

A successful decorating scheme depends on the blend of colors and the proportions in which they are used, as well as how the patterns, styles, and textures of items used in a room work in combination. Before decorating a room, most interior designers create a mood board to assess how colors, fabrics, and patterns work together.

A mood board is a thin piece of cardboard or foam board with paint color swatches and samples of rugs, wallpaper, and fabrics that will be used. They are easy to assemble and help you avoid making the expensive mistake of buying items that do not fit into your decorative scheme. They allow you to experiment with your scheme by adding and subtracting elements until you are happy with your choice. When making a mood board, lay out the swatches in proportion to the space they will occupy in the room. For example, wallcovering normally occupies the largest area, so it should take the most space on the board. Cushion fabrics and other accents should take less space.

In addition to making a mood board, draw a floor plan of the room (see pp.74–75); attach photographs of furnishings and decorative elements that you want to keep, along with pictures of new design schemes that you like. These storyboards will help you to assess the proportions of a room and to visualize how existing elements will work with new decorative schemes.

▶ The color of the mood board should match the color that you intend for the walls, which are the largest individual component of the room. Include a cutting of the wallpaper or paint sample, and number it for the key. Mark lines on the rear of any samples and trim them in line with any design. Use pinking sheers for fabrics to keep them from fraying. Where possible, try to position cuttings on the board to show where they will appear in the room. Overlap them to get an idea of how different colors, patterns, and textures will work together. A swatch for an area rug, for example, should be placed next to, or on top of, a carpet swatch. Do the same with a cushion fabric to see how it will look with a couch.

Taking up the largest area of the board, a swatch of wallpaper shows how a warm, neutral background color will offset the rest of the room.

Three different shades have been chosen for the paintwork. The darkest is for the baseboard to anchor the color scheme to the floor.

A soft tint has been chosen for the ceiling, instead of a pure white, so that there is less contrast with the color of the walls.

A faded-red paisley fabric with splashes of green has been chosen for the curtains and a few cushions to inject accents of color into the scheme.

The natural fabric used for the window shade provides a change of texture and color.

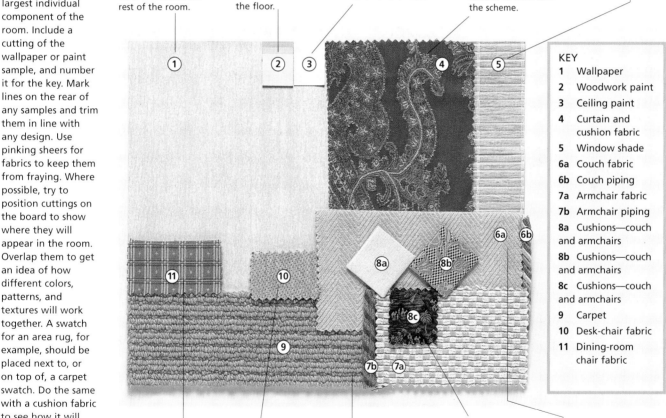

KEY
1   Wallpaper
2   Woodwork paint
3   Ceiling paint
4   Curtain and cushion fabric
5   Window shade
6a Couch fabric
6b Couch piping
7a Armchair fabric
7b Armchair piping
8a Cushions—couch and armchairs
8b Cushions—couch and armchairs
8c Cushions—couch and armchairs
9   Carpet
10 Desk-chair fabric
11 Dining-room chair fabric

A bright textured plaid fabric, instead of a neutral one, is a practical choice for the dining-room chairs, the strong colors complementing their wooden frame.

A chenille fabric has been selected for the desk chair, echoing the color of the couch and armchairs.

A twilled carpet in a warm neutral shade helps to anchor the scheme and creates another layer of texture.

All rooms need a splash of black, here provided by the patterned cushion fabric.

A textured weave in a herringbone design is used for the couch and sets off the cushions. The piping chosen for the fabric picks out the tones of the fabric used on the dining-room chairs and curtains.

COLOR EFFECTS

COLOR CHARACTERISTICS

● **Red:** Red is the warmest color there is and in its pure form, it is often associated with danger and excitement. Pink and the other lighter tints of red are less aggressive. Darker shades, such as burgundy, are rich and sumptuous.

● **Blue:** Fully saturated blue is the coldest color and has the opposite impact to red, producing a sense of calm. Tints of blue have a fresh, clean feel, while its darker shades, such as navy blue, are dignified and dependable.

● **Yellow:** At its maximum intensity, yellow is a striking and joyful color. Light tints of yellow are luminous and refreshing, while its shades are more earthy and restrained.

● **Violet:** A combination of blue and red, violet is a challenging color. Violet's darker tones, such as purple, have long been associated with royalty, while its tints have a nostalgic quality.

● **Orange:** A vibrant combination of red and yellow, orange is a warm, friendly color that in its pure form is used as the international safety color. Orange's darker tones have a warm, earthy quality, while its tints are cheerful and relaxing.

● **Green:** A soothing combination of blue and yellow, green has strong associations with nature. Its dark tones have a restrained, traditional quality, while its tints tend to be more lively and playful.

● **Gray:** An uncompetitive neutral color, gray can be successfuly used to calm down color schemes employing bright, contrasting hues.

Color not only changes the mood of a room, it can also change its optical appearance. Warm colors, such as red, which have a long wavelength, or dark colors, which reflect only a small proportion of light, appear to advance and make a room seem smaller. Conversely, cool colors, such as blue, which have a short wavelength, or light colors, which reflect a high proportion of light, appear to recede and make a room seem larger. Colors of contrasting hues or different tones can be used in combination to alter the optical proportions of a room. Lighting also has a major impact on the appearance of a room. Bright sunny rooms look larger than dim rooms that receive no direct sunlight.

THE EFFECT OF LIGHT

Daylight is made up of a spectrum of hues—red, orange, yellow, green, blue, indigo, and violet—and its cast (color) changes through the course of the day. Daylight has a warm glow in the early morning, is neutral at noon when the sun is at its brightest, and becomes more blue as daylight fades. Artificial lighting also has different casts: Incandescent light is yellow, fluorescent light is blue, and halogen light is a bright white.

◄ The type and intensity of light alters the look of paint and fabric colors. In a room that receives direct sunlight at noon, the colors in the room retain their original hue and subtle gradation of colors can be seen. Further interest is provided by the pattern of shadow and light that is produced.

◄ In a room lit by incandescent light, a distinctive yellow cast is produced. This has the effect of warming neutral and pale colors, making a room look more intimate. Fluorescent and halogen light work best with strong colors. They can have a draining effect on neutral or muted colors.

OPTICAL TRICKS USING TONE

The most dramatic transformations to the optical appearance of a room are achieved by changing the tonal balance. All pale colors, including warm ones, make a room look bigger. Conversely, all dark colors, including cool ones, make a room look smaller. Below, a room is decorated using a light and a dark color in different proportions to show some of the ways tone can be used to alter our perception of space.

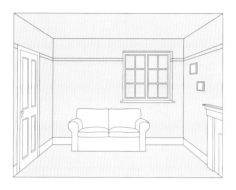

Using the same tone of color throughout a room preserves the proportions of that room. If a light color is used, the room will look bigger than if a dark color is used.

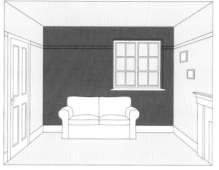

Painting one of the walls a dark color makes that wall appear to advance. This effect can be used on end walls to optically shorten long, thin rooms or corridors.

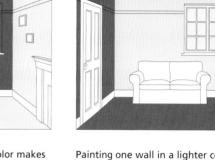

Painting one wall in a lighter color than the other surfaces will make that wall appear to recede. This effect can be used to prevent square rooms from looking too boxlike.

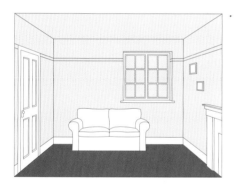

Dark colors make a floor look smaller, while light colors make it look larger. A small room with dark floors can look cramped even if the walls are painted in a light color.

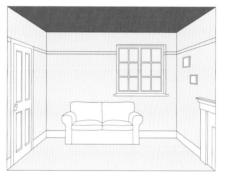

To make a ceiling appear lower, paint it in a darker color than the walls. This effect is useful in rooms where the ceiling appears too high for the dimensions of the room.

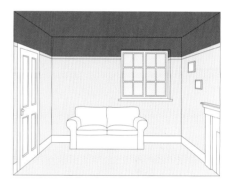

To optically reduce the height of a room still further, take the dark color down to the picture rail. Using a light color below the picture rail makes the room seem broader.

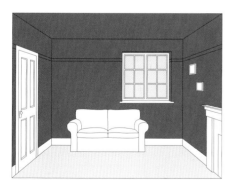

In a room where the walls and ceiling have been painted a dark color, a light floor color can be used to prevent the room from looking cramped and oppressive.

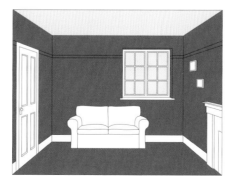

To make a room appear taller, the ceiling should be painted in a lighter color than the walls. Using dark colors on the walls draws them closer together.

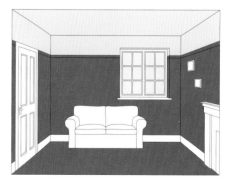

The heightening effect of using a light color on the ceiling is diminished if that color is taken down to the picture rail. This lowers the line of sight to the height of the picture rail.

USING STRONG COLORS

Once you've learned enough about color to conquer your fear of it, you'll want to make full use of this resource in all its diverse hues and intensities. Deep, rich, or vivid shades are not always an obvious choice, but they can make a powerful impression when used over large areas. Because strong colors dominate their space, they can transform a featureless room into an irresistibly inviting one.

Strong colors will inevitably absorb more light than pale tints and can make a room look slightly darker and smaller than it would with a more conventional treatment. Remember, though, that many stunning design schemes focus on coziness, intimacy, and drama instead of on size and brightness.

◀ In this living area, glowing tones of pink establish a strong design personality while creating an atmosphere that is not only warm, but supremely relaxing. Note the choice of soft coral on the architectural details such as the molding and baseboard—a bold change from the standard white or cream, and a choice that also reinforces the room's exotic look.

USING THE PALETTE

Intense color is more suitable for some decorating styles than others. If you long to fill your home with radiant hues, explore sympathetic sources such as tropical, Asian, Oriental, Moorish, Mexican or any style that has its origins in a warm, sunny climate and, therefore, uses colors such as bright pink, sea blue, crocus yellow, palm-leaf green, and strong, bright salsa shades. Re-create Provençal interiors, using earthy reds and browns, yellows typical of sunflowers, greens found in the trees, vines, and hills, and blue to reflect the intenses shades of the sky. Or consider bright retro looks based on the trends of the 1960s and 1970s. Be inspired by the fabrics, furniture, ceramics, and art that were around at that time.

◀ The rich shades of terra cotta and forest green that dominate this striking scheme work well together, partly because they (or their base hues, red and green) are complementary colors (they lie opposite one another on the color wheel), and partly because they create an effective balance in terms of depth and intensity, so neither of them overwhelms the other or the rest of the furnishings. Wisely, neutral floor coverings and simple shapes allow the color scheme to take center stage.

◀ Enjoy all your meals in a carefree holiday mood for the cost of a few cans of sky-blue paint and simple curtains in sunny seaside stripes.

▶ For maximum drama, set off intricately carved furniture painted snowy white against the velvety darkness of navy walls and ceiling. Small cushions with a lime-green theme provide an additional layer of color.

USING PASTEL COLORS

Gentle, relaxing, and easy on the eye, pastel hues are popular color palettes for the home. In design terms, one of their most useful qualities is that, as long as they are all equally pale, they always look good together. For this reason, never rely on commercial labeling when choosing your furnishings ("pastel rose" could mean anything from off-white with a slight blush to candy pink). Instead, use your own eye to assemble a collection of chalky hues that mix effortlessly in every combination and are ideal for setting off natural materials such as wicker, stone, unbleached cotton or linen, and light or medium-tone wood (heavy dark timber can overpower pastels and destroy the visual balance of any scheme that features them).

◀ Large expanses of soft powder blue are guaranteed to look cool, fresh, and light. In this large family bathroom, the scheme has been kept simple and traditional, with classic white towels, fixtures, and architectural detailing. The mellow tones of the natural wood floor add a touch of warmth to the blue-and-white scheme.

USING THE PALETTE

☐ If you favor the tranquil prettiness of pastels, look to the following sources for inspiration: country-cottage schemes in which faded tints look

☐ wonderful on everything from color-washed walls and hand-painted furniture to homespun, vegetable-dyed textiles; period-inspired schemes based on late-18th- to early-19th-century styles,

☐ such as Rococo, which suits feminine shades, such as pink, soft blue, and cream, perfectly; modern styles that feature such hues as soft pistachio, eau-de-nil,

☐ lilac, and pale lemon. Pastels look particularly refreshing when teamed with white. Use white in a two-color scheme or use additional pastel shades to

☐ create more variation. Keep the tonal values the same for the best look.

◀ Pastels are infinitely versatile—the appealing powder-blue shade that transforms this scheme creates a look that is fresh and energizing. Any hint of coldness is dispelled by the cozy woolen carpet and upholstery, and subtle accents in pale lemon and mauve.

◀ Without dominating the space, a band of soft yellow between the countertops and ceiling helps soften the hard edges of a modern kitchen.

▶ Use pastels to anchor monochrome schemes that feature several different tones of the same hue. The blue used on the walls of this country bedroom falls midway between the palest and darkest shades on display.

USING NEUTRAL COLORS

O ften resorted to as a safe, lackluster option in place of anything more adventurous, neutral colors can look dingy and uninspiring. However, embraced with enthusiasm and skill, they can represent the ultimate in cool, natural design sophistication.

To make neutral hues work, remember that they have to be chosen as carefully as any other colors. An undisciplined mix of greenish taupe, yellowy cream, and pinky beige, for example, will not blend magically just because all three are vaguely "neutral." To ensure success, stick to one basic version of each neutral color you use (brown with a yellow instead of a red or blue cast, for example), and vary the tone, patterns, and texture on each surface.

◄ Pale neutrals work well with generous proportions and graphic shapes to create an undemanding contemporary look. Here, a subtle scheme focuses attention on the outsized furnishings and fireplace and their richly textured surfaces. The jumbo scatter cushion helps to reinforce the room's chunky look and provides maximum comfort.

USING THE PALETTE

Neutral shades feature widely in many contemporary styles such as: international modernism, the classical architectural look that features white walls, natural textures and materials, and shiny surfaces, including chrome and glass; eco-chic, with its handwoven textiles, hand-thrown pots, waxed timber, and natural stone, all set off against walls brushed with distemper; and minimalism, a stark uncompromising style from which all extraneous detail, ornament, and color have been eliminated. The neutral palette creates a calming atmosphere, across a variety of styles, depending on the color contrasts used. For the most noticeable contrast of all, use black to create a harder, smarter, urban-chic style.

◄ Carefully chosen for their warmth, the scrumptious coffee, cream, and chocolate tones that dominate here mean that the atmosphere runs no risk of being sludgy or dull. The medium tone on the fireplace wall has a particularly appealing tendency to take on subtly different casts with the changing light. The earthy tones of the decorative scheme are enhanced by the natural wood floor.

◄ Many people find the purity and calm of a white bedroom perfectly conducive to rest and relaxation. However, introducing accents of color, provided here by a jazzy throw, will ensure that the look does not become too cold and clinical.

▶ The stark contrast of dark-oak beams against dazzling white plaster highlights the soaring pitch of this dramatic loft space.

COMBINING COLORS

O ne of the least intimidating ways to approach color combining is to choose types or moods of color before you consider hues. Colors can be grouped in different ways—those found together in nature have a natural affinity with one another, as do color families created by chemical dyes. Pale tints mix effortlessly, as do deep ones such as wine, navy, and bottle green. Once you've settled on a general type of color, it's easier to make individual choices.

Using sample cans, swatches, and cards will help you see how colors can work together. To make your task easier, look for a paint range that provides help in the form of cross-referenced swatches or lists of recommended color coordinations.

◀ Striking blocks of typically Art Deco color (warm and slightly muted peach and lilac) define this strongly 1930s-inspired loft, with its graphic, gridlike windows, sleek leather seating, and low, clean-lined storage unit.

USING THE PALETTE

If you don't know where to start when it comes to mixing color, try to identify a general color family you particularly like. Think about: bright, citrus shades of orange, lime, and lemon; Fall shades of gold, russet, and brown; ice-cream tints such as rose, eau de nil, banana, and aqua; earthy ocher, terra cotta, chestnut, and copper; and intense jewel shades such as ruby, topaz, sapphire, and amethyst. If you want a particularly sleet, contemporary look, introduce accents of strong bright colors, such as bright turquoise, fuchsia pink, or the primaries, into a black and white scheme. For a softer look, choose more mellow shades, such as pretty pinks, and use a softer neutral interior based around cream and coffee shades.

◀ Vivid tropical hues can be cleverly combined to create a cool, exotic scheme. Here, intense azure blue, palm-leaf green, and lavender are punctuated with warm accents of crocus yellow and crimson to produce a look that is stimulating but not jarring. Neutral tints on the ceiling and floor provide the necessary contrast and balance.

◀ In this open, airy space, fondant-hue walls define different activity areas. Contemporary art and modern furniture ensure that the overall effect is far from sugary.

▶ An old-fashioned garden provided the inspiration for this delightful scheme. The dominant colors are rose pink, crocus yellow, and wisteria blue, accented with blocks of leafy green.

WORKING WITH PATTERN

Like colors, the patterns you choose for a room can alter your visual perception of it, change its mood significantly, and help create a wide range of design periods and styles. Fresh plaids suggest a country theme, for example, while rich paisley swirls embody the Victorian era. When working with different patterns, the trick is to find a harmonious middle ground between the sterile and dated look of obsessively coordinated fabrics and wallpapers and the aesthetic mayhem that results when poorly matched patterns cover too many surfaces. If you're lacking in experience, remember that starting with plain walls and floors will allow you to experiment with pattern elsewhere and reduce the risk of expensive design disasters. Keep in mind, too, that most rooms contain large areas of informal patterns that are easy to overlook when you're putting a scheme together—a wall of shelves filled with books or collectibles, for instance, or a wooden floor made up of intricate parquet tiles.

▲ Simple black-and-white motifs help create a 1950s look in this contemporary Swedish living room. Note how skillfully the scale of each pattern has been linked to its use—small doodlelike shapes for the throw-pillow covers, and big bold circles woven into the striking sunshine-yellow rug.

▶ Country stripes in soft shades of gray-blue adorn almost every surface in this inviting bedroom, including the walls, the windows, the high-hinged screen, and the narrow rug beside the bed. The painted floorboards subtly reinforce the striped theme, while providing a welcome expanse of solid color.

WALLS

Use pattern to change the apparent proportions of a room or disguise architectural awkwardness. Vertical stripes will make a room look taller, while horizontal lines can make it seem wider. Stripes don't have to be in the form of wallpaper. In fact, if your walls or ceiling are not perfectly straight, the unforgiving geometry of printed stripes will make it more obvious. For a more flexible alternative or to create a less formal look, use painted lines or tongue-and-groove paneling (mounted vertically or horizontally) to achieve a similar effect.

To camouflage sloping ceilings or projecting corners, use one pattern with a small design throughout the room. Treating walls and ceiling separately in oddly shaped rooms tends to highlight irregularities.

◄ In this Moorish-inspired bathroom, ceramic wall tiles in harmonious tones of blue create a subtle underwater effect. Tiles offer numerous options for creating pattern, from the simplicity of plain white tiles with a grouting of similar tone to the complex designs produced by large arrays of hand-decorated squares.

▶ The unique and stylish detailing on these plain pale walls has been achieved with only a few sample cans of paint and a steady hand. The vertical lines were drawn using a plumb line, then painted over. The rectangles were outlined in pencil and marked with masking tape before they were filled in.

FLOORS

In most homes, floor coverings use a higher proportion of the decorating budget than any other element. It is also true that patterned floors present more design problems than plain ones, so if your confidence is failing, you should stick to plain flooring materials. If you opt for pattern, do so only as a positive choice, not as a misguided attempt to disguise stains on floorboards—any design that is complex and colorful enough to do this is unlikely to flatter your room, and small, regular motifs make stains more, not less, obvious. There are two ways to use pattern on the floor:

● As an overall design;

● On a made-to-order surface that defines the room using central panels, borders, and corner motifs.

▲ The richly colored stone tiles that cover the floor (and the walls) of this bathroom provide subtle visual interest and focus attention on the intricate mosaic insets.

◄ An op-art variation on checkerboard tiles, this practical vinyl floor sets the scene perfectly in a retro 1960s kitchen. The bold design of the flooring is offset by the plain colors and clean lines of the furnishings.

COMBINING PATTERN

The skillful mixing of patterns that are all different, yet complement each other and their setting perfectly, is one of the hallmarks of a stylish room. Developing a sure and instinctive eye for pattern takes time, but you can't go far wrong if you begin by limiting your choices to patterns that feature the same types of color. For example, spring rose, leafy green, daffodil yellow, and bright blue are all clear, fresh tints; while russet, bark, flame, and ginger are all autumnal shades. Vivid pink, orange, and yellow are all bright funky hues, while fawn, lavender, gray, and silvery green are subdued shades.

It is also important that the patterns you combine have broadly similar personalities. For instance, down-home ticking stripes have nothing in common with stylized period ones and should not be combined. However, patterns do not necessarily have to have similar motifs. Ordinary plaids and stripes, for example, work well together with similar patterns or with simple country florals. Varying the scale slightly between patterns displayed together will add interest to the combination, but don't go too far; tiny delicate shapes beside huge bold ones are much more likely to look disastrous than decorative.

◀ Strict adherence to ice-cream tints and straight-edge shapes gives this pattern-filled room a mellow, harmonious feel. A geometric theme is established with the customized paint treatment on the walls, which is then carried through in the designs of the framed prints, the cubical storage unit, and the rug.

▲ At first glance, the only large area of pattern in this lofty bathroom seems to be provided by a Roman shade. In fact, the kaleidoscope of light and shadow made by the glow of a pierced hanging lamp falling upon trailing ivy, sinuous shelf brackets, and decorative glass bottles also creates intricate patterns.

WINNING COMBINATIONS

Although they weren't chosen from coordinated selections, the patterns in each of the groups below work well together because they share color families (although not precise hues) as well as general characteristics. The stripes, for example, with their muted, broken colors, have closer links with a formal living room than a circus tent or a beach hut.

Sophisticated stripes

▲ The textiles that dress this brass bed are linked by their rich warm colors and stylized floral motifs. A Persian rug behind the headboard acts as an opulent wall hanging, while oriental cushions supplement the traditional pillows.

Country flowers

◄ In this fairy-tale child's bedroom, a vibrant upholstery fabric dominates the scheme. Tiny yellow plaids on the bed linen and curtain borders and the pattern on the walls add interest. Dotted among these are painted flowerpots that have been painstakingly copied from the fabric.

Playful plaids

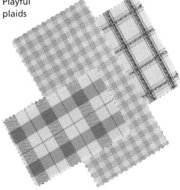

USING TEXTURE

Introducing one or two tactile elements allows you to experience the space through touch as well as sight. Some materials, such as stone, brick, plaster, sisal, and unbleached linen, have pleasing natural irregularities that create a reassuring three-dimensional effect. A mellow wooden floor will bring color and warmth to a room decorated in a neutral palette, while such accents as smooth velvet cushions, a luxurious chenille throw, a shag rug, a terra-cotta pot, or a piece of gnarled driftwood will add further textural interest.

FABRICS

From shiny silk, satin, and taffeta to coarser materials, such as burlap, felt, and tweed, fabrics offer a wealth of textural interest. Think about the other furnishings and furniture in your room when choosing new fabrics. In the same way that certain colors work well together, so do different textures. Silk, for example, works very well with smooth, shiny materials such as dark wood or chrome.

▲ Always consider where different textures are placed in relation to each other. In this bedroom, the bed's wooden frame and headboard help to offset the opulent texture of the bedspread, pillows, and curtains.

▲ Our response to texture is not always as immediate as it is for such things as color or pattern, but our senses do instinctively register how the surfaces of different materials look and feel, whether they are warm or cold, rough or smooth, fine or coarse. In this neutral scheme, the chair cover, curtains, and tablecloth are counterbalanced by the pottery, pebbles, and wooden picture frames to create interesting layers of different textures.

▶ Textural variation is particularly important in rooms where there is little background color. In this white bedroom, subtle contrasts of texture are provided by the floaty voile at the window and the crisp white bed linen. Further injections of texture are provided by the low wicker table and vase of dried grasses.

WALLCOVERINGS

Your walls are an intrinsic part of your interior decoration. Use them as a neutral background for the colors and textures that you have chosen for the rest of your room, or make them a central, textural feature, either by putting up wall hangings or paneling, or using textured wallpapers or paints. You can also add interest to your walls, particularly in older buildings, by dividing them with features such as a chair and picture rails.

▼ In a cavernous loft space carved out of a converted warehouse, the exposed brick walls bring a warmth and textural interest that wouldn't be possible if they were smoothly plastered. The rough texture of the walls contrasts with the smoother surface of the mezzanine area.

◄ Wood has an inherent tactile quality that invites you to reach out and touch it. In this dining room, the cheerful yellow on the walls helps pick out the different grains of the wood flooring and pine furniture.

FLOORING

Floors provide a large surface area on which to experiment with different materials such as wood, slate, stone, or vinyl. However, practicality, as well as style, should govern your choice. Think about how much use the room will get and whether you will be happy with certain textures. Ceramic tiles, for example, are a hardwearing choice in a bathroom, but if you hate having cold feet, you may want a warmer option such as vinyl.

▼ In a sparsely furnished living room, an expanse of hardwearing textured carpet becomes a main feature. The pots and fireplace add another textural dimension.

▼ Suggesting Scandinavian country style, white-washed floorboards make an informal, low-maintenance floor covering that sits comfortably in either a traditional or a contemporary room. Placing a rug over a hard floor provides not only welcome warmth and comfort underfoot, it also creates another layer of texture.

TEXTURAL CONTRAST

Hard or soft, rough or smooth, shiny or matt, variations of texture can have a profound impact on the overall look and feel of a room, especially in neutral schemes where there is little color or pattern, or where decorative elements are kept to a minimum. Natural materials, including unpolished wood, wicker, seagrass, terra-cotta tiles, cork, and wool, generally have warm, comforting properties and can help to inject some color. Hard, shiny surfaces, such as glass, marble, and stainless steel, help to reflect the light and make rooms appear brighter and cooler.

TEXTURED WALLS

Walls provide an ideal canvas on which you can experiment with variations of texture, from rough plaster to smooth, silky latex paints. The new generation of textured paints offers subtle metallic, chalky, and sandy finishes that enhance the walls and reflect the natural light. These tactile paints can be used on whole walls to create solid blocks of texture or combined with flat paints to create interesting contrasts.

▲ A variety of tactile elements, including leather, marble, wood, stone, cotton, and wool, have been cleverly combined in a living room that is coolly understated yet welcoming.

▶ A patchwork of jewel-like velvet squares on the wall, pillows, and bedspread bring a touch of opulence to a bedroom.

◀ In a rustic bedroom, an antique bedspread and wall-hung rug complement the muted tones of the wood, earthenware, and wicker.

▲ The mellow tones of a terra-cotta pot teamed with a collection of tribal masks are all that is needed to bring textural interest to a neutral scheme.

▶ Chosen for their light-reflecting properties, the chrome fixtures, glass basin, vitrified ceramic tiles, and mirror have transformed a small, awkward space with no natural light into a bright, stylish bathroom. The matt texture of the wooden floor provides an interesting contrast to the shiny surfaces.

FABRIC FURNISHINGS

● Shiny fabrics, such as silk, taffeta, and moiré, reflect the light and can be used for pillows, throws, and curtains.

● For a tactile, natural floor covering, consider coarse textures, such as jute, sisal, coir, seagrass, or rush matting; carpets that have similar textural qualities include cord and some of the more rugged wool weaves. For a smoother finish, you can choose from linoleum, rubber, and vinyl.

● Rugs, throws, kilims, dhurries, and rag rugs can all be used to introduce small touches of texture into a room.

● Patterned fabrics include tartan plaid, brocade, damask, chintz, embroidered tapestry, crewelwork, bouclé, and toile.

PROPORTION

When most people are faced with designing a room or buying an item of furniture, they think first of the style, color, and size of any potential purchase. But even when a chair or a cabinet meets your requirements in all these areas, it will still look out of place if its proportions don't work with the other objects around it and the room itself.

When it comes to home design, proportion is just as much a matter of common sense as strict rules (see box, opposite). Many architectural styles dictate, to some degree, their own requirements. Victorian reception rooms, for example, tend to have higher ceilings than those in newly built houses and can, therefore, showcase large, imposing items of furniture that would look wrong in a low-ceilinged ranch house.

◀ The owners of this lofty Victorian living room have ignored the kind of high, formal furniture intended for it in favor of an exotic, laid-back Eastern style. The theme is established with low daybeds that accentuate the room's vertical proportions and free the walls for prints and pictures that would otherwise look too large. The warm color scheme reinforces the ethnic look and helps to create a cozier, more relaxed atmosphere than would have been the case with either cool whites or pale blues.

◀ A large, modern bed is in scale with the proportions of a tall, contemporary interior. Introducing items of different heights, such as the pair of lights, helps to make the room feel less imposing.

▲ Large seating units can work well in a small space. Here, a large daybed occupies an entire wall of a box-shaped room. The child's armchair and stool create visual tricks with the proportions of the space.

▼ To accommodate a large-scale, ornate bed, this modest-size bedroom has been given a simple, yet strong color treatment on the walls, and the rest of the floor area has been left clear.

HINTS AND TIPS

● Never furnish a large or high room with lots of small, spindly pieces of furniture; they will always look out of place.

● King-size storage items (cabinets, shelf units, cupboards, or armoires) can look fabulous filling a whole wall; if they're not valuable antiques, consider giving them the same paint treatment as the walls to achieve an almost built-in look.

● High-ceilinged rooms should be balanced with one or two pieces of tall furniture.

● Low furniture can make rooms look higher, so if you find your ceiling oppressive, choose your seating and storage accordingly.

● To expand a small, low room visually, hang curtains from floor to ceiling and from wall to wall instead of stopping them at the window frame.

LIGHTING

No matter how much time and money you spend on decorating your home, if the lighting doesn't come up to scratch, then a room will never really look or feel right. Making sure you have enough of the right type of illumination should be one of your main priorities when you are planning the room. Begin by looking at the space from different angles and at different times of the day. Even a room that gets plenty of sunlight will need some backup on cloudy days. Think about what the room will be used for, and at what time of day or night, and whether there are any decorative features or pieces of furniture that you would like to highlight. Consider, too, how light will affect the room's proportions and the perception of space. A high-ceiling roomed will feel cozier and less imposing if the source of light is directed downward, whereas in a low-ceilinged space, the light should point up. Placing candles in front of mirrors also helps to create a feeling of spaciousness.

▲ Simple votive candles make an unusual and decorative floor-level lighting display. The ceramic pots and pieces of volcanic lava help reflect the light.

▶ Intense sunlight needs to be controlled. Here, floor-length semi-opaque curtains help filter out the sun's rays without throwing the living room into darkness. Venetian blinds, available in a choice of finishes, would also work in this modern setting, allowing the level of light to be adjusted as needed and creating an attractive dappled effect. Note the two stylish freestanding uplighters that bathe the ceiling in light at night. Overhead, a skylight lets in more light.

▲ Natural daytime light can become an important decorative feature in its own right. In a high-ceilinged loft space, sunlight flooding through the windows creates an alluring display of silhouettes on the large expanse of white wall.

▶ In a modern bathroom with no natural light, recessed ceiling spotlights provide the right amount of task lighting without making the room feel cold and clinical. Glass, metallic, and ceramic surfaces help reflect the light. Bathroom lights should be enclosed if they are likely to get wet (an electrician is the best person to ensure that bathroom lighting is properly wired, following safety standards).

NATURAL LIGHT

The intensity of daylight, and its partner, shadow, changes at different times of the day and with the seasons. The play of light affects the mood and color of a room, a fact that should always be taken into account when planning a scheme. If possible, choose a room's function according to the quality of light it gets and at what time of day. In rooms with no natural light, such as a bathroom, you may consider having a skylight or window put in. Choose materials that have light-reflecting properties such as mirrors, clear glass or plastic shelving, chrome, and pale wood flooring. Use an oil-base paint, and choose a finish that catches the light. This helps create a more open feeling in the room.

▲ A large arched window prevents this top-floor room in Brussels from being thrown into gloom during the day. The light, airy effect is reinforced by the paintwork, wooden floor, and large, arched mirror. Outside shutters allow the window to be left free of curtains. Artificial light is provided by Art Deco lamps.

◄ A predominantly white scheme looks fresh and energizing in a spacious attic that is bathed in natural light for most of the day. In a room that gets little sun or loses the best light after early morning, a warmer tone, such as dusty pink or pale yellow, might be a more appropriate choice.

ARTIFICIAL LIGHT

A single bulb suspended from the ceiling is seldom adequate, nor is it the most flattering option for the room or its occupants. Ideally, you should incorporate a combination of the three main types of lighting. Ambient light, in the form of hanging fixtures or up- or downlighters, throws light over a large area and provides the main background illumination in a room. Task lighting includes desk lamps or halogen spots to concentrate illumination on a specific activity, such as cooking; the best task lighting is adjustable, allowing you to direct the illumination to where it is needed. Accent lighting picks out interesting features, such as a painting, and is provided by spots, strips, or picture lights.

◀ Skillfully arranged downlighters bring pattern and tonal variation to a spare minimalist hallway. Concealed lighting throws the stairs into relief. For safety, always light the top and bottom steps of a staircase.

▲ In an old-fashioned hall, the red shade on a traditional table lamp casts a mellow glow that complements the staircase and beams, and a wall-mounted light highlights a display of plates.

LIGHT BULBS

● Tungsten bulbs have a soft, slightly yellow cast, making them suitable for illuminating colors.

● Fluorescent bulbs have a long life and emit little heat, but their cool blue light can be somewhat harsh and hard on the eyes.

● Halogen bulbs are much smaller than the alternatives. They produce a strong, clear light, without either a warm or cool cast.

FURNITURE

Whether it is an antique or stylishly modern, a family heirloom or a junk-shop find, a piece of furniture should appeal to the senses, inviting us to look at it and use it. Think about the furniture you have—or intend to acquire—when you are planning a room's layout and consider how its shape, style, historical, and cultural references can be woven into the decorative scheme. A beautiful art deco dressing table could be the starting point for a period bedroom or a set of 1950s chairs the inspiration behind a retro-style kitchen. Think, too, about the size of your furniture in relation to the proportions of your room. For example, the couch should be comfortable for the number of people who will usually use it—often two or three—but not too large or small for the size of the room.

▲ Choose furniture that reflects the room's function. A large three-seater couch massed with plump cushions and teamed with occasional tables helps inspire a feeling of comfort and relaxation.

◄ The couch, chairs, and ottoman have been upholstered in restful, neutral fabrics to harmonize with the rest of the living room.

▶ Arranging tables and chairs in groups in different parts of the room, instead of clustered together in the center, can help to make a large, high-ceiling room feel cozier and less imposing. These elegant Gustavian-style dining chairs have been pushed back, helping to make a feature of the tall window.

▶ Antique furniture can have an inherent charm that endures, where contemporary pieces can easily look dated. Here a fourposter draped in attractive toile fabric brings elegant 18th-century style to a bedroom.

HINTS AND TIPS

● Moving furniture around can breathe new life into a scheme. You could bring seasonal changes to a living room, for example, by arranging the chairs around the fire in winter, then turning them to face the windows in summer.

● Buy the best-quality bed that you can afford and, ideally, one that is at least 6 in (150 mm) longer than the tallest person sleeping in it. The mattress should offer good support and be covered in a natural fabric. Always lie on the bed to test it before you buy it.

● Make sure a dining table is big enough—or can be extended—to seat the right number of people.

● When you buy a new piece of furniture, always have a copy of the room's measurements and a tape measure with you. Check that a bulky item, such as a couch, will fit through the doors and up the stairs if necessary.

● Allow sufficient clearance between individual pieces of furniture so that people can move easily around and through a room.

FINISHING TOUCHES

It is often the small touches that can do so much to bring life, warmth, and unity to a room, so always think about how you can incorporate treasured possessions and appealing details when you are planning a scheme. An heirloom quilt, a favorite vase, or one or two well-chosen scatter cushions might, for example, help create a visual link with the walls, furniture, and textiles. Observe the colors of a painting and think about how they can be repeated elsewhere—as accents on cushions or rugs, perhaps, or in larger amounts on walls or floors. You may want to pick out a particular shade with flowers or fruit. Interesting architectural features, such as an intricately tiled fireplace or ornate molding, can also provide a wealth of inspiration for a decorative scheme.

▲ In a bedroom with a distinctly Oriental flavor, an amber-colored glass vase picks out the mellow tones of the wooden headboard and curved bedside table with its integral reading lamp.

▼ Flowers, chosen to match the stunning shade of purple on the couch, and carefully arranged paintings help to reinforce the strong interplay of color and symmetry in this living room. Note how the shape of the glass vases helps to define the sculptural form of the couch.

▶ In a calm, minimalist interior, a simple arrangement of twigs is not crowded out by other pieces, but given plenty of space to breathe. The colors and textures are echoed in the wooden floor and table and wicker chairs.

▶ The small, gilt-framed bird painting in the top left-hand corner was the inspiration for this scheme. The electric blue has been alluded to on the elegant regency-style sofa and is highlighted with gold pillows. The colors are also picked out around the window and on the cushions on the floor.

▲ The hand-painted base of a wooden-topped kitchen table presented a decorative starting point for the rest of the scheme. Teamed with the whites and watery eau-de-nil shades used elsewhere, the repeated fish motif and casual arrangement of shells and pebbles help to conjure up a distinctly nautical theme. By hanging the two large pictures stacked one on top of the other, they become focal points, instead of being dwarfed by the proportions of the high-ceilinged room. Notice how a simple bowl of oranges on the side table below the pictures adds a welcome splash of vibrant color to the scheme.

HINTS AND TIPS

Faced with an awkward design problem, many of us are tempted either to ignore it altogether, or to splash out on a redecoration project that may not be necessary. In many cases, a new surface, a change of use, or simply a fresh way of looking at the situation is enough to transform a boring, awkward, or wasted corner into a stylish and practical feature.

TINY TILES

One of the most ancient forms of decoration, mosaic tiles can add color, pattern, and texture to walls, floors, furniture, or work surfaces. Most complex mosaic designs are sold on a backing of paper or net so they are easy to install, but the tiles are also sold loose so you can build up your own patterns and choose your own colors to create a variety of pictorial motifs or abstract designs.

Over large areas, mosaics can be an expensive option, but they are much more affordable for walls or floors in small spaces like bathrooms, or as a way of giving a personal finish to a humdrum architectural feature or item of furniture, such as a table (see pp.162–163). If you like working with mosaics, create unusual pattern-on-pattern effects using fragments of broken china (odd or chipped plates are ideal for this) instead of standard tiles. (But remember that this treatment is unsuitable for floors or work surfaces.)

▲ If you have an unattractive view from your window, hang translucent curtains or shades to preserve modesty and admit light, then add interest with a trim. Here, red gerberas spots adorn the middle of three panels in pale voile and provide an unusual touch.

◀ Blend a traditional fireplace into a modern scheme by painting it to match the walls (paint the inside only if the flue is blocked off). Use brightly colored mosaics to decorate the edges.

▼ An exquisite mosaic floor with classical scroll border makes this tiny bathroom look larger than it is. The overall color treatment also enhances this effect.

UNDER THE STAIRS

If you have stairs rising from an entrance hall or a ground-floor room, the area underneath them can be difficult to utilize to its full advantage. Restricted in height and cut off from natural light, this space usually tends to get boxed in to form a cavelike cupboard, or is treated as a semipermanent dumping ground for bulky possessions in need of a home.

To maximize the potential of this awkward triangle, either draw up a room plan specially designed to accommodate its limitations (by locating a seating, dining, or working area here, for example), or invest in a purpose-made storage system that allows you to see—and to reach—all the contents easily, instead of having to explore shadowy nooks and crannies to find what you want. At its most basic, such a system could involve a simple row of hooks for coats and jackets or a set of hooks mounted at increasing distances from the floor to follow the line of the staircase with a few stylish bags suspended from them to hold unlovely necessities. For items that are too heavy or bulky to hang, add a roomy wooden, metal, or wicker chest. A built-in cupboard featuring different-size shelves could be used for storing items such as shoes.

▲ As part of an open-plan reception area, the corner under the stairs is an ideal place for a small dining table; this round one with its neat central pedestal makes it easy for diners to slip in and out of the inside chair. Overhead, a pendant downlighter relieves the gloom and casts a flattering glow on the setting and the food.

▶ Custom-built and mounted on an ingenious track system, these stepped, wood-frame shelving units store a wide range of household items from shoes to bed linen. Note the unobtrusive finger holes that take the place of conventional handles.

STORAGE SOLUTIONS

If your rooms are overrun with clutter, investigate the storage potential of wasted spaces.

● Put up a shelf at molding height across a small room or along a corridor to store items such as out-of-season clothing, family archives, and old correspondence. Hide messy collections inside stylish boxes, baskets, and files.

● In a tiny bathroom, install a high shelf across one wall for toiletries and towels; you can tuck a compact stool under the basin to use for easy access.

● If you need a new bed, buy one with drawers built into the base or with a hinged mattress with a roomy compartment underneath.

● Insert freestanding internal shelves in your kitchen cabinets so you can use the wasted space above a single layer of tin cans, jars, or glasses.

STOLEN SPACES

When it's not possible to create the storage provision you need from completely dead space, you should consider carving it out of an existing room. If you're clever, you'll hardly notice the loss of space, and the extra storage capacity you gain may just swallow up all your excess possessions.

A dramatic example of this tactic would be a proprietary closet organizer system (shelves, hanging rails, hooks, racks, baskets—whatever fills your needs) mounted wall-to-wall and floor-to-ceiling across a room. Concealed behind large doors (folding or sliding) or inexpensive curtains or shades (made from muslin, sheeting, or ticking, for example), a capacious unit like this can be designed to complement any decorating style and allow even the most persistent hoarder to live in a cool, clutter-free environment.

On a smaller scale, consider framing a doorway with a deep shelf unit that can hold anything from china and foodstuffs in the kitchen to toys and games in a child's bedroom or a small library of books in the living room.

◀ This elegant shelving arch, with its casing border, a deep baseboard, and a witty mock keystone over the door, merges seamlessly into the room's traditional structure.

▲ One wall of this kitchen has been turned into much-needed storage, its sleek sliding doors giving easy, compact access. Internal lighting reveals the entire contents at a glance.

SMART SHELVES

No matter how much you spend on furnishings, flimsy shelving sagging under the weight of its contents will make any room look cheap.

● Make sure all your shelves (particularly those intended for books) have plenty of support in the form of strong brackets, wooden supports, or concealed rods set into the walls (see pp.166–175).

● Use chunky wood (reclaimed railroad ties, for example, make sensational shelves) or man-made board, such as MDF (medium-density fiberboard); or add a decorative strip along the front of each shelf to add visual weight and a quality finish.

CAMOUFLAGE TRICKS

One of the most useful decorating skills is the ability to disguise or hide inelegant—yet indispensable—features with ingenuity and flair. Whether you use folding screens, *trompe l'oeil* brushwork, fabric panels, specially designed curtains and shades, judiciously positioned furniture, or custom-made carpentry, these will help you to make the most of the space and resources you have to work with. However, make sure that any concealment involving utilities, such as plumbing and electricity, allows quick access in an emergency.

▶ While open-plan living allows you to take advantage of light and space, it does limit your ability to hide mess. In this fresh, citrus-bright studio, a permanent semi-circular screen made of plywood retains the sense of space while separating the main activity areas; on the kitchen side, a deep work surface allows you to leave dirty plates and saucepans out of sight of guests.

◀ Unless you can afford sleek, sculptural radiators, or you're lucky enough to have chunky, old-fashioned ones, radiators are charmless parts of your décor. Here, one of the offending objects is neatly boxed in, its warmth escaping through a row of curvy cutouts.

▲ Built-in closets are one of the best storage solutions available, but in a tiny bedroom, they can appear to be overwhelming. To render it almost invisible, this closet has been concealed behind a flush door that is papered to match the walls, and has an unobtrusive handle. Floral prints continue from the wall across the door.

DESIGN IN PRACTICE

Having thought through how you would like your interior to look, and armed with ideas about how you can use elements such as texture and color, you can now set about the exciting task of transforming your home. Whether you are planning a complete overhaul, or would simply like to make one or two decorative improvements, this chapter will show you how it can be done, room by room. Inspirational photographs, before-and-after shots, and practical floor plans show you what can be achieved, often for a limited outlay of time, effort, and money. Helpful information boxes will guide you through tried-and-tested design solutions and steer you through some of the common pitfalls. There is advice on everything from safety and ergonomic planning to choosing the right flooring, furniture, and wallcovering. You will also see how improving the lighting and storage systems in such rooms as the kitchen or bathroom, providing for a utility area, and making sure that your home office is as comfortable as possible will add immeasurably to your quality of life.

CREATING YOUR ROOM PLAN

Before you settle on a final arrangement for any of your rooms, you will probably resort to a certain amount of trial-and-error furniture shifting. To keep this to a minimum, however, and to avoid any costly mistakes when it comes to buying new items, take the time to make an accurate room plan on which you can try out all the possibilities and eliminate those that are completely unworkable.

To do this, draw a scale plan of each room on a large sheet of graph paper, marking on it not only all the relevant measurements, including such things as fixed furniture, but also the position of things like radiators, fireplaces, power and telecommunications points, plumbing facilities where relevant and clearance required for any doors or windows that open into the room.

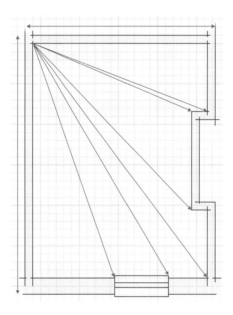

PLACING THE FURNITURE

Once you have created a basic floor plan, you can then decide where pieces of furniture – either built-in or freestanding – are to go. Take measurements of existing pieces as well as any you intend to buy, and on another sheet of graph paper, and using the same scale, draw and cut out a template that can be positioned on your floor plan.

◀ For general purposes, a simple floor plan will do. If precise information about recesses and projections is required (for fitted cupboards, perhaps), a system of diagonal measurements can be used.

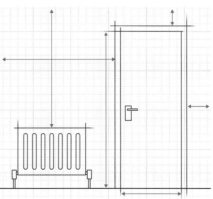

▲ Sketch a wall plan (an elevation), indicating fixed features and noting all relevant measurements, such as the height and width of a door, and the height of a radiator.

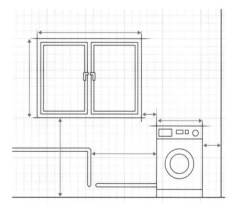

▲ With complex elements such as water, waste and domestic appliances, it's vital to record the exact position of existing plumbing and features such as windows.

◀ Poor planning can have dire consequences. In this ill-considered kitchen, heat from the oven puts enormous strain on the refrigerator and wastes energy. Open drawers hinder access to the oven door, while cooking utensils are kept in a dangerous position above the rings.

SPACE PLANNING

▲ Clever planning allows you to make full use of the space you have. Relieve pressure on a bathroom by turning the understairs area into an extra cloakroom. A conventional toilet fits neatly into the angle of the stairs, while a miniature basin is less bulky than a standard model.

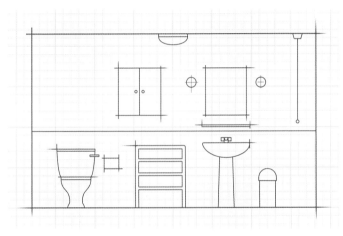

▲ For a hard-working space such as a bathroom, an accurate elevation diagram will help you to position wall-fixed items logically in relation to fixed elements such as the toilet, washbasin and towel rail (see p.101).

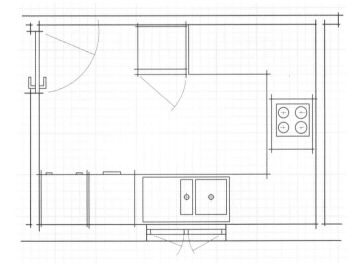

▲ A floor plan should record the position of all major furnishings and appliances. Seen here in aerial view, this kitchen has been designed around a classic, work triangle (4 m/13 ft 3 in maximum) formed by the refrigerator, the hob and the sink. Door and window swings are also indicated (see p.77).

▲ Hanging the door to open outward leaves enough space inside the room for a neat storage area beside the basin. To reduce the clearance necessary, however, a folding door has been fixed rather than a solid one; translucent glass panels ensure privacy while admitting some light.

PLANNING YOUR KITCHEN

The kitchen is perhaps the most important room in a house, and regardless of whether you have a tiny galley kitchen or a spacious kitchen/dining room, making sure the layout is well organized will add to your enjoyment of your home. First you must consider how you live and what type of kitchen you want. Look at the available space and decide what furniture, storage, and equipment you will require. You may need to make adjustments to the plumbing, lighting, or ventilation, or install additional outlets. Careful planning will help make sure that your kitchen functions efficiently and is a safe, comfortable, and enjoyable place to be in.

KITCHEN CHECKLIST

● How large is your kitchen? Is it a living and entertaining space, as well as somewhere to cook? How much time do you spend there?

● How many people use the kitchen? Will more than one person be preparing/cooking, serving, or clearing up at one time?

● Are you a family? Will there be children running in and out? Even if your kitchen is small, do you need space for a baby's highchair?

● Could bulky items, such as a washing machine or a freezer, be put elsewhere?

● Is a dishwasher a priority? Do you have space to stack and unstack without being cramped?

● Is the current lighting system adequate? Do you have enough task lighting and is it positioned in the right places?

● Do you want to look out of the window when preparing food or when you are at the sink?

● Do you want a single or double sink? Have you got enough space on each side to stack and drain your dishes?

● Do you need to reposition the plumbing and electrical outlets or put more in?

● How much storage do you need? Are there any wasted spaces that could be better used?

● Do you often entertain friends or relatives? Are you happy for your guests to be in the kitchen while you are preparing a meal?

CASE STUDY: SMALL OPEN-PLAN KITCHEN
Tucked into the corner of a combined living and dining area, this compact kitchen makes very good use of space and has been cleverly designed to blend with the rest of the room. The island unit has storage on both sides and can be used for preparing and serving meals. The unit also helps screen off the main cooking area without isolating the cook. Introducing a different floor surface also serves to divide off the room's different functions. There is a good combination of open and closed storage, including drawers, cabinets, and shelves. The wall cabinets have been custom-built to fit the available space and feature shelves of different heights. The kitchen also has plenty of easily accessible outlets. Note how the refrigerator, sink, and stove are all in easy reach of each other.

KITCHEN ORGANIZATION

There are two main principles to follow when planning the layout of your kitchen. One is the "work triangle" (13 ft 4 in/4 m maximum), which places emphasis on the need for an unobstructed path between the three main activity areas—sink, oven, and refrigerator. The second can be best understood by the motto "store, prepare, cook, wash, serve, door," which explains the linear working practice of preparing and serving a meal. Plan your storage, countertops, and appliances according to where you use them in this sequence. There are many space-saving solutions, such as corner sinks, that can help you make the most of a small kitchen.

◀ ▼ The original units in this galley kitchen have been given an instant face lift with a coat of paint and new handles. The glass shelving, tiling, and countertop all make the kitchen feel lighter and less enclosed. Replacing one of the cabinets with open storage for pans and other utensils has also helped to open up the space.

KITCHEN PLAN

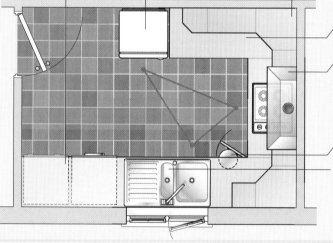

Washing machine and dishwasher next to sink, so all your plumbing is on the same wall.

Refrigerator is positioned well away from the oven so that it works more efficiently.

Overhead cabinets above countertops are placed at a comfortable height for easy access.

Ample countertops in near both the fridge and oven.

Hood removes all smells.

Trash can in cabinet is within easy reach of sink and stove. Note the space needed for it to swing out safely.

Second smaller sink allows access to water when large sink is filled.

KITCHEN PLANS

When planning the layout of your kitchen, you should look carefully at the space and think about the process of what you do and where and when you do it; then try to place everything in a logical location so that you never have to go far for anything.

Place your cabinets at a comfortable reaching height for you and other adults.

Narrow galley
A narrow galley allows for only units and appliances placed along one of the longer walls. Use the "store, prepare, cook, wash, serve, door" theory.

Wide galley
A small rectangular kitchen may allow you to have units along two sides, in which case, follow the "work triangle" theory.

L-shape
The "work triangle" works well in an L-shape. It can be used in a kitchen/dining room, with one arm of the "L" separating the two areas.

Horseshoe
The "work triangle" works best in a horseshoe shape. The cook has to move only a small distance from stove, sink, and refrigerator.

Island unit
Islands suit large kitchens, where they can literally be the center of activity. They can be used for storage and dining, depending on the design.

KITCHEN STYLE

KITCHEN WORK SURFACES

Choose a material that suits your needs in terms of durability and the level of maintenance required.

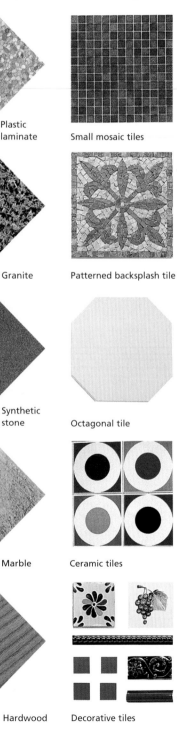

Plastic laminate

Granite

Synthetic stone

Marble

Hardwood

Small mosaic tiles

Patterned backsplash tile

Octagonal tile

Ceramic tiles

Decorative tiles

Once you have decided what you need in your kitchen and how major appliances and other items should be positioned, you can consider the style and precise details. The planning work you have already done should have helped you visualize your new kitchen and may suggest a style to you. For example, if you have a small kitchen you might choose light colors, which give a greater impression of space, or a streamlined, modern style that makes a virtue of a small space, with lots of high-tech, space-saving devices. Always remember to think about who will be using the kitchen—even when you are considering the look. The ergonomics of your work space are very important, so think about the height of the sink, the countertops, the oven, the storage units, and the dishwasher.

▲ This spacious kitchen and eating area has been designed to recall the décor of a 1950s American diner, an effect achieved by the central "bar" area with integral sink, the gingham-covered stools, the hanging lamp, the woodwork and the kitch accessories. The other island unit features ample space for food preparation on top and drawers for storage underneath.

▶ This basement open-plan kitchen-dining room receives very little natural light. To combat this, a bright, uncluttered, modern scheme has been used to reflect the light as much as possible. The touches of cool blue create interest and help make the space look larger. Recessed spotlights in the ceiling provide overhead lighting.

◀ A stylish, modern kitchen-dining room enhances the available space by using bright, white walls that reflect the light. The touches of blue on the cabinets create a feeling of freshness. Natural wood, glass-front cabinets, modern steel chairs, and an industrial-style oven keep the effect light and bright.

▲ This country-style kitchen achieves a charming, old-fashioned effect. The warm green and yellow décor, the checked gingham curtains and storage covers, the old-fashioned sink, the wooden countertop and draining board, and the blue-and-white stove all conjure up a cozy, unhurried feeling.

STORAGE

Having enough easily accessible storage space is one of the main ingredients of a smooth-running kitchen. The most flexible storage systems usually feature a combination of built-in and freestanding furniture, as well as a mixture of open and closed storage. Movable furniture, such as a butcher's block on castors, is another useful option. Think about the things you will need to store and how often you will use them—in addition to food and cooking utensils, you may have to find a home for appliances such as food processors, cleaning equipment, and oversized items such as an ironing board.

If you are not planning to overhaul your kitchen storage, but would like a new look, you can achieve a great deal simply by preparing and painting or spraying the old doors and attaching new handles. You can also update old cabinets with new doors—this is also useful if you decide you want to hide away items such as the dishwasher or washing machine.

◄ Plenty of open storage is a boon to the busy cook, who can see and access ingredients and utensils in an instant. This stylish island unit features work surfaces on top and plenty of storage, so that pans and other kitchen implements can be kept conveniently close to the integral burners.

▲ A slimline, floor-to-ceiling slide-out cupboard makes good use of the available space and provides ample storage for kitchen paraphernalia, which can be tucked away out of sight when it is not in use. The shelves at the top of the unit are useful for storing items that are not needed on a daily basis.

STORAGE SOLUTIONS

● Look for cabinets that incorporate pull-out trays or drawers; some corner units have revolving carousel fittings that utilize the space more efficiently. Louvered doors allow air to circulate and are a good choice for cabinets where food is stored.

● Make sure you incorporate plenty of cabinets and shelves of different heights so you can accommodate items of varying sizes.

● Narrow open shelves for single-line storage make good use of any dead wall space.

● An old-fashioned plate rack mounted over the sink is a simple and time-saving storage option.

● Look for an island unit that features plenty of storage space and can double up as a table.

● A wall-mounted stepladder for pots and pans makes good use of dead wall space.

● Hang utensils, pans, and other frequently used items from hooks attached to a simple stainless steel or wooden pole.

▲ As an alternative to cabinets, where items can be difficult to access, a set of wide drawers with special dividers makes finding things easy. Drawers should be positioned close to the sink or dishwasher so that clean dishes can easily be returned to their places. Deeper drawers are useful for storing bulkier items such as pans, large dishes, or electrical appliances.

◄ A combination of different storage requirements are catered for in this large family kitchen. The handsome old pine hutch and high open shelving running the length of one wall mean decorative pieces can be left on display, while other items are swallowed up by closed built-in storage units.

WALLS AND FLOORS

Choosing the right wall- and floor coverings can make a dramatic difference to the overall look and feel of a kitchen. Materials should be selected for their practical, as well as aesthetic, qualities. Surfaces should be easy to clean, durable, and resistant to water, steam, and grease. For flooring, the climate and the people in the house will also help to influence your choice. Surfaces, such as slate, stone, terrazzo, and quarry tiles, are hard-wearing, but they can be cold to walk on if there is no underfloor heating. If you have children, you may want to opt for a softer material such as linoleum or cushioned sheet vinyl. Polished wood is a good-looking, long-lasting choice, but floors that are not sealed properly will be damaged if spillages seep through.

For walls, choose washable paint and paper. Other options include cork, ceramic tiles, wood, and vinyl, which will help to insulate against heat loss.

◀ The attractive lavender used on the walls offsets the harder, shiny surfaces of the floor, countertop, and utensils. With their light-reflective properties, such materials as glass, zinc, and chrome are a good choice for a room that gets little or no natural light.

▲ If you have already chosen your furniture and fixtures, use them as a starting point for your decorative scheme. Here, deep blue was used on the walls to counterbalance the striking yellow of the retro-style units. A pale floor covering helps throw the table and chairs into dramatic relief.

▼ Neutral walls and wood flooring have been chosen for an open-plan space that has been designed along the lines of a professional caterer's kitchen. Although the room gets plenty of natural light, the wall lights provide artificial backup.

▼▼ Choosing different types of flooring helps to define the two areas of activity in this kitchen-dining room. The tall, backless hutch, which is used for storage and serving food, also helps to screen the kitchen without closing it off.

HINTS AND TIPS

● Ventilation can be a problem in kitchens. Even if you have a big window, you will probably need a fan and a hood, which are very effective in containing and minimizing cooking smells.

● Use a fungicidal adhesive to hang wallpaper—it will prevent mold from forming.

● Conventional radiators can take up a lot of valuable space, so think about installing a system of floor, wall, or ceiling heaters.

DINING ROOMS

TABLEWARE

Choose dishes, glassware, and flatware that are appropriate for the occasion. Team them with a tablecloth, place mats, and napkins in a complementary color.

Traditional silverplate

Blue-handle stainless steel flatware

Beige-handle stainless steel flatware

Ornate crystal wineglass

Turkish tea glass

Two-tone wineglass

Plain dinner set with decorative edging

Allover pattern, floral dinner set

When planning a dining area, think about the room and how you want to use it. Is it to be a place for regular family meals or will it be reserved for more formal occasions? Is there scope for extending the dining table to accommodate more guests? Will you be eating there during the day or mainly after dark? You will also need to make sure there is safe and easy access to the kitchen.

Whether you have the luxury of a separate, self-contained dining room or have to commandeer a corner of the living room, the surroundings should be relaxed and welcoming. A sturdy table and some comfortable chairs are essential, and there should be enough light without it being too harsh and glaring; a table lamp or candles will help create a congenial atmosphere at night.

▲ Wood is a practical and aesthetically pleasing choice for a dining room. Here, a simple table, unupholstered chairs, and a bare wooden floor suggest an informal approach. The artifacts on display provide diners with plenty of scope for conversation.

▶ A modern version of the traditional sideboard and a freestanding unit keep dishes, flatware, and table linen organized and close at hand. Alternatively, a traditional hutch, armoire, or simple chest of drawers would serve the same function.

◀ For comfort and easy access, this dining table is set in the middle of the room, just close enough to the fire on cold days and with the window to the side so that diners are not sitting facing or with their backs to the light.

▲ The furniture, fabrics, and finishing touches in this wood-paneled dining room all create a mood of cozy informality.

HINTS AND TIPS

● For maximum comfort, choose chairs with gently sloping, instead of upright, backs.

● Look for folding or drop-leaf tables that can be extended when you have extra guests. A pair of simple trestle legs and a piece of wood can make a useful extension. Consider coffee tables that rise to form full-height tables. Invest in a few folding chairs that can be stowed away.

● For an informal approach, group odd chairs of a similar style or shape. You can revamp thriftshop finds with

a coat of paint, or impose unity by recovering any drop-in seats (see pp.238–239). Simple slipcovers in the fabric of your choice will transform a set of dining chairs (see pp.240–241).

● Place candles in front of an uncurtained window or a mirror to create a dramatic effect and double your "curtain power."

● Be aware that warm-colored light from candles adversely affects cool color schemes in rooms used for evening dining.

PLANNING YOUR LIVING ROOM

LIVING ROOM CHECKLIST

• How large is your room? How many people do you expect to be in it at any one time?

• What kind of living room would you like? Is it a family/TV room? A calm, meditative retreat at the end of the day? A room that you want to impress people with?

• How much direct natural light does the room get, and when? What type of artificial light will you be using?

• How much stuff have you got? Do you need to keep all of it?

• Do you like to have books or objects on display? If you prefer to hide them, think about having shelves behind closet doors that blend with your walls.

• Are you fed up with your furniture? Do you have enough of it? Or too little? Can you buy new items, or can you upholster or alter what you already have?

• What style of architecture is your home? If features have been taken out, would you like to put them back in? Does anything need to be removed? Do the proportions need to be altered structurally or decoratively?

• How does the style of your home relate to what you envision? For example, if you want flamboyant 17th-century rococo, you might think twice if your home is modern with small, low rooms.

• What looks do you like in other people's homes or in magazines? Analyze the look—it may not cost you a lot to create a similar look.

Your living room is one of the most important areas of the house. It's primarily a place to relax—whether with friends and family or alone—so the comfort factor is all-important. Before you embark on major purchases or decorating schemes, think about the atmosphere that you would like to create, the elements that you want to include—such as books, storage, or ornaments—and who is going to be using the room. Take your time over making decisions, because errors can be costly and time consuming. Always test colors on your walls and live with them for a while before choosing; if you are buying rugs or new carpet, borrow them for a few days and see how they "grow" on you. Make sure you measure properly for furniture, and consider its size in relation to the rest of the room.

CASE STUDY: HOW TO COPE WITH SPACE
Large, tall rooms can be just as difficult to plan as more confined spaces—you don't want to feel lost or overwhelmed. The owners of this lofty gable-ceilinged living room have maintained its natural feeling of airiness and spaciousness, while at the same time creating a sense of intimacy. The fireplace provides a focal point. Bookshelves fill the space on each side to a height level with the top of the window; this means that the eye stops before it follows the diagonals of the roof upward. The effect is enhanced by hanging a large, bold poster (on the right) at the same level. The fireplace mantelpiece and shelving, which is broken up into small compartments, extend into the room, reducing its apparent length.

MAKING YOUR SPACE WORK FOR YOU

Moving is often the catalyst for a major home overhaul. Think about what you like and dislike about the structure and decor. You might want to build around an existing feature, or you might need to remove something before you can start work. Analyze the elements carefully, and be patient. You may decide to build up the look of your living room over a period of time, buying furniture as and when you can afford it; even so, to avoid mistakes you'll need to have an idea of what you want at the start. Think about the room's layout: What is the focal point? What do you like to look at when you are sitting down? How about the view from the window—do you want to gaze at it or away from it? Decorate with these points in mind.

◀ This living room is part of an open-plan space; the ottoman in the foreground creates a "wall" on one side. The main focal points are the fireplace and the tall windows; the lack of curtains means the beautiful view cannot be ignored.

▲ Although this Mediterranean-style living room is used as a thoroughfare, it has been made into a cozy, intimate space by placing focus on the fireplace. The mantelpiece area is filled with plenty of visual interest.

▼ The large, square-shape canvases on the walls of this tall, cool room prevent it from becoming overwhelming, despite its size. The comfortable and informal furniture helps to create an atmosphere that is modern and relaxed.

FLOORING

The treatment you give your living room floor is just as important as what you do with your walls. In terms of color, see the floor as a fifth wall. A dark floor will make a small room seem smaller. In terms of color, many designers stick to shades that are naturally found in nature, beneath your feet. Brown, green, gray, shades of gold, copper, and ocher are all good choices, while bright red and yellow might be considered jarring. What kind of flooring do you already have? Can you strip and varnish or paint your existing floorboards? If you live in an apartment, you may find that stripped floorboards are unsuitable because noise will travel to the unit below unless you have effective soundproofing. Laminated floors, consisting of thin strips of wood glued to backing board, might be the answer. Or would you prefer something softer such as a large rug or wall-to-wall carpet? Think about your floor in relation to the furniture. And don't forget to consider the texture—in terms of the look, the feel on your feet, and how much wear and tear you expect it to receive.

LIVING ROOM STYLE

CURTAIN POLES

Available in a selection of materials and diameters, and in styles ranging from antique to modern, curtain poles are a decorative way to hang curtains.

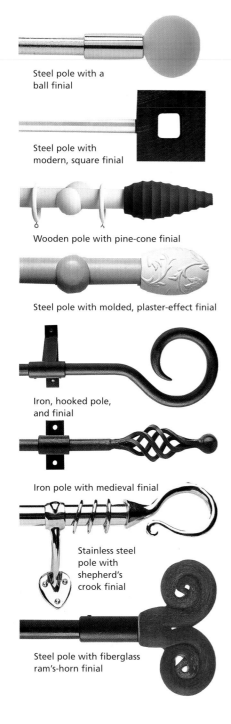

Steel pole with a ball finial

Steel pole with modern, square finial

Wooden pole with pine-cone finial

Steel pole with molded, plaster-effect finial

Iron, hooked pole, and finial

Iron pole with medieval finial

Stainless steel pole with shepherd's crook finial

Steel pole with fiberglass ram's-horn finial

With thought and careful planning, your living room can be whatever style you want it to be—regardless of size. To create the look you want, however, you will need to consider your living room as a whole. Think about unifying factors such as color, textiles, and the general shape and style of your furniture. And be brutal—too much furniture, or too many decorative pieces, can ruin the look, so put away anything that detracts from the desired effect. You may even want to build cabinets to hide the TV or hi-fi when not in use. Don't forget to consider the lighting. Natural light, or lack of it, will affect the way in which you design your space.

▶ A combination of traditional, contemporary, and ethnic elements creates an attractive, semiformal room. The neutral color scheme acts as a unifying factor and allows the objects and furnishings to make an impact.

▼ The design of this cheerful living room is simple yet effective. The pale décor reflects the natural light, while the various checked patterns create a strong but not overpowering effect.

WALLS AND WINDOWS

The way you treat your walls and windows depends on your taste and the architectural space. The style of your curtains should be in keeping with the proportions of your room. Heavy velvet and damask, for example, look better in larger, more opulent surroundings. Don't forget to think about what the curtains will look like when they are both open and shut. Team your curtains with your wall color, and consider the fabric in both natural and artificial light. If privacy is not a consideration, consider leaving your windows bare—but make sure your woodwork is spotless.

Walls can make or break a room, so think about them with care. In choosing a wall color, consider the room's proportions, how much light it receives, what time of day you generally use the room, what colors you respond to, and how your walls might complement your furniture. Wallpaper is an option, but think carefully about patterns— they are difficult to get right in relation to everything else. You also need to consider what you might place on the walls such as pictures and shelving. Fabric, stone paneling, and industrial materials all help to create a different feeling.

▲ Large amounts of light stream into this large, double-aspect modern interior. The tall windows and doors have been left free of detailing and curtains to avoid detracting from their geometric simplicity. Natural wood and simple contemporary furniture create a refreshing ambiance.

▶ Floor-to-ceiling window shutters enhance the angular, modern look of this living room. Panels on each side of the fireplace project from what would have been recesses; this unusual feature adds interest and is in keeping with the hard, clean lines of the interior.

CURTAIN HINTS

• Your window treatment can help alter the proportions of the room. Using a longer track can make a window look wider.

• Valances should be well above eye level and the tracks placed so that the fabric does not hang over the glass at the top.

• With tab-top curtains, you can create a vibrant effect by hanging two pairs together, using voile or sari fabric in contrasting colors. Use a "white-out" window shade to block out the light.

SHELVING AND STORAGE

The clutter of daily life is what gives a room its sense of life and prevents it from being a sterile, unlived-in space. Disorganized clutter, however, detracts from the style of a room, so it needs to be streamlined and contained. When it comes to storage solutions, the possibilities are almost endless. Your things can be hidden away in window seats or box-type coffee tables, or behind doors and paneling. Or you can make your storage requirements into a stylish feature—whether it be transparent open cubes that stack together, shelving made from interesting materials, such as glass or reclaimed floorboards, or more traditional items of furniture such as chests of drawers, highboys, and linen chests. If you prefer a unified look, consider having storage built in to fit your space exactly—this is especially useful for recesses and other awkward corners. Details are important, too—a modest piece of furniture can be transformed by replacing the handles with more expensive, stylish alternatives. And do not forget the little things, such as CD racks, that can introduce a stylish note into your living room at relatively little expense.

▲ This modern built-in boxed storage fills an awkward space under a sloping roof. Because it has been designed on two "stepped" levels, it does not make the room feel smaller, which a long built-in closet would have done. The useful wicker baskets are an attractive feature that could be put anywhere.

◀ Storage is always a challenge in studio apartments such as this one. Here, the closet behind the sofa acts as a "wall" between the living room and the kitchen area—an effect underlined by hanging pictures along the back of it. The pale colors and glass-front storage unit help to maximize the overall sense of light and space.

▼ Custom-built furniture can be designed to suit your exact storage requirements. This stylish unit features a good combination of open and closed storage, as well as surfaces for display.

▶ Shelves behind wooden panels provide display space in this grand country-house-style drawing room. The doors can be open or closed—a concept that can translate to modern interiors.

CHOOSING STORAGE

You need to think both creatively and practically when choosing storage for your living room.

● Consider your lifestyle: Will you dust and look after items on open shelving? Some modern looks, such as glass shelves, need to be kept clean for a streamlined effect.

● Think about color and materials. Be daring and treat the back walls, or interior, of a storage area in a more dynamic way than the rest of the room—the objects on display will break up the color.

● Decide how often you use your things and what can be stored. Box storage is most useful for items that you do not use regularly.

PLANNING YOUR BEDROOM

BEDROOM CHECKLIST

• How many people will occupy the room?

• Do you spend much time in your bedroom during the day? Do you need to use part of the room as a home office?

• Are there any things, such as noise, that irritate you about the room? Would it be possible to relocate to another part of the house?

• Will you need to replace the bed now or in the near future?

• At what time of the day does the room get the best light?

• Which colors would you feel happiest being surrounded by first thing in the morning and last thing at night?

• Do you like to wake up in the dark or in a bedroom filled with direct or diffused light? This will affect the type of window covering that you choose.

• Do you like to be surrounded by possessions or do you prefer a pared-down, uncluttered look?

• How much storage space do you need? Do you prefer built-in or freestanding furniture? Can any items, such as out-of-season clothes, be kept elsewhere?

• Do you like to read in bed? Do you need a bedside table and a light that can be turned off when you are in bed?

• Would you like to install a connecting bathroom?

The way your bedroom looks and feels can have a profound effect on the quality of your life. A bedroom is the most personal place in the house; it is where you go to relax and escape the pressures of the world, and this should be reflected in how the room is arranged and decorated, and in the choice of furniture and textiles. Choose lighting that will create the right ambient mood at night and organize a storage system that will help to make your daily routine run more smoothly. Small rooms in particular need careful planning; with too much furniture they can easily begin to look overcrowded and chaotic, so assess exactly what you will need. If a bedroom is to do double duty as a work space, you might want to screen off the two areas of activity.

CASE STUDY: THE ATTIC BEDROOM
Tucked away from the home's main areas of activity, an attic room can make an ideal location for a peaceful bedroom. Here, a dormer window was added to help open up the space and allow sun to stream in during the day, while the bold blue on the walls helps to create a cozy, intimate nighttime atmosphere. Painting the whole room in the same color helps to mask the room's awkward proportions. A useful cabinet has been built into the wall, freeing up valuable floor space, while the choice of light furniture, textiles, and flooring helps prevent the room from feeling claustrophobic. The wall-mounted adjustable lights provide plenty of backup illumination at night.

CHILDREN'S ROOMS

● Always put safety first when planning a young child's room. Furniture should conform to national safety standards. A nursery needs to be situated close to the parents' room. Never position a bed or chair under a window, and do not put shelves directly above a bed. Windows should be equipped with safety catches, outlets with safety covers.

● Providing enough accessible storage is essential. Look for modular units that can expand or be adapted as the child grows. Low-level storage options such as trunks, blanket chests, and freestanding bookshelves help to keep items within a child's reach and should make clearing up easier. Crates, boxes, and pullout drawers make useful under-bed storage for toys and out-of-season clothes.

● Consider a bed that combines storage and a play/work area.

● For walls, choose washable wallpapers and paints. Avoid heavily patterned wallpaper that a child will quickly tire of or outgrow.

● Have fun with color and pattern. Customize furniture, walls, or even floors (see above) with paint.

● Where two older children are sharing, a screen such as a low bookcase will help to divide up the room into separate areas.

● A teenager's bedroom will need plenty of outlets and a flexible lighting system, including a good task light for study.

▲ Simple fitted shelves and a desk have transformed an alcove in a small, spare bedroom into a quiet writing corner. The daybed has been specially built to fit the length of the wall. The furnishings and painted furniture suggest Swedish country style.

THE COMFORT ZONE

Sometimes a few simple changes can be all it takes to transform a dull, lifeless bedroom into a warm, inviting space that is full of personality. The bedroom on the right had plenty of potential, but the original decorative scheme made the room look rather cold and gloomy. A light-enhancing white was chosen for the walls and ceiling, which has helped to camouflage the room's awkward angles. Swapping the curtains for a blind has also helped to make the room feel lighter and airier. Replacing the carpet with a wood floor has given the room a stylish, contemporary edge.

▲ ▶ With a new headboard and fresh linen, the bed is now the main focus of attention. The utilitarian clothes rail has been banished in favor of a stylish full-length mirror, transforming a dingy corner. Moving the blanket chest away from the center of the room has also helped to enhance the overall feeling of spaciousness.

BEDROOM STYLE

BEDSIDE LIGHTING

Shaded lamps help to set an ambient nighttime atmosphere. Make sure the light is easy to reach from the bed and is bright enough if it is to be used for reading.

Art deco steel and glass bedside-table lamp

Contemporary bedside-table lamp

Japanese-style bedside-table lamp

Contemporary bedside-table lamp

Tiffany-style bedside-table lamp

Contemporary bedside-table lamp

Iron-based standing lamp

Whether your preference is for a traditional look, perhaps with an antique bed draped with an heirloom quilt, or you favor the pared-down minimalism of a Japanese-inspired room, the decorative scheme should be conducive to rest and relaxation, inspiring you to retreat there at the end of the day. The main item of furniture is undoubtedly the bed itself. You will spend about one third of your life lying on it, so buy the best-quality mattress and base that you can afford. The style of bed—an elegant iron four-poster, say, or one with a handsome painted headboard—can dictate the overall look of the room. Storage is another important factor—if you do not have enough, and in the right place, your bedroom will be hidden by clutter, and you will not enjoy your peaceful haven.

▲ Cool blue walls complement the mellow tones of an elegant bed, while elements of the decorative scheme are picked up in the pair of modern table lamps on the side tables. The room's restful atmosphere is enhanced by the rug and crisp white bed linen.

▲ With its imposing paneled headboard, this antique bed takes center stage in a 16th-century country house with low, exposed beams and whitewashed walls. The cozy bedside lamps and cheerful bedspread help dispel any hint of austerity.

◄ In a suburban house built in the 1920s, decorative flourishes, such as the cherub motifs and dreamy voile curtains, conjure up the style of an 18th-century boudoir.

► Delightful floral-patterned wallpaper makes a feature of the awkward proportions of an attic bedroom and creates a fresh invigorating backdrop for the feminine furniture and fabrics.

STORAGE

Having enough space to store things so they are not all piled in a messy heap on the floor will help you feel organized and will change the look of your bedroom. Think about what you will need to store and how much space you have. Decide whether you would prefer built-in units or freestanding pieces of furniture. Could some items, such as out-of-season clothing, be kept elsewhere in the house? Explore the potential of any unused spaces—for example, items that are not needed on a daily basis can be stored in baskets, boxes, or crates under the bed. You will also need one or two flat surfaces, such as a bedside table, for a lamp or night-time reading material.

▲ In a walk-in closet leading off the bedroom, clothes are stored in a tower of pullout crates (these are actually laundry boxes made of cardboard).

◀ Custom-built modular units provide capacious storage inside and ample surface space on top.

▼ Versatile, low-level storage in a children's room allows favorite items to be easily retrieved—and put away again at the end of the day. Here, shelves for books and toys, and a chest of drawers for clothing, have been customized with bright blue paint.

FURNITURE

The bed itself must be chosen with comfort firmly in mind, but you should also choose a framework that is in tune with your style. Think about how each item of furniture works with other pieces in the room in terms of size, materials, and proportion—a small table next to a single bed, a larger chest of drawers at the side of a fourposter. Make sure you have enough room to move around and position storage where it is easily accessible and will open properly. Look at ways in which you can maximize the storage potential of a piece of furniture. You can double the amount of hanging space in a closet, for example, by adding another, lower clothes rail.

◄ Crisp white and apple-green paintwork provides a perfect background for the wrought-iron bed. Other furniture has been kept to a minimum so that the bed is the room's main focus of attention. Picking up the Gothic theme, the Roman shade links the walls and bed linen.

▼ Contemporary beechwood furniture is given plenty of space to breathe in this well-proportioned room. Note the small console table used as a dresser and the freestanding, movable shelves that can be accessed from both sides.

WALLS AND WINDOWS

The most dominant surfaces in any room are its walls, so the treatment you choose for them will set the scene for all the other elements. This is not the place to experiment with garish hues (no matter how fashionable) or clashing patterns. Instead, take advantage of the powerful influence color has on mood by basing your scheme on one you really love, then finding a tone or shade of it that encourages serenity and relaxation; soft eau-de-nil instead of acid lime, subtle terra cotta instead of fiery orange. Once you've established a color theme, explore all the possible ways of interpreting it on your walls—as a plain paint finish, a textured or printed wallpaper, a layer of fabric, or a subtle decorative effect.

For the windows, choose a covering that provides privacy and reinforces the style you're trying to create—full-length curtains in a traditional room, for example, or sleek window shades or venetian blinds in a contemporary one.

FABRIC-COVERED WALLS

As a stylish alternative to paper or paint, try lining your bedroom walls with fabric. There are several ways to do this:

● Mount strips of wood top and bottom, seam your chosen material into the required width, stretch it taut, and anchor it in place with a staple gun. For extra heat and sound insulation, first line the walls with insulation batting.

● Invest in a specialized track system that allows the fabric panels to be removed for washing and replaced quickly and easily.

● Gather your material gently onto curtain wire or rods at the top and bottom of each wall, or only at the top for a less formal effect.

◄ The dramatic arched window that dominates this chamber has inspired a host of ingenious paint effects, from the blue color wash on the walls to the *trompe l'oeil* molding and imposing classical column on the projecting wall.

► Expanses of pale wall establish space and light as the principal design features of this first-floor bedroom. The old sash window has been replaced with doors to the yard, and a glazed area above it lets in dramatic rays of sunshine.

◄ Here, broad blue stripes establish a fresh seaside look and pull the pitched ceiling into scale with the rest of the room. The roughly plastered end wall cleverly suggests a chalky cliff face.

▶ Solid shutters block light well, take up little space, and suit the simple lines of this rustic bedroom. On the walls, a coat of paint in warm dusty rose sets off the natural wood furniture.

▲ Avoid hanging elaborate, multi-colored pictures on busily patterned walls. In this room, a set of simple framed prints sits elegantly against a traditional wallpaper design of subtle stylized blooms on a muted gray-green ground.

PLANNING YOUR BATHROOM

- How often is your bathroom used and at what time of the day?

- Could you install additional facilities elsewhere in the house—a shower next to the bedroom, perhaps, a separate powder room, or a downstairs toilet?

- Is the existing plumbing system adequate? Is the water supplied at a high enough pressure and do you have enough hot water?

- Would it make sense to relocate the bathroom to another room?

- How much storage space will you need?

- Would you like to install new bathroom fixtures (bathtub, basin, and toilet)?

- What type of lighting will be appropriate for the room?

- Are there any special features, such as a new shower or a heated towel rack, that you would like to install?

- Does your bathroom have adequate heating and ventilation?

- Do you need to install another electric outlet?

- Do you need to make any special provisions for young children or an elderly person?

- Would you prefer a separate bathtub and shower?

- In a large bathroom, do you want to move the bathtub into the middle of the room, or install a raised floor for a sunken bathtub?

Often tucked into a tiny, awkward space and feeling cramped and claustrophobic, many bathrooms are a long way from being the havens of function and relaxation that they should be. Further design challenges are posed by inadequate storage, lack of natural light, and poor ventilation, making the bathroom one of the trickiest rooms in the whole house to get right.

Creating a bathroom that is right for you might mean overhauling the entire space—redesigning the original layout or installing new fixtures or flooring. You might even decide to relocate to another room. Sometimes, though, you can give your bathroom a new lease on life by making just one or two changes. Inject some color with a fresh coat of paint on the walls and some complementary tiles (see pp.154–155), replace the existing fixtures and add some stylish accessories to give your bathroom an instant facelift.

CASE STUDY: A PLACE FOR EVERYTHING
A functional, streamlined bathroom has been carved out of a narrow, awkwardly shaped space. The corner bathtub tucks neatly into the area in front of the window, while the vanity unit features plenty of storage space, including drawers that let you see their contents at a glance. There is also plenty of surface room on each side of the basin, a useful feature that is often overlooked, even in more spacious bathrooms. Enclosing the toilet tank and pipework has created an additional surface on top. The neutral decorative scheme and simple window shade help create a light and airy atmosphere. The chrome hardware, glass shelf, and large mirror also help to catch the light. Cheerful accessories bring welcome splashes of color and reinforce the mood of relaxation.

◀ Adding an internal window of glass bricks has helped open up a small bathroom that gets no natural light.

▶ In a bathroom occupying what would have once been a bedroom, the bathtub takes center stage. The heated towel rack is positioned so that warm towels are easily accessible from the bathtub.

BATHRROM PLAN

Maximizing all the available space, both horizontal and vertical, is the key to creating an efficient bathroom. With careful planning, a bathtub, shower, and storage space can all be tucked into the most compact space.

A central ceiling light provides overhead illumination. The bulb is enclosed for safety.

A shower stall with a space-saving inward-opening door has controls that are easily accessible and a showerhead that can be adjusted to suit the height of each user.

Ceramic tiles are used for protection by the bathtub; easy-to-wipe vinyl wallpaper has been hung above them.

A built-in floor-to-ceiling storage unit includes a lower cabinet for concealed storage and open shelving for items in regular use.

A compact bathtub with a nonslip surface tucks neatly between the shower and storage unit. A sturdy handrail has been installed.

A lockable wall-mounted cabinet keeps medicines and other items out of children's reach.

A heated towel rack keeps warm towels within easy reach of the bathtub and basin.

Mirror with lights positioned on each side to illuminate all the angles of the face. The shelf below keeps the edge of the basin clear of toiletries.

A deep, wide basin with a single-handle faucet has been positioned so that there is plenty of space to maneuver.

ORGANIZING THE SPACE

● To position a bathroom basin at the right height, cup your hands together in front of you, with your arms extended toward the floor and your shoulders straight. The height from the floor to your hands is the correct position for the plughole.

● A bathtub requires clearance equal to about its width.

● There should be an adequate gap between the rim of the toilet seat and a wall or other obstacle.

● Curved bathtubs and corner basins are designed to fit into dead spaces and awkwardly shaped rooms. Wall-hung toilets and basins free up valuable floor space.

Basins
Make sure there is enough space in front and at the sides so you can wash in comfort.

BATHROOM STYLE

FAUCETS

If you don't want to replace your fixtures, you can update your bathtub or basin with new modern or reproduction faucets available in a variety of styles and finishes.

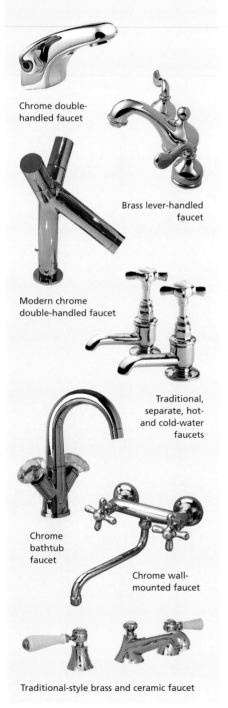

Chrome double-handled faucet

Brass lever-handled faucet

Modern chrome double-handled faucet

Traditional, separate, hot- and cold-water faucets

Chrome bathtub faucet

Chrome wall-mounted faucet

Traditional-style brass and ceramic faucet

Enhancing the perception of space and light is a consideration in any decorating decision. In a bathroom that has no natural light, you might consider adding an internal window or skylight, or even replacing a non-load-bearing wall with glass bricks. Reflective paint finishes, such as oil-base glossy or eggshell paint in cool, receding tones of aqua, blue, green, or lilac, will help to make a small, dingy bathroom appear brighter. You can also inject light with mirrors, ceramic tiles, chrome fixtures, and other shiny surfaces.

▲ Suggesting purity and cleanliness, a white scheme enhances the sense of airiness in a sunny bathroom, occupying what would originally have been a bedroom. Simple pieces of furniture dispel any hint of the sterility that can be associated with all-white bathrooms.

▶ The combination of brick trellis, slate, glass, terra cotta, and cool white cotton fabric at the main window brings interesting tonal and textural variation to a serene Mediterranean bathroom; vibrant color is provided by the red geraniums.

WALLS AND FLOORS

Practicality is the key when you are choosing wallcoverings and flooring for your bathroom. Wall treatments should be easy to clean and able to withstand the hot, steamy atmosphere. Paint is the easiest and most affordable option, but, to withstand the condensation, you must use a semigloss or glossy finish instead of a flat latex paint. Ceramic, glass, and mosaic tiles provide a good waterproof surface for walls, and they can be used in smaller amounts as protection around the bathtub and basin. Tongue-and-groove paneling is another good-looking choice and can be painted or treated with polyurethane varnish. Bare plaster walls sealed with a flat-finish varnish has a warm, rustic quality.

For floors, you should choose moistureproof materials, such as cork or cushioned vinyl, instead of jute-backed carpet, which can quickly show water marks and may rot if it gets wet. Some synthetic, foam-backed carpets and carpet tiles are specifically intended for bathroom use, but make sure they can be lifted up easily to dry if necessary. A non-slip rug or bath mat placed next to the bathtub or shower will provide warmth underfoot and help absorb any splashes.

▲ Although expensive, marble is a cool, sumptuous, and hardwearing material. In this pared-down bathroom, the marble bathtub and floor blend seamlessly together.

▶ Blue and white is a classic color combination for a bathroom. Here, a swimming-pool look is achieved by using small mosaic tiles on the floor and on the wall behind the walk-in shower. Although the bathroom is tucked into a small space with no windows, recessed ceiling halogen spotlights, a clear shower screen, and plenty of reflective surfaces create a bright and welcoming feeling in the room.

▲ Durable, waterproof, and warm underfoot, linoleum is available in sheet or tile form and in a host of colors and patterns. The colors of this geometric design have been chosen to complement the old-fashioned tub.

STORAGE

Every bathroom, regardless of its proportions, will function more smoothly and be more relaxing to be in if there is adequate storage for toiletries and other items. Things that are used on a daily basis should be kept close to where they are needed, on a stable surface so they won't topple over and spill. A built-in cabinet on the wall or under the washbasin will keep clutter out of sight, but some open storage, such as shelves or even a freestanding table, is also useful and can be used to display a collection of pretty bottles, ornaments, or plants. A mirrored bathroom cabinet near the washbasin is another practical option. Available in a range of styles and materials, some cabinets have additional features such as a fluorescent light or a small heater behind the mirror that prevents condensation from forming on it. Drawers are useful, since they allow you to see the contents easily. Medicine and disinfectant should always be stored well out of the reach of children, preferably in a cabinet with a childproof catch or lock.

◀ Floor-to-ceiling open storage featuring glass shelving makes good use of space in a compact bathroom. Other paraphernalia is swallowed up by the capacious mirrored cabinet.

▲ A built-in storage unit featuring cupboards and drawers uses up every inch of dead space underneath the basin.

STORAGE IDEAS

● Look for washbasins that feature integral storage. Some have drawers, a towel rod, and plenty of surface space on top.

● Built-in bathroom furniture conceals unsightly plumbing and provides useful storage.

● Organize bathroom toiletries in a rack hooked on a shower door.

● A slimline, mirror-fronted wall cabinet will swallow up plenty of bathroom clutter.

● Look for compact units that double as a laundry hamper and storage for towels.

● Attach clothes hooks or a wire storage rack to the door.

FIXTURES

Bathroom fixtures come in a huge choice of styles and finishes to suit every taste and budget. There is also a wide choice of fixtures that have been specifically designed to fit into small or awkwardly shaped rooms. If you are combining a bathtub and shower, choose a wide, flat-bottomed tub with a nonslip surface; a glass bath screen must be shatterproof. Otherwise, attractive plastic shower curtains are widely available and can be wiped clean or replaced easily. A wall-mounted chrome towel rack combines function with good looks.

▶ Compact matching sinks can be a worthwhile addition in a busy household. A large mirror such as that shown here serves both a practical and aesthetic role in a bathroom. Lights, with their bulbs enclosed and operated by a pull cord, should be positioned on each side of a mirror over a sink so they illuminate all the planes of the face.

◀ A lovely old roll-top bathtub with claw feet, an antique chair, and tongue-and-groove paneling combine in an elegant period bathroom. If you can't find original fixtures, good reproductions are on the market. A shelf and paneling can be used to hide the plumbing.

▲ You can give your bathroom an instant facelift with colorful accessories that help create a visual link with the overall scheme. Here, towels and other finishing touches have been carefully chosen to pick out the zingy colors of the wall tiles and cabinet.

HALLS AND STAIRCASES

DOOR HARDWARE

Breathe new life into a tired door with a choice of traditional or modern hardware.

Plastic lever handle and key plate

Chrome knob

Chrome and brushed aluminum lever handle

Brass knob

Pewter knob

Classic brass lever handle and key plate

Pewter knob

Wood and steel knob and key plate

Modern steel and plastic lever handle

Brass lever handle

Steel and plastic door pull

Classic brass door plate

Classic brass door pull

As the main artery of a home and usually the first thing you see on entering, a hallway can set the tone and atmosphere for the rest of the house. Assess the impact your hall makes by looking at it from different angles—from the front door, from the top of the stairs—and at different times of the day. Decide whether it is warm and inviting or cold and unwelcoming. Does the decorative scheme tie in with the rooms leading off it, or does the space feel disconnected from the rest of the house?

Are there any interesting decorative features that can be capitalized on—an appealing archway or balustrade, perhaps, or wood paneling, fretwork, or molding? Elements such as these can make eye-catching focal points and can often provide inspiration for the whole scheme. Where halls flow into open-plan living spaces, it might be sensible to carry color through. However, because halls are spaces to pass through, instead of linger in, you can use stronger colors than you might in other areas of your home.

◄ The tiled floor is in keeping with the period feel of this Victorian hallway, but carpet is a safer and less noisy choice for the stairs. The sunny half-landing with its uncurtained sash window serves as a pleasant stopping point when you are going up or down the stairs.

► A light, simple decorative scheme helps to open up a small, windowless hall, and it allows the elegant spiral staircase to become the main focus of attention. Note how the framed pictures pick out the wood of the banister and have been carefully arranged to follow the curve of the staircase.

◄ With a table and chairs, welcoming table lamps, and flowers and paintings lining the way, this wide galleried hall leads you from the outside world into the main area of the house.

▲ Continuing the same color scheme and flooring in the rooms leading off the hall helps to create a visual link between the different areas of the house, so there are no jarring contrasts.

Removing some of the doors has also helped to open up the space, making the rooms an extension of the hall. The shiny chrome coatstand is a lighter, stylish alternative to a wooden version.

STAIRCASES

● Hard floor surfaces are durable and relatively easy to keep clean, but they can be noisy. Polished wood stairs can be slippery, and they can be dangerous in homes where there are young children or elderly people.

● Carpet is soft underfoot and has sound- and heat-insulating properties, but make sure it is designed for heavy traffic and is firmly tacked to the stairs. Many types of carpet quickly show marks, so avoid very pale colors; a softly patterned carpet will show less dirt than a plain one.

● Light the top and bottom of the stairs for safety.

● Changing levels with a single step can be dangerous. Two steps are safer. Consider changing the color or texture of the floor to help the eye notice the difference. Where three or more stairs are needed, there should be a handrail for safety.

● Do not position uplighters on a staircase or lower landing where the source of light can cause dangerous glare when descending the stairs.

PLANNING YOUR HOME OFFICE

Once you have assessed your requirements, you need to organize your space for maximum comfort and efficiency. Try to choose a spot that is quiet, with enough room to house your equipment and storage, as well as your desk and chair. If you can set up an office in a separate, dedicated room, it is a good idea to accommodate an additional work surface. It's also a bonus to have somewhere that gets plenty of natural light, although you will still need to provide adequate artificial lighting. In dual-purpose rooms, where an office is tucked into the corner of a bedroom, for example, a screen will help to separate the two areas. Items that are in constant use need to be easily accessible from your desk, and for every item of furniture, always allow enough space for convenient use and clearance.

CASE STUDY: ATTIC ROOM

A compact but ergonomically sound home office has been tucked in an awkward space under the eaves. The desk, which has been custom-built to fit the full width of the attic, offers a good, deep work surface on top and plenty of legroom underneath. Instead of built-in drawers, sleek box files store office paraphernalia and fit neatly under the sloping ceiling. Dormer windows have been added to allow natural light to flood into the room, while a wall-mounted spotlight provides additional light for evening work.

ORGANIZING YOUR SPACE

Once you have decided on your priorities, you need to design a practical and comfortable working area. With thought, this is possible in even the most confined space and need not be prohibitively expensive. Create a floor plan of the space, indicating where all the main pieces of furniture are to go (see pp.74–75). You should mark on your plan such things as light fixtures and electrical outlets, and indicate the position of windows, doors, and items attached to the walls such as cupboards and shelves. Arrange storage so that frequently used items are easily accessible and remember to allow at least 40 in (1 m) in front of a filing cabinet or shelves for easy access.

HOME OFFICE PLAN

Plan your office with your working practices in mind, with easy access to furniture and accessories.

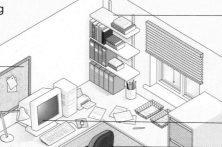

Place a bulletin board for notes in easy sight of your desk.

Uplighters provide wide-angle light that reflects off the ceiling.

Outlets are required for all your equipment.

A desk lamp is a vital part of equipment. Its light should not reflect off your screen.

Place your telephone on the left of your keyboard if you are right-handed, on the right if you are left-handed.

Easy-access shelves are important for books and files that you use every day.

Your computer screen should be directly behind your keyboard and straight in front of you.

An ergonomically sound office chair is vital. If you have a model with arms, you should make sure they will fit comfortably under the desk.

A tall filing cabinet is a very useful item for files and reference material that is not in daily use.

Keep your wastebasket close by, but not so you bump into it.

▲ The desk in this stylish, sun-filled home office has been correctly positioned at a right angle to avoid glare, while a gooseneck lamp provides good task lighting on dark days. As the desk has no integral drawers, day-to-day storage is housed in the portable deep boxes on the floor.

WORKING IN COMFORT

Paying attention to the ergonomics of your home office will help povide long-term comfort, health, and productivity.

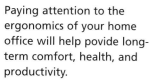

● Invest in a good, adjustable chair that will support your lower back. For stability, choose a model with five legs.

● For easy access, allow at least 3 ft (90 cm) between your chair and a wall or piece of furniture so you can get in and out easily.

● The height of a work surface should be between 23 and 28 in (58 and 71 cm). If you use a computer, make sure the desk is deep enough for both keyboard and monitor to be in front of you instead of on one side, which can cause neck strain.

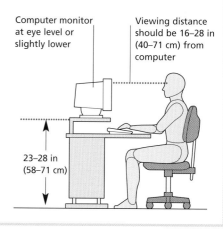

Computer monitor at eye level or slightly lower

Viewing distance should be 16–28 in (40–71 cm) from computer

23–28 in (58–71 cm)

HOME OFFICE STYLE

STORAGE

Office furniture suppliers are a good source of flexible storage for a home office. You can change the color of some units, such as a filing cabinet, with car spray paint.

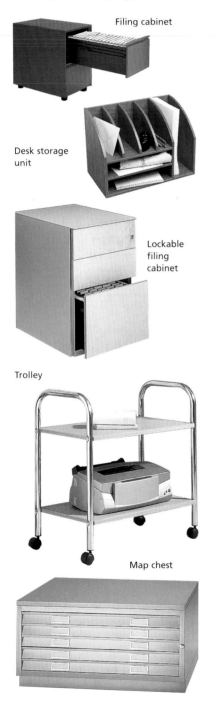

Filing cabinet

Desk storage unit

Lockable filing cabinet

Trolley

Map chest

The way your home office looks and the impression it creates are an important consideration. However, you need to strike the right balance between comfort and practicality. Garish colors and fussy furnishings are not conducive to hours of concentrated work, but you do not want to reproduce the gray functionality of a corporate office. For walls and ceilings, neutrals and such shades as soft greens or pale blues are easy on the eye and will complement traditional and modern office furniture. Choose a plain, hardwearing surface, such as wood or flat-pile carpet, for the floor covering. You can personalize your space and inject splashes of more vibrant color with stylish storage and accessories or an eye-catching rug.

◄ The storage requirements in this well-organized home office have been cleverly thought through. Papers and other office paraphernalia are stored in box files, which have been chosen to match the calm, neutral tones of the room. An aluminum can houses rolls of oversized papers.

▲ This compact cabinet has been custom-made to house a mini office, complete with computer, fax machine, and plenty of storage space. Even a wastepaper basket has been tucked inside. At the end of the day, the keyboard tray slides away and the doors are closed to conceal the contents.

▲ In an office set in a separate building in the backyard, splashes of color teamed with pictures and photographs provide inspiration during the working day. A pedestal unit can be wheeled out to provide an additional surface.

◄ A home office has been tucked into an alcove under the stairs. The strong blue defines the office area, and complements the surrounding scheme. Color-coordinated accessories are stored on the open shelves and trolleys.

UTILITY ROOMS

USEFUL STORAGE

There are plenty of attractive, sensible storage options available, including modular shelving, which is inexpensive and allows you add to it as your needs change.

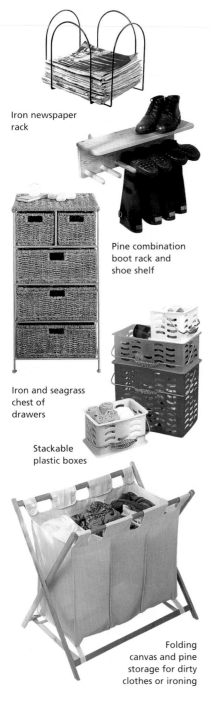

Iron newspaper rack

Pine combination boot rack and shoe shelf

Iron and seagrass chest of drawers

Stackable plastic boxes

Folding canvas and pine storage for dirty clothes or ironing

If there is no obvious place for a utility room, explore the potential of underused areas such as a cellar or shed. A cool, dry garage could be the ideal place to store wine, foodstuffs bought in bulk, recycling boxes, or even out-of-season clothes. If you are altering the layout of your home, dividing a bedroom into a bathroom and a utility/laundry room is a useful arrangement. If your utility room is on the first floor, an adjoining "mud" room allows you to separate dirty shoes and outdoor items from cleaner, indoor items.

▲ Sometimes a utility area can share quarters with other activities. Here, a quiet corner of a study is used as a place for ironing. The large wicker baskets, whichallow air to circulate, and gingham-covered ironing board have been chosen to blend with the rustic style of the room.

▶ Open storage allows you to see at a glance where objects are and reach them easily. Industrial-style shelving such as this can be adjusted to accommodate different-size items. Wall brackets keep the ironing board away from the floor where it could easily topple over.

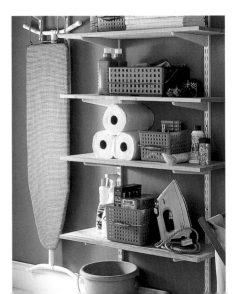

◄ Having a separate space where you can attend to the laundry or store household items, such as a vacuum cleaner, ironing board, and cleaning products, can be an invaluable addition to a busy household, helping to take the strain off the kitchen and keeping other areas of the house free from clutter. This well-organized laundry room features plenty of closed storage, with a large surface on top for folding clothes, a double sink with wall-mounted faucets, and an overhead drying rack.

▼ Laundry facilities are housed in a compact cupboard, built to ceiling height to provide space for storing towels or clothes on top. When not in use, the stacked washing and drying machines are hidden from view by the door.

SAFETY

● Never attempt to reroute wiring or install plumbing yourself. Always use a professional electrician or plumber.

● Electric outlets should be positioned well away from water.

● Make sure plenty of cool air can circulate around electrical appliances.

● An iron should have a separate, easily accessible outlet positioned at the same height as the ironing board to make sure wires don't trail and that the plug can be easily disconnected when not in use.

● Floors must be level and structurally sound to carry the weight of heavy appliances such as washing machines or freezers.

● Store tools, detergents, and cleaning products well out of the reach of children, ideally in a locked cupboard. It might be a good idea to have a lock installed on the utility-room door itself.

TOOLS, MATERIALS, AND TECHNIQUES

ARMED WITH FRESH INSPIRATION for transforming your home, and with a clearer idea of the style you would like to achieve, you are now ready to put your ideas into practice. This chapter will guide you through the stages of home decorating, showing you how to tackle essential techniques such as painting, wallpapering, and tiling. Illustrated with clear photographs and accompanied by easy-to-follow instructions and expert advice, there are step-by-step instructions covering everything from color washing and laying vinyl tiles to making your own window shades or slipcovers. Directory spreads give a summary of each of the projects, highlighting the tools that will be needed and offering guidance on how long the work will take and the level of skill required.

Covering painting, wallpapering, tiling, flooring, working with wood, and textiles, this chapter gives pertinent advice on preparation and planning for each task to make sure the projects run smoothly and are completed successfully.

PAINTING DIRECTORY

PAINTING: PREPARATION AND PLANNING

SKILL LEVEL Low
TIME FRAME 1 day per room
SPECIAL TOOLS Electric sander
SEE PAGES 120–121

Preparing and planning for any painting project ensures that the finish is hardwearing and attractive. Preparation is always the least appealing part of any type of home improvement project, but it is essential and must be looked on as part of the project. In most situations where a painting project does not live up to expectations, it is the result of poor planning and preparation. You should plan the order of the work before you start painting, so that you can plan efficiently and make use of any labor-saving items such as electric sanders to reduce the amount of time necessary for preparation.

You should make sure that paint cannot be splashed or sprayed onto areas that are not supposed to be painted. To prevent this, remove as much of the furniture as possible from the room, and cover any furniture that has to stay with drop cloths. Take up and remove any rugs and carpets, or cover them with drop cloths. Make sure that drop cloths extend to the edge of the floor, taping them to the baseboards if necessary.

Fill any holes or cracks with the appropriate filler for the job, and wash down all the surfaces—this may need to be done before and after filling—to remove any impurities that could react with the paint.

If there are any stubborn stains or marks that cannot be removed, cover them with a shellac-base primer to stop the marks from bleeding through the new paint finish.

PAINTING SEQUENCE

SKILL LEVEL Low
TIME FRAME 1 day (depending on room size)
SPECIAL TOOLS None
SEE PAGES 122–123

When painting a room, you should first prepare the wall surfaces (see pp.120–121) before you plan the order of painting. You can save time, and achieve a better finish, by following a simple order of work. Begin with the larger room surfaces—the ceiling, then the walls. Once these have been painted, you should turn your attention to the smaller, more ornate surfaces, including the doors, windows, and any moldings such as baseboards, picture and chair rails, and door frames. It is usually easier to paint clear defining lines between wooden features and walls and ceilings if the wooden features are painted last.

Always start at the top of the room and work down, because, no matter how careful you are, some overspray is inevitable and it will always fall toward the lower surfaces. By working from the top down, any spills from above will be covered as you paint the lower areas.

As well as following the correct order for the room as a whole, features such as doors and windows require a specific order of work to make sure that no sections are missed as you apply each coat of paint. Applying the paint correctly will guarantee a consistent finish and ensure that each of the different sections or parts of the door or window are clearly defined.

PAINTING AWKWARD PLACES

SKILL LEVEL Low to medium
TIME FRAME Depends on the size of the job
SPECIAL TOOLS Extension pole, radiator roller, paint shield
SEE PAGES 124–125

Inevitably, not all areas in a room are easy to reach. You will, therefore, have to devise various mechanisms and techniques to get into awkward spaces. To paint these areas successfully, you need to improve your access to them, and to make sure that you have the correct equipment and tools for the job, often ones that are designed to deal with detailed or precision painting.

Many access problems are due to height, either of walls, ceilings, or windows, so you may need to use a stepladder or other type of ladder, some

Paintbrushes

Soft-bristle brush

Artist's paintbrush

Masking tape

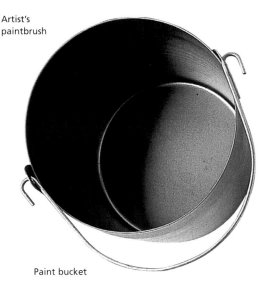

Paint bucket

of which can fold into a platform. If you want to avoid or limit the use of ladders, tools such as extension poles can help you extend your reach. You can attach a pole to a paint roller in order to gain access to high areas and ceilings while you remain standing safely on the floor.

If you are unable to remove the radiators in a room before painting, a custom-made radiator roller is ideal for painting the wall surface behind them. Another labor-saving device that helps improve accuracy and detail is a paint shield. This tool is particularly useful when you are painting next to glass because any paint overspill will hit the shield, not the glass. This can save time and energy that would otherwise be spent removing paint from the glass.

PAINTING FURNITURE

SKILL LEVEL Low to medium
TIME FRAME 2 hours
SPECIAL TOOLS Stamps
SEE PAGES 126–127

The rules for painting walls and woodwork apply to painting furniture; the only difference is that the project is on a much smaller scale. To achieve the best possible paint finish, remember to follow the order of work and ensure that the item of furniture receives the correct number of coats of paint.

Preparation is just as important so that the paint you apply is readily accepted by a smooth surface. You may need to remove all traces of previous coatings, especially if the furniture has been waxed or varnished in the past.

You can choose a paint color to link the furniture to other areas of the room. Painting your furniture is an ideal way of integrating the items into the room scheme as a whole.

Stamps and stencils can be used as decoration, and will give greater interest to the finished effect. You can also give the furniture a special paint effect to make it look aged or distressed. This will give a more lived-in look. For the best results, you should protect the painted finish with wax or a coat of varnish. To maintain a lasting finish on furniture that receives a lot of everyday wear and tear, such as kitchen chairs, it is a good idea to apply extra coats of wax or varnish to the surface from time to time.

METALLIC PAINT CRAFTS: ANTIQUE METAL

SKILL LEVEL Low to medium
TIME FRAME 2 hours, not including drying time
SPECIAL TOOLS
SEE PAGE

The development of metallic paints has opened up a new area of decorative painting techniques. You can use these paints to completely change the appearance of household objects, although you should consider the relatively high cost of metallic paint, which makes it more desirable to use it sparingly on small features or items instead of across wide, open surface areas such as on entire walls and ceilings.

You can leave a metallic finish as plain metal, or create a further effect by adding a craqueleure finish to give it a more distressed appearance. Enhance the craqueleure finish by painting on burnt umber to highlight the cracks in the finished surface, if desired. When applying burnt umber to the craqueleure, take care to wipe away any excess color before it dries, so the burnt umber is left only in the cracks in the finish.

METALLIC PAINT CRAFTS: VERDIGRIS

SKILL LEVEL Low to medium
TIME FRAME 4 hours for an average-size room, not including drying time
SPECIAL TOOLS Stencil brushes
SEE PAGE 129

Verdigris is different from most metallic paint effects in that you are trying to re-create the effect of oxidized or weathered metal instead of shiny, polished metal. The effect is particularly well suited to ornamental or strongly molded features such as a cornice in a room at the junction between the walls and ceiling. By using a number of different coats of glaze, applied in the correct order, you can produce a verdigris effect that looks like the genuine deterioration of copper, brass, or bronze.

Many manufacturers supply the different paint colors required for this finish in kit form. You can, however, mix your own colors by using normal acrylic glaze and standard colorizers. If you are mixing your own colors, take time to examine a picture of verdigris in order to accurately match the different shades and tones of the real thing.

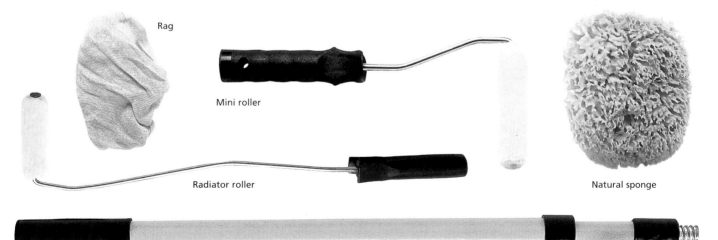

Rag

Mini roller

Radiator roller

Natural sponge

Extension pole

STENCILING WALLS AND FLOORS

SKILL LEVEL Low to medium
TIME FRAME 1 day for an average-size room
SPECIAL TOOLS Wax pencil, utility knife, stencil brushes
SEE PAGES 130–131

Using stencils on both the walls and floors in a room is a simple way of producing a well-integrated scheme. Much of the pleasure of stenciling can be derived from making your own stencils. To make a stencil, simply draw a design onto a sheet of acetate, using a wax pencil, then carefully cut out the design with a utility knife.

Border stencils are particularly effective used around the lower levels of walls or the perimeter of floors, where they can act as a frame for other decoration in the room. There are any number of combinations of stencils and patterns that you can use on walls and floors, and you can use one or more colors. It is worth experimenting with various colors on some scrap paper so that you are sure of your choice before you start on the wall or floor surface.

STENCILING FURNITURE

SKILL LEVEL Low to medium
TIME FRAME ½ to 1 day
SPECIAL TOOLS Stencil brushes, artist's paintbrush
SEE PAGES 132–133

A furniture stenciling project needs to be approached in much the same way as you would any other painting job. You must carefully prepare the surfaces and apply the correct number of coats of paint to give a sound base for the stencils. Only then should you think about applying your stencil design.

Many manufacturers produce groups of stencils that are designed to be used together to form an overall stencil picture or pattern. However, there is a certain amount of flexibility in this design idea—you can either follow the manufacturer's instructions exactly, or you can vary them to add your own personal touch. Whatever choice you make, it is important to take time to position the stencils before applying the paint and to pay careful attention to detail. Using color with a greater intensity in particular places on the stencil can create a more three-dimensional effect, and employing an artist's paintbrush for fine detailing can be very effective.

COLOR WASHING WALLS

SKILL LEVEL Low
TIME FRAME 1 day for an average-size room
SPECIAL TOOLS Badger-hair or soft-bristle brush
SEE PAGE 134

Color washing is a relatively simple paint effect that uses a tinted glaze to produce a restful and textured color tint on a wall surface. You create texture by the method used to apply the glaze, and its coarseness depends on how much you soften this application.

Color washing requires a light color base coat of emulsion paint, which works as the background for the glaze. It is a particularly good paint finish for rough or uneven wall surfaces, because the color tends to be picked up more clearly within the grainy texture of such walls. To increase the depth of this effect, you can apply more than one coat of color wash.

COLOR RUBBING WOOD

SKILL LEVEL Low
TIME FRAME 1 day for woodwork in an average-size room
SPECIAL TOOLS None
SEE PAGE 135

This paint effect is similar to color washing, except that color rubbing is applied to wooden surfaces. Diluted water-base paint or a tinted glaze is applied to bare wooden surfaces, allowing the grain of the wood to pick up the pigment of the glaze. In this way, a stained-wood appearance is achieved, with the grain highlighted in your chosen color.

When color rubbing items such as wooden picture rails, try to color rub them before securing them to the wall, because the color rubbing process will be much easier. Once decorated, use bonding adhesive to attach the items, so no mechanical fasteners are required, which might spoil the effect. Color rubbing is a particularly good paint effect to use in combination with color washing—the two together provide a well-integrated decorative scheme.

Paint roller handle and sleeve

Stippling brush

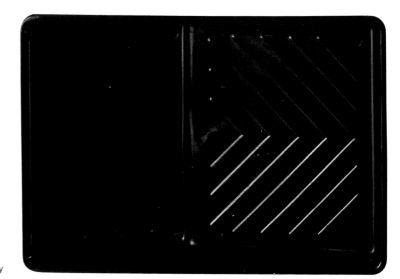

Roller tray

MARBLING

SKILL LEVEL High
TIME FRAME 1 to 2 days for an average-size room
SPECIAL TOOLS Stippling brush, soft-bristle brush, artist's paintbrush
SEE PAGES 136–137

Marbling is a difficult paint effect to achieve. However, with practice, you can use it to produce very decorative finishes throughout your home. You should always follow the step-by-step instructions carefully. Never be tempted to skip any of the steps, otherwise, you will not be able to produce an authentic marbled finish. Before attempting a large area, it is best to master the technique on a slightly less ambitious project.

As with many paint effects, it helps to have an extra pair of hands to help with the marbling—if the glaze dries before you have time to apply the effect, you may have to start the process all over again. You will need to use several types of brushes to produce a marbled effect, so make sure you already have them at hand before you start the project.

RAGGING AND RAG ROLLING

SKILL LEVEL Low to medium
TIME FRAME 1 day for an average-size room
SPECIAL TOOLS Cotton rags
SEE PAGES 138–139

Ragging or rag rolling uses tinted glaze. Like most paint effects, the glaze may be applied with rags or painted on the wall with a paintbrush before the rag is applied to the surface to create patterns or impressions.

Although both ragging and rag rolling are created with the same tool—rags—the two effects are markedly different. Ragging alone provides a highly textured paint finish, whereas rag rolling turns this finish into a more directional effect. To make decorative striped patterns on wall surfaces by rag rolling, mask off areas before applying the glaze; then remove the masking tape to reveal the striped pattern. The masking technique illustrated on page 139 is just one example of how this design works. The same principle can be applied in various other ways to produce a variety of very individual finishes.

STIPPLING

SKILL LEVEL Low to medium
TIME FRAME 1 day for an average-size room
SPECIAL TOOLS Stippling brushes
SEE PAGES 140–141

Stippling is a simple textured paint effect produced by using a specially designed brush to make small impressions in a glazed surface. It can mimic the textured look of velvet. You can use more than one color on a wall surface—blend or change them according to your personal choice.

Patience is required to achieve an even finish when using a stippling brush. Corners need particular care; it is easiest to use a smaller stippling brush to get right into the corner.

CREATING DECOUPAGE

SKILL LEVEL Low to medium
TIME FRAME 2 to 4 hours (depending on project size)
SPECIAL TOOLS None
SEE PAGES 142–143

Although not strictly a paint technique, decoupage wall effects tend to require a painted background in order to show them off to their best advantage. You can add your own completely individual touch to a room's decoration with decoupage.

Secure your design on the wall with spray adhesive, then cover the design with several coats of varnish to protect it. Or, instead of using spray adhesive, adhere the designs to the wall with a standard wallpaper paste made up in a diluted consistency (similar to the mixture required for hanging lining paper).

As well as creating designs on walls, you can use decoupage on items of furniture. This option is especially attractive if you want to link the pattern or design on the wall surfaces with the furnishings in the room to integrate the whole room scheme. For example, copying the design used on wall surfaces onto the top of a coffee table looks great. If you do this, you should cover the design on the tabletop with a sheet of glass (have a glazier make it for you) to give the decoupage finish added protection. If you do use a sheet of glass, make sure that it has a beveled edge so that there are no sharp edges.

Sanding block

Sandpaper

Caulking gun

Electric sander

Stippling brushes

PAINTING: PREPARATION AND PLANNING

With all painting projects, it is vital to take time to prepare and plan the procedures so that you achieve the best possible finish. Although preparation and planning are undoubtedly the least interesting aspects of decorating, they are the processes that frequently make the biggest contribution to the quality of the end result. As well as preparing the surfaces you want to paint, it is equally important to protect those surfaces that you want to keep free from paint. You should clear the room of as much furniture and upholstered furnishings as possible, cover items that cannot be moved with drop cloths, and mask items such as outlets to protect them from splashes of paint.

A poor finish on a newly painted surface can be the result of various factors, but in the majority of cases it is due to lack of filling and sanding, or inadequate washing down of the surfaces before starting to paint. Dirt and grime cannot simply be covered over with a coat of paint, because they will always bleed through the paint eventually and spoil the finish. Washing down walls and woodwork will ensure that you have a sound surface for painting before you begin.

Another consideration is whether any major construction work needs to. be carried out before you paint. Any rerouting of pipes or cables is better done before you start to redecorate—this type of work will leave patches on the walls that will need redecoration.

In the same way, decide whether pictures or shelves will be staying in the same place on the wall. If they are going to be moved, take them down, remove any hardware from the wall surface, and fill the holes as necessary before you start painting. The shelves or pictures can then be repositioned once the decorating is finished.

MASKING UP

1 If carpets have to remain in place during decoration, ensure that they are well covered with drop cloths. It is worth securing the cloths to the baseboards by using masking tape around the edge of the room, so that there is no danger of the cloths creeping away from the walls.

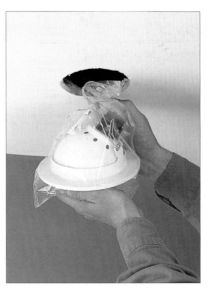

2 You should mask light fittings before painting near them, but first turn off the electricity at the service panel. Ceiling spotlights can often be lowered and covered; mask them in a plastic bag while you are painting. Remove door handles, or mask them and other fittings such as electrical outlets, using masking tape.

FILLING AND SANDING

1 All small holes and cracks in wall surfaces should be filled with an all-purpose filler. Cut away the crumbly edges of wall cracks using a utility knife. Dust out any loose material and wet the crack and edges with some water applied with an old paintbrush.

2 Mix up some all-purpose filler to a smooth but firm consistency. Load the filler on to a putty knife and apply it to the crack. The flexibility of the knife blade should allow you to press the filler firmly into the crack. Do it as neatly as possible to reduce the amount of sanding needed once the filler has dried.

3 When the filler is dry, sand the area to a smooth finish. A hand-held electric sander is ideal for this purpose, making the job much faster. For deep holes in the wall surface, you may need more than one application of filler.

WASHING DOWN

All surfaces must be washed down before painting. This can be done before or after filling. Use a mild detergent solution to remove any dirt or grime from the surface. After this, wash down and rinse the surfaces with clean, warm water.

FLEXIBLE FILLING

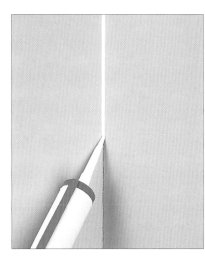

Where cracks have appeared in corners, it is best to use a flexible filler instead of an all-purpose one. Use a caulking gun to apply the filler (which comes in a tube) to the crack. Smooth the filler with a wet fingertip before it dries (you cannot sand this type of filler).

STAINING

Occasionally, you will come across areas or stains on the wall surface that do not disappear during the washing down. These must be sealed before painting, or they may bleed through the new paint. Spray or brush on a proprietary sealer in these areas to neutralize the stain.

PAINTING SEQUENCE

Following a specific order of work when painting a room will ensure the best use of both your time and energy. As a rule, it is best to work from the top down, painting the ceiling and wall surfaces before moving on to the other surfaces such as doors, windows, and baseboards. This is because it is much easier to paint a straight line along woodwork edges at the junction they make with ceilings or walls instead of the other way around. In order to achieve a good finish on your painted surface, always allow enough drying time between the coats of paint. When painting doors and windows, follow a regimented order, particularly when applying two or more coats of paint—in this way, you will not miss any areas because you cannot remember, or cannot see, which ones have been painted several times and which still need another coat.

ROOM ORDER OF WORK

One of the most important reasons for beginning at the top of a room and working down is to avoid repeating work marred by paint splashes. By painting the ceiling first, especially if you are using a roller, any paint that falls on adjacent surfaces can be painted over when you reach them. If you work the other way around, finishing the lower levels first, you will probably spill paint on the finished areas when you paint the ceiling, which could ruin the finish on the lower levels. A good order of work avoids this problem. The diagram on the right shows the order in which you should paint the features.

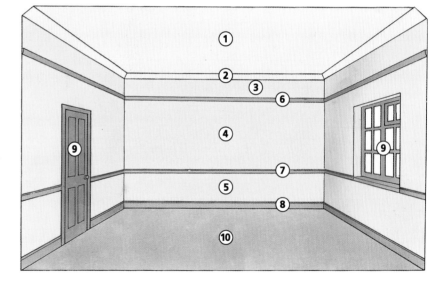

HELPFUL HINTS

When estimating the quantity of paint needed for a job, always refer to the manufacturer's guidelines on the side of the can. Unsealed surfaces such as new plaster walls will require more paint to cover them than repainting a painted surface. The first coat of paint on a surface will use more than the second or subsequent coats. The amount will also vary according to the type of paint you are using. As a rule, water-base, or latex, paints go much further than alkyd ones.

1 Begin with the ceiling. If using a roller, start on one side of the ceiling and work to the opposite side. Cut in (paint into the angle) with a paintbrush around the edge.

2 Continue on to the coving or cornice. Cut in precisely on the top edge along the ceiling, the lower edge can overlap onto the wall.

3, **4**, and **5** Once the ceiling is done, work down the walls. Cut in a precise line with the wall and coving and do the same at the chair rails, baseboards, and other moldings.

6, **7**, and **8** Paint or stain picture and chair rails and baseboards, working down the wall surface. Cut in at the junction with the wall surface.

9 Paint doors and windows. Cut in around the junctions of moldings and window frames with the wall.

10 If required, paint the floor surface last of all.

HOW TO PAINT A PANEL DOOR

Panel doors are a common door design, and, as with other surfaces, you will need to follow a strict order of work when painting one. In this way, all the areas will be painted with an equal number of coats of paint, ensuring the best possible finished result. Remove the door handles or any other door hardware before you start painting. This also gives you the opportunity to clean them before you reposition them on the door after the paint has dried. Or mask off the hardware, using plastic bags and low-tack masking tape.

The illustration at right shows the order in which all the separate components that make up the door structure should be painted to provide the best results. As you progress across the door surface, keep inspecting for runs or drips of paint, especially at the corners of the panels. Brush them out as necessary.

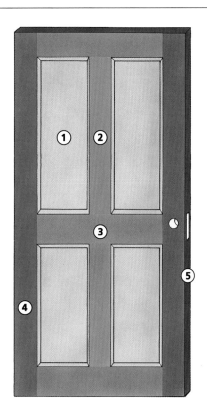

1 Start by painting the panels, working from the top down. Paint the panel moldings at this stage. Some doors may have more than the four panels shown here. Simply begin at the top levels and work down.

2 Continue on to the central vertical stiles, thus linking the panels.

3 Move on to the horizontal rails, working from the top down, thereby finishing the central area of the door.

4 Finish the face of the door by painting the two outer stiles.

5 Finish by painting the top and side edge of the door as required. Once these are painted, you can paint the door frame.

HOW TO PAINT A CASEMENT WINDOW

Windows require even greater precision than doors because there should be a well-defined dividing line between the rabbets and the glass surface. The best plan is to divide the window into sections. Start each section with the rabbets next to the glass and gradually work away to the outer areas of the window frame.

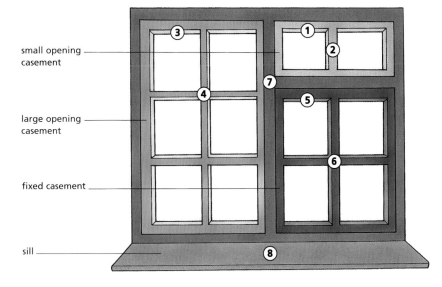

small opening casement

large opening casement

fixed casement

sill

HELPFUL HINTS

● There are various tools, such as window shields (see p.125), on the market that make painting windows easier. There are also brushes with angled heads, which make it easier to paint window rebates—the shape allows better access into the corner of the rebates, next to the glass.

● If any paint does splash onto the window surface, allow it to dry and then remove it with the aid of a specially designed window scraper.

1 and **2** Start with the rabbets on the small casement window at the top, then paint the rails.

3 and **4** Paint the rabbets, then the rails on the large opening casement window.

5 and **6** Paint the rabbets, then the rails on the fixed casement.

7 Paint the main frame.

8 Before painting the sill, wipe with a cloth dampened in mineral spirits.

PAINTING AWKWARD PLACES

YOU WILL NEED

Extension pole and brush
with extended handle
Scrap cloth and masking
tape
Radiator brush, cardboard,
and low-tack masking tape
Thin cardboard or paint
shield
Small paintbrush
Artist's paintbrush

Not all surfaces are easy to paint, either because of limited access or a problem with the actual surface itself. Many of these problems can be overcome by simply applying a very methodical approach to your work. However, there are also a variety of different tools available that can help to deal with restricted access and unusual surfaces. It is also worth considering using products that can speed up work such as items that will shield or protect areas that you do not wish to come in contact with the paint. You should try to plan ahead of time so that you'll have on hand any of the devices that will help you to tackle your project.

DEALING WITH HEIGHT

1 Extension rods are an ideal labor-saving device, because they eliminate the need for a ladder when you have to paint ceilings or the top area of wall surfaces. Before buying an extension rod, you should make sure that its threads are compatible with the roller handle you are using for painting.

2 Once the top area of a wall has been rollered, it is still necessary to finish off around the edge. The technique for this procedure is known as "cutting in." Brushes that have extended angled heads are ideal for this purpose, because you can continue to paint while still standing at floor level.

PROTECTING WALLS

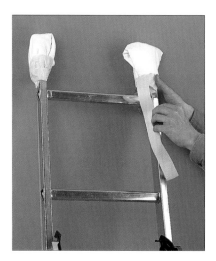

In particularly high areas, such as stairwells, you will almost certainly need to use a ladder to gain access to the higher points. Protect wall surfaces from the top edges of the ladder by binding them with cloth and securing them in place with masking tape.

HELPFUL HINTS

Ladder technology has now reached the stage where it is no longer necessary to purchase a number of separate ladders for different uses around the home. For exteriors you may still need to use longer extension ladders, but for interiors you can now buy combination ladders that are specially designed to fold into stepladders, normal extension ladders, or even working platforms. It is worth spending extra money on these items to ensure good quality, and the time-saving and space-saving benefits will far outweigh the burden of the initial investment.

RADIATORS

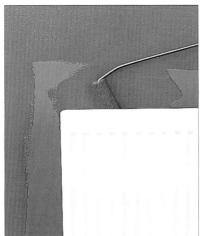

1 Ideally, radiators should be removed so that you can decorate behind them, but this does require plumbing knowledge. Also, in many cases, the radiator may be too awkward to move. In these instances, use a proprietary radiator roller to paint the wall surface behind it.

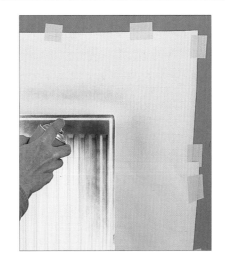

2 Make sure the radiator is turned off before you start painting it. Aerosol paints are quick and easy to use on radiators, but be sure to wear a respirator mask, and protect the wall from any overspray by taping an oversize sheet of cardboard behind it.

SHIELDING TIPS

Speed up the painting of pipes that are next to the wall by using a piece of cardboard to protect the wall surface as you move along the pipe. Move the cardboard with one hand as you apply paint with the other.

Windows are always time-consuming to paint, mainly because it is necessary to cut in neatly around the edge of the glass. Speed up the process by using a paint shield, holding it at the woodwork/glass junction, so that any overspill goes on the shield instead of the glass.

DEALING WITH DETAIL

1 Picking out any particular details in architectural features within a room, such as the detail found in a cornice or coving, can take a long time. You can speed up the painting process by using the base coat or undercoat as a background color for all additional colors used.

2 Use a small artist's paintbrush to paint in the detailed features, completing one color at a time as you progress across the molded surface. This type of painting does take time, but the attractive finish is certainly well worth all the effort.

PAINTING FURNITURE

YOU WILL NEED
....

Coarse and fine-grade
sandpaper
Cloth
Paintbrush
Stamp(s)
Stamp roller
Fine-grade steel wool

MATERIALS
....

Latex paint
Stamp paint
Clear wax

A coat of paint is a simple way to revive an old piece of furniture or provide a different effect for a new one. There are a number of options available when considering painting. Depending on the look you want, these range from using several coats of paint to produce a precise new finish to achieving a distressed appearance by masking and/or sanding the piece of furniture between coats. In this example, the distressed look has been used to revive an old painted chair.

Stamps can be used as an additional embellishment to give a decorative finish. Choosing colors and the stamp design is a matter of personal preference, but always consider the color scheme in the room where the piece of furniture will be placed. It is very easy to get carried away with stamps and "overdo" their use, so try to refrain from covering the whole chair with stamps—using a simple design and pattern often produces the best result on furniture.

Painting furniture is a perfect way to soften a room's color scheme and integrate chairs and other items into the overall design.

1 Sand the whole chair completely with coarse-grade sandpaper, then with a finer grade. This removes any flaky or loose old paint layers and provides a key for the application of new paint. Wipe down the chair with a damp, clean cloth to remove any dust from the surface.

2 Working from the top down, apply a coat of emulsion paint to all parts of the chair, ensuring good, even coverage. Once the first coat has dried, apply a second coat to even out the finish. During application, keep inspecting the work to ensure that there are no runs in the paint finish. Brush them out, if necessary.

3 Apply stamp paint to the stamp using a roller. Ensure that the whole face of the stamp is covered with an even coat of paint. Before applying the stamp to the chair, test the impression on a scrap piece of paper to check that the paint is evenly distributed.

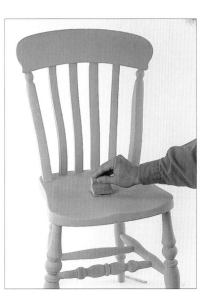

4 Position the face of the stamp in the desired position on the chair surface. Apply steady, even, downward pressure. Be careful not to allow the face of the stamp to move across the surface of the chair and smudge the image.

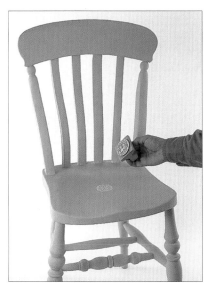

5 To avoid any smudging, remove the stamp from the surface with a perfect vertical action. Reapply paint to the stamp before applying the stamp to the next position on the chair. Build up your own pattern or design, varying the size of the stamp, if required, as shown here.

6 Once the stamp paint has dried, use a piece of fine-grade sandpaper to gently distress areas on the chair. Pay particular attention to the edges and high points in the molded areas of the furniture, because these would be the first places to wear naturally over time.

7 Finally, with some fine-grade steel wool, apply a coat of clear wax to the furniture surface to protect the finish. This will also rub away a little more paint, including some of the stamped areas, which will add to the overall distressed effect.

NAUTICAL THEME

Furniture that has been personalized with a decorative paint finish can become the starting point for the look of the room, as in this spacious kitchen, where the colors of the wood-topped table are echoed elsewhere (see p.67). The table base was given several coats of soft green paint to create a distressed look, then a stamp was used to add a fish motif.

METALLIC PAINT CRAFTS: ANTIQUE METAL

YOU WILL NEED

Paintbrush
Cloth

MATERIALS

Metallic paint
Craquelure (basecoat and topcoat)
Burnt umber (available from an artist's supply store)
Varnish (optional)

Applying a metallic finish to household objects is a simple way to revamp an item, giving it a new look and texture. This finish may be given an aged look by painting it with craquelure to create an older, distressed, or antique appearance.

Metallic paints are now more widely available, and the latest types can provide an increasingly realistic metallic effect to items made of other materials. There is a good selection of colors or "metals" to choose from, catering for all types of personal preference. In this example, a pewter effect has been chosen to change the appearance of a simple terra-cotta pot. However, equally impressive finishes may be achieved in such colors as gold, brass, or copper, again with a craquelure effect added to produce the "aged" or antique appearance.

1 Apply an even coat of the metallic paint to the terra-cotta pot with a paintbrush. Check the manufacturer's directions for the particular paint you are using, but generally only one coat is required because metallic finishes often have excellent covering properties.

2 Once the metallic paint has dried, apply one layer of craquelure basecoat to the pot, following the manufacturer's directions. Make sure that it is well brushed out, with no drips or runs in its surface. The initial milky coating will eventually dry to a slightly sticky but clear finish.

3 Apply one layer of craquelure top coat, again using a paintbrush, and make sure that the entire pot surface is covered. As the topcoat dries small cracks will begin to appear in its surface. The thicker the layer of topcoat applied, the deeper the cracks will be.

4 To highlight the cracks in the finish, rub over the pot surface with a rag that has been dipped in a small amount of burnt umber. The burnt umber will become stuck in the cracks that have been created by the craquelure finish and provide the final antique effect. Varnish the pot, if required.

METALLIC PAINT CRAFTS: VERDIGRIS

YOU WILL NEED

Stencil brushes
Paintbrush
Cloth

MATERIALS

Latex paint
Acrylic glaze
Colorizers

Verdigris is a crystallized substance that forms on copper, brass, or bronze surfaces, due to atmospheric action forming a coating of carbonate of copper. However, the characteristic shades of green produced by verdigris can be replicated on other surfaces to give a highly decorative "aged" finish. Reproducing this effect on interior surfaces is effective, particularly when applied to surfaces that have relatively intricate or ornate detail such as the cornice around a room. To produce a good verdigris effect, you will need to make glaze mixtures in two or three shades of green by mixing acrylic glaze and colorizers, following the manufacturer's instructions. Some manufacturers produce verdigris kits, eliminating the need for you to do your own mixing. Apply the different shades to the surface one at a time.

1 Apply a basecoat of latex paint to the cornice and allow it to dry. Using a large stencil brush, apply the palest of the green mixes to the cornice. Try to get the bristles into most areas of the design without saturating the surface with color.

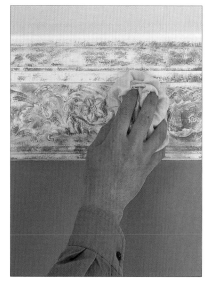

2 Before the green dries, wipe over the cornice surface using a slightly dampened cloth. This removes some of the paint from the cornice high points while leaving a much greater concentration of the paint in the lower depressions of the molding.

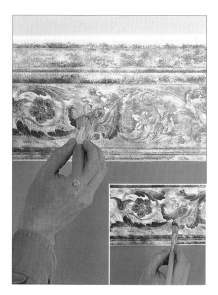

3 Add the second, much darker, green to the cornice, again using the large stencil brush (after cleaning it first), but concentrate your efforts on the high points of the molding in the cornice. Once this has dried, use a smaller stencil brush to add a slightly darker green to these "high" areas. Leave this to dry.

4 Finally, dilute the darkest green mix with some more glaze to make it a much lighter color and a more transparent consistency. Apply a coat of this diluted glaze over the entire cornice. This helps the "aged" effect and also fills in any areas where the basecoat may still show through.

STENCILING WALLS AND FLOORS

YOU WILL NEED

Paper
Pencil
Cutting board
Acetate
Wax pencil
Craft knife
Tape measure
Stencil
Paintbrush
Masking tape
Stencil brushes

MATERIALS

Stencil paint
Latex paint
Varnish (optional)

Ethnic designs always make effective stencil finishes, with subtle color variations adding to the finished look of the stenciled wall or floor.

Stenciling is a versatile decorative effect for bringing color and pattern to all types of surfaces. The technique is the same whatever the surface being stenciled, whether it be walls, floors, or articles of furniture (see pp.132–133). There is a wide range of manufactured stencil designs to choose from, but it can be very rewarding to make your own, which adds a more individual touch to the stenciled surface. Stencils can be made from pieces of thin cardboard or acetate. Acetate stencils will last longer and are easier to clean than stencils made of cardboard.

MAKING A STENCIL

1 Draw your design on a piece of paper, ensuring that the outline is clearly defined. For the less artistically inclined, a picture can be traced instead of drawn. It is worth noting that the simplest designs are often most effective.

2 Transfer the design to a piece of acetate and use a wax pencil to trace the picture onto the acetate. Place the acetate on a cutting board and cut out the traced design with a craft knife, carefully following the lines of the design.

USING A STENCIL

1 Adding a background color to a stencil design can enhance the finished effect. In this case, a border stencil is being used to run around the perimeter of the floor in the room. Measure the width of the stencil to calculate the correct positioning on the floor.

2 Transfer the width measurement to the floor, then apply masking tape around the entire floor perimeter. Using a small paintbrush, apply latex paint as a background color in the masked-off area, taking care not to let any brush strokes extend onto the main part of the floor.

3 Once the painting is complete, remove the masking tape to reveal a perfectly painted border around the room. If there are any areas where paint has seeped under the masking tape, sand them back to the floor color so that the lines of the border are sharp and precise.

4 Apply the stencil over the painted border, using a stencil brush to paint the design. Remove excess paint from the bristles before application, and keep the brush perpendicular to the floor at all times while stenciling, "pouncing" the brush up and down. Move the stencil along to continue around the whole room.

5 The same border design may be applied to the walls, if desired. In this case, a homemade stencil has been used to highlight the corners in the room. Applying the color more densely around the edge of the pattern gives the finished design a more three-dimensional effect.

6 The homemade design may also be used to accent the floor finish and link the two designs. Wash the stencils in warm water from time to time to remove any excess paint. This ensures that a neat finish is achieved with each new application of the stencil. Once the paint is dry, apply a coat of varnish to protect it, if desired.

STENCILING FURNITURE

YOU WILL NEED

Sandpaper
Cloth
Paintbrush
Stencil set
Masking tape
Large stencil brush
Small stencil brush or artist's
paintbrush

MATERIALS

White latex paint
Acrylic glaze
Colorizers
Stencil paints

A simple piece of furniture, such as a small, plain chest of drawers, can be given an elaborate decorative effect with a series of striking individual stencils that create a well-coordinated theme.

Stencils are a good way to add a decorative edge to simple pieces of furniture. Stencil designs can be as simple or as intricate as you want. They can be applied to older pieces of furniture to add interest or to disguise a worn surface. Alternatively, as in this example, a new, but unfinished, chest of drawers can be painted and customized by the stencil pattern of your choice to make a highly decorative piece of furniture.

1 Lightly sand the chest to smooth any rough areas, then wipe it down with a damp cloth to remove any dust and debris from the surface. Pay particular attention to the drawer faces and top and sides of the chest, because this is where the stencils will be positioned.

2 Remove the drawers. Paint the chest with a basecoat of white latex paint, then paint the drawers separately. If the wood is particularly resinous, it is advisable to prime it first, but in most cases a standard latex paint will act as an adequate primer for the acrylic glaze.

3 Mix up two glazes, adding a colorizer as needed. In this example, acrylic glaze has been tinted to produce a pale green and a mid-blue glaze. Apply a coat of the pale green glaze to the outside of the chest, applying it evenly to produce an overall but semi-transparent finish.

4 Apply the pale-green glaze to four of the drawers, and use the blue glaze on the other four. The sides of the drawers and their edges must be painted. The inside of the drawers can be painted with glaze, or not, as you desire. Allow the glaze to dry.

5 Decide on an overall design for stenciling the chest and begin with one drawer. Place it on its back so that the front of the drawer is facing upward. Place the required stencil onto the drawer face, using some masking tape to hold it in position.

6 Begin to apply the stencil paint, using a large stencil brush for the larger areas of the pattern. Always keep the stencil brush perpendicular to the drawer face, "pouncing" it in an up-and-down motion, and remove excess paint from the bristles on a scrap piece of paper before applying it.

7 Clean the brushes regularly, ensuring that different colored areas of the design are not contaminated by paint from other areas. For the more detailed work, and specifically for highlighting, as shown here, use a small stencil brush or even the end bristles of a small artist's paintbrush.

8 Once each design is complete, carefully remove the stencil and continue on another drawer or part of the chest. Build up your designs until all the stenciling is done. Once the paint has dried, the chest can be given a coat of varnish for added protection before you use it.

COLOR WASHING WALLS

YOU WILL NEED

Large paintbrush
Badger-hair or soft-bristle
brush

MATERIALS

Latex paint
Acrylic glaze
Colorizers
Varnish (optional)

Color washing is one of the easiest paint effects to achieve. Strokes made by the bristles of the brush create a textured finish that combines with the color of the basecoat to form a three-dimensional, semitransparent finish. The intensity of the effect depends on the basecoat color and the number of glaze coats applied.

Combining color washing on the walls and color rubbing on the woodwork is a dramatic way of using two paint effects in one room.

1 Apply a latex basecoat to the wall surface, and allow it to dry. In this example, a pale blue has been used. Apply glaze to the wall surface, spreading it evenly with a large, relatively coarse-bristle brush. Move the brush in all directions across the wall surface.

2 While the glaze is wet, use a badger-hair or other soft-bristle brush to take the harshness out of the brush strokes and blend the glaze color across the surface of the wall. Use very light strokes in all directions, making sure that the bristles of the brush barely touch the surface of the wall.

3 Once this coat has dried, apply a second, slightly darker coat of glaze and, again, use the badger-hair brush across the wall surface. Further coats of glaze may be added, and softened, to create greater depth and dimension in the finish. Seal the wall surface with a coat of varnish, if you desire.

CREATING MOOD

Color washing creates a subtle paint effect, but it can have a great impact in terms of adding warmth to a room, depending on the colors you choose. Color washed walls make an excellent backdrop for the other features in a room. For a Mediterrean courtyard, a color wash of faded terra cotta has been applied to roughly plastered walls (see p.23).

COLOR RUBBING WOOD

YOU WILL NEED

Paintbrush
Cloth
Clear wax
Caulking gun
Pencil
Carpenter's level

MATERIALS

Acrylic glaze
Colorizers
Bonding adhesive

Color rubbing is a similar effect to color washing, except that once the color has been applied to a surface it is rubbed away. The effect is similar because the glaze provides an overall effect that has no particular pattern, but simply highlights different areas in a random fashion. Although color rubbing can be used on wall surfaces, the technique is generally used to create a finish for wood surfaces. The procedure involves tinting a bare wood surface, which highlights the grain and provides a decorative stained appearance to the wood. The best effect is achieved on a wood that has a relatively prominent grain, because this gives a greater variation in color and a more defined finish. A latex basecoat is not required. The acrylic glaze is mixed to the color of your choice with one or more colorizers, and then it is painted straight onto the wooden surface.

1 Mix the glaze with the colorizer of your choice, and apply it directly onto the surface of the wood with a paintbrush, covering it evenly. Here, a chair rail is being coated. Where possible, color rub items before they are attached to the wall—this makes it easier to achieve a neat edge once in position.

2 Before the glaze dries, use a clean cloth to rub over the rail length, removing excess glaze from its surface. The glaze left on the wood will become ingrained in the surface and highlight the grain of the wood. Once dry, rub a coat of clear wax over the rail to provide a decorative and protective coat.

3 Instead of nailing the chair rail to the wall surface and running the risk of damaging the color-rubbed effect, use a proprietary bonding adhesive. This is usually supplied in a tube that fits into a caulking gun, and it is easy to apply to the back of the chair rail.

4 To act as a guideline, draw a pencil line on the wall surface, along the top of a carpenter's level. Press the rail in place. Remove any excess adhesive from around the edge of the rail with a damp cloth before the adhesive dries.

MARBLING

Marbling is one of the more difficult paint effects to achieve with any high degree of authenticity and you should practice before applying it to wall surfaces. In order to achieve a realistic result, it is worth copying a picture of marble or a piece of the real thing.

Marbling is a good mood-creating finish for walls. Its appearance can vary according to the light source in a room and its intensity.

One of the benefits of practicing the effect is that it will allow you to experiment with colors and design before committing them to the wall. Varying intensities of color and the number, angle, and prominence of the veining in the marble all need to be practiced if you are to achieve an attractive finish that fits into the room's overall color scheme.

Depending on your level of skill, the finish can be applied to entire wall surfaces, although maintaining an even effect over large areas is difficult. The easier option is to decorate smaller areas such as the panels below a chair rail. Whichever option you choose, a well-executed marble effect provides a stunning addition to the decoration in a room. It is often easier if two people work together—one can apply the glaze while the other uses the various tools needed to produce the marbled finish while the glaze is still wet, each concentrating on their own particular tasks to maintain a consistent finish.

1 Apply a white latex basecoat to your surface and allow it to dry. Then apply two different colored glazes using a 1-in-(25-mm-) wide brush. Apply the glazes in a random strokes that fall in a similar direction, across the wall surface, leaving the basecoat showing in some areas.

2 Use a large stippling brush across the glazed surface, pressing the tips of the bristles into the wet glaze and allowing them to blend the two colored glazes into each other. Allow the stippling brush to spread the color onto the unglazed white areas, so the whole surface will have a stippled glaze finish.

3 Take a soft-bristle brush and gently draw the bristles across the glaze surface, removing any harsh brush marks from the glazed effect. First, draw the brush against the direction in which the glaze was initially applied; then draw the brush in the same direction in which the glaze was applied.

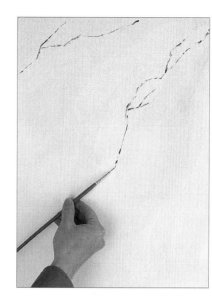

4 Use an artist's paintbrush to apply thin veins of raw umber to the glaze surface. Rotate the brush between thumb and index finger as you draw it across the glaze. Try to keep the veins running across the wall in the same direction as the initial glaze application.

5 Draw the soft-bristle brush over the vein surfaces, blending them into the overall effect. Initially, work the brush gently against the vein direction, then apply the brush in the same direction as the veins to produce the most authentic effect.

6 Once the glaze and raw umber have dried, sand the wall surface gently with fine-grade sandpaper. Take care not to make scratches in the wall surface. The function of the sanding is to flatten the finish and raise a little dust on the surface without damaging the effect.

7 Do not remove the dust with a cloth—instead apply a coat of lacquer directly onto the wall. Allow it to dry, sand again, and apply another coat. This alternate sanding and lacquering provides the final marble effect, softening the marbling and giving a very solid-looking, flat finish.

HELPFUL HINTS

● Marble is a naturally occurring material, and it is important to try to accurately mimic its appearance if you want the finish to look authentic. It is difficult to produce a perfect replica, but a picture or a piece of marble will certainly help your efforts. A piece of natural marble will also provide a good guide for the color you use.

● You do not have to restrict a marbling paint effect to walls. You can apply the finish to other items that could be made of marble such as coffee-table tops, lamp bases, and shelves.

RAGGING AND RAG ROLLING

YOU WILL NEED
....

Protective gloves
Paintbrush
Paint bucket
Cotton rags

Masking options

Masking tape

MATERIALS
....

Latex paint
Acrylic glaze
Colorizers

A ragged paint effect, whether completely random or more directional, as shown here, can create a strong, dramatic look on wall surfaces.

Using cloths or rags to create paint effects is a popular way of adding a textured finish to wall surfaces. The two main techniques are ragging on—this involves applying glaze to the wall with the rag—and ragging off, where the glaze is brushed onto the wall and impressions are made in its surface with the rag. A third method, rag rolling, involves brushing the glaze onto the wall, then rolling rags down the wall surface in one direction. Using masking tape with rag rolling produces a flowing, striped effect.

RAGGING ON

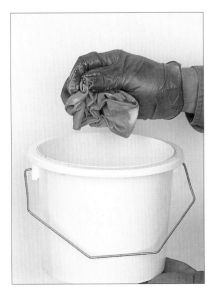

1 It is advisable to wear gloves for all ragging; otherwise cleaning your hands can be a lengthy job. Apply a basecoat of latex paint to the wall surface and allow it to dry. Mix the glaze and colorizers. Dampen a rag and, holding it in a crumpled position in your hand, dip it into the glaze. Squeeze out the rag to remove excess glaze.

2 Apply the rag to the wall surface, still holding it in a crumpled ball in your hand. After each impression, alter your hand and wrist angle to create a random instead of uniform pattern. Once the impressions start to become less defined, reload the rag with more glaze.

RAGGING OFF

1 Apply a basecoat of latex paint to the wall surface and allow it to dry. Apply glaze to the wall surface, using a large paintbrush. Ensure that the entire basecoat is covered, working in areas of 1 sq yd (1 sq m) at a time, or the glaze may dry out before you create a ragged effect.

2 With a crumpled, dampened rag, create impressions on the glazed surface by pressing the rag into the glaze. After each impression change your hand and wrist angle. Once the rag is clogged with glaze, wash it thoroughly in clean water. Continue the process over the entire glazed surface.

RAG ROLLING

1 Cut up a number of rags into squares of 10 in (25 cm), and roll them up into sausage-shaped cylinders. For each rag, fold in both ends to make the rolls a uniform length and to ensure that there are no frayed pieces of material.

2 Apply the glaze as in step 1 of *Ragging off*. Dampen the cylindrical rags and roll them down the glazed surface in as vertical a direction as possible. After each run, slightly overlap the next roll onto the previous impression. Clean or change rags once they become clogged with glaze.

MASKING OPTIONS

1 Use masking tape to divide up the wall surface into a vertically striped design. Apply glaze between the masked-off areas. Then roll the rags down between the masked-off areas, making sure that the rag length does not extend beyond the tape guidelines.

2 Once the rag-rolled impression has been made, remove the masking tape on either side to reveal a patterned stripe. Continue applying the striped effect to the other areas on your wall surface, as required.

STIPPLING

YOU WILL NEED
....
Paintbrush
Stippling brushes
Cloth

MATERIALS
....
Acrylic glaze
Colorizers
Varnish or glaze coat

Stippling is a subtle paint effect that breaks up the finish on a wall surface to give a more textured look than that produced by flat paint colors. As with most paint effects, glaze is used to produce the finish, so the texture of the stippling is slightly translucent. Stippling is not difficult, but great patience is required while using the stippling brush across the entire wall surface—any missed areas will show up and ruin the effect. In terms of color, it is always best to apply a coat of light latex paint before the glaze, because this provides the most suitable background for showing off the texture. Walls can be stippled with a single color, or, as in this case, two colors can be used and blended into one another to give an unusual decorative effect. The stippling technique can also be used to create random stripes on the wall surface, or to color the edges or corners of the room a slightly different shade than the central wall areas.

A stippled textured finish on the walls provides a mellow, warming backdrop for the overall decorative scheme of a room.

1 Apply glaze to the wall surface, ensuring a good even coverage. The brush marks can be either left going in random directions, or, once the surface is covered, you can use some light strokes with the brush to "lay off" the glaze in a vertical direction, so that all brush marks are pointing one way.

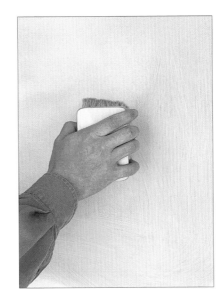

2 Use a large stippling brush across the glaze surface, "pouncing" it in an up-and-down motion, allowing the extreme ends of the bristles to press into the wet glaze surface. After each impression, move along to the next area, shifting your wrist position slightly in order to apply random brush impressions.

3 As you progress across the wall surface, use a cloth to remove excess glaze from the bristle ends after every few applications of the brush. Failure to do so will cause the bristles to become clogged with glaze, which will smudge and affect the stipple finish.

4 If using two colors, apply the second color once you have stippled one section. Apply the color up to the first color, leaving a small gap between them where the basecoat on the wall surface will continue to show.

5 Stipple the second color using the same technique as for the first one. If using the same stippling brush, clean it very thoroughly before using it for the second color; otherwise, the first color will contaminate the second glaze and take away from the effect.

6 At the dividing line between the two colors, use the stippling brush to blend along the junction. The subtlety of this joint depends on how much glaze you applied to the wall and the amount of white you left showing between the two colors when applying the glaze.

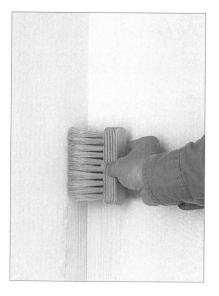

7 Deal with corners using a smaller stippling brush, which is designed precisely for this purpose and makes access into these junctions much easier. Once stippling is complete, allow it to dry thoroughly before applying two coats of varnish or a protective glaze coat.

HELPFUL HINTS

● When stippling, apply glaze to the wall in areas of 1 sq yd (1 sq m) at a time; if you do a larger area, you risk the glaze drying out before you apply the effect.

● Use silk latex paint as a basecoat. The glaze takes longer to dry on this type of surface than on matte finishes, giving you a longer working time on the glaze.

● Build up depth of color and texture by applying more than one stipple coat. Applying a slightly darker shade over a lighter one will produce a more three-dimensional finish.

CREATING DECOUPAGE

YOU WILL NEED

Thin cardboard
Pencil
Cutting board
Craft knife
Straightedge
Carpenter's level
Cloth

MATERIALS

Photocopied musical score
Spray adhesive

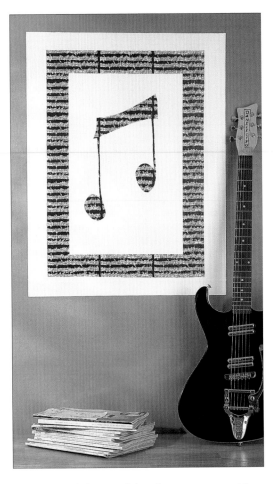

The musical theme of this decoupage provides a decorative, framed picture effect on a plain wall surface.

Decoupage literally means "to cut up," and it is a way of producing a decorative collage effect on walls and furniture (or even household items such as vases, trinket boxes, and table mats) by cutting out paper images and adhering them onto the chosen surface. All types of paper materials can be used such as photocopies of your favorite pictures, old writing scripts, or old wallpaper motifs. In this example, a musical score has been photocopied, then the center portion has been removed and a large musical note has been cut from it. The musical note has then been adhered onto a white surface surrounded by the border of the black-and-white photocopied score. If preferred, it can be adhered straight onto the wall. Although a musical theme has been used here, you can adapt this idea to any subject of your choosing. Framed cutouts of vegetables and fruit work well for a kitchen wall, while fish and seashells look good in a bathroom.

1 Draw a musical note with a pencil on a piece of thin cardboard. If you are not confident enough to do this freehand, photocopy a picture of a note and enlarge it on a photocopier to the size that you want for your project.

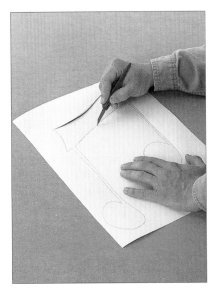

2 On a cutting board, cut around the edge of the note, using a sharp craft knife, to separate the note from the main body of the cardboard. Be careful when using a sharp knife, and never position your free hand in front of the blade.

3 Position the note you have cut out in the center of your photocopied musical score, aligning it with the design. Measure a border or frame around the edge of the note, and mark it with a pencil. Cut around this line with the craft knife to remove the center of the photocopied score, leaving just an outer frame.

4 On the central cutout portion of the photocopy, position the cutout cardboard note once more. Using the craft knife, cut around the edge of it until you are able to lift out a replica of the note design.

5 Decide where you want to position your decoupage on the wall. Use a carpenter's level and pencil to draw a guideline on the wall surface. This guideline should be drawn to the width of the photocopy frame, where you want the bottom edge of the frame to sit.

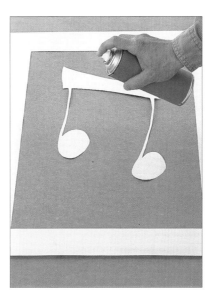

6 Using a spray adhesive, spray the back of the photocopy frame and the back of the note cut from the photocopy. Follow the manufacturer's guidelines—most of them recommend leaving the spray to soak into the paper for a short while before applying it to the wall.

7 As soon as the adhesive is ready, place the frame on the wall, following the pencil guideline marked on the wall. Secure the note in the center of the frame to complete the picture. Using a slightly dampened clean cloth, flatten the design into place, removing any air bubbles from the paper surface.

HELPFUL HINTS

● Instead of using a spray adhesive, you can use ordinary wallpaper paste or slightly diluted PVA glue to adhere the decoupage designs to the wall. For the beginner, a PVA solution is often easier to use, because it will take longer to dry on the wall surface than the other adhesives, which will give you more time to move the decoupage image around and reposition it if necessary.

● Once they are dry, decoupage images can be protected with several coats of clear varnish.

WALLPAPERING DIRECTORY

WALLPAPERING: PREPARATION AND PLANNING

SKILL LEVEL Low
TIME FRAME ½ day for an average-size room
SPECIAL TOOLS None
SEE PAGES 146–147

Just as you need to prepare before painting any surfaces, preparation and planning are needed before you start wallpapering. Remove old layers of wallpaper, then fill, sand, and seal bare walls, as required, before applying new paper. Carefully measure up the room to find out how much paper is needed and where to start papering.

WALLPAPERING A ROOM

SKILL LEVEL Low to medium
TIME FRAME 1 day for an average-size room
SPECIAL TOOLS Paste brush and table, paperhanging brush
SEE PAGES 148–149

Check whether the wallpaper you are using is prepasted or if it will need pasting. Whichever type of paper it is, the application technique is very similar. When hanging wallpaper, you'll need to begin from a completely vertical starting line, and always butt lengths together; trim to fit at ceiling and baseboard level with a utility knife. Have a good supply of blades for the knife as they usually become blunt very quickly when cutting wallpaper.

WALLPAPERING PANELS

SKILL LEVEL Low to medium
TIME FRAME 2 hours
SPECIAL TOOLS Metal ruler, paste brush, paperhanging brush
SEE PAGES 150–151

Making panels out of wallpaper creates an effective decoration for the walls, especially when a border is applied around the perimeter of the panels. Precise pattern matching and accurate application techniques are necessary to create the best effect. Take time to plan the panel size so that you achieve a balanced effect on the wall surface. Be sure to choose wallpaper and borders with suitable designs for this technique, because the borders will require need to be mitred at each of the corners.

USING BORDERS AND FRIEZES

SKILL LEVEL Low to medium
TIME FRAME 2 hours for an average-size room
SPECIAL TOOLS Paste brush, paperhanging brush
SEE PAGES 152–153

Borders and friezes may be hung at any level on the wall surface. You will need to be sure that you match patterns in corners and that the border is level. Some borders and friezes are self-adhesive, others require pasting. Use border adhesive on unpasted borders before applying them. If you use wallpaper paste, the edges of the border or frieze may lift away from the wall surface after a relatively short time. Border adhesive is much stronger and creates a more secure bond between border and wall.

When applying a border, don't make the common mistake of forgetting to keep both the border and the wall surface clear of excess adhesive during and after the application process. Adhesive dries very quickly, so you will need to have a bucket of clean water and sponge ready. As soon as a length has been hung, wipe off any excess adhesive, especially on the border edges. Once adhesive has dried on a wall surface, it is almost impossible to remove it, and characteristic shiny patches are left on the wall or border surface, which spoil the finished look. If, despite all your precautions, you do get a shiny area, wiping the surface down with a mild detergent solution followed by rinsing in clean warm water will sometimes make it less shiny. If the border has been applied over a painted surface instead of wallpaper, it may be possible to paint over any shiny areas with the wall color, but take care that no paint spills onto the border surface.

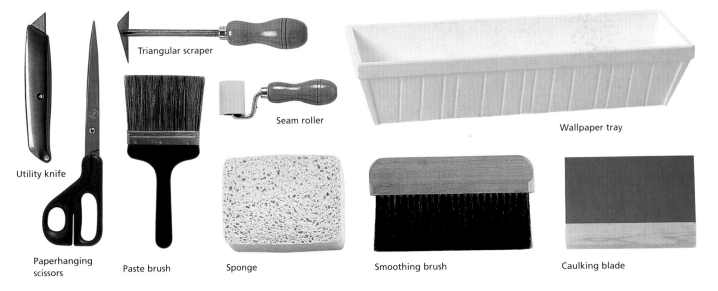

Utility knife

Triangular scraper

Seam roller

Wallpaper tray

Paperhanging scissors

Paste brush

Sponge

Smoothing brush

Caulking blade

TILING DIRECTORY

TILING A WALL

SKILL LEVEL Low to medium
TIME FRAME 2 to 4 hours for an average-size wall
SPECIAL TOOLS Adhesive spreader, tile cutter, grout spreader, grout shaper
SEE PAGES 154–155

Tiling is a straightforward process as long as you have a solid, level starting point. Furring strips are generally required to provide a sound base. Careful planning is essential, as are accurate cuts to deal with the edges of the design. Good grouting will add the necessary final touch.

USING DIFFERENT PATTERNS AND DESIGNS

SKILL LEVEL Low to medium
TIME FRAME 2 to 4 hours for an average-size wall
SPECIAL TOOLS Adhesive spreader, tile cutter, grout spreader, torpedo level
SEE PAGES 156–157

The basic tiling technique can be adjusted to deal with tiles

of different sizes and patterns to produce any number of unusual finishes. Experiment with different designs by laying out the tiles dry before applying them to the wall.

TILING A BACKSPLASH

SKILL LEVEL Low to medium
TIME FRAME 2 hours
SPECIAL TOOLS Adhesive spreader, tile cutter, grout spreader
SEE PAGES 158–159

Backsplashes are nearly always tiled. They give you a great opportunity to add some interesting design elements and make a feature of what is basically a very practical area of wall space. For greater impact, you can apply border tiles around the edge of the backsplash. Always make sure that you make a good seal with silicone sealant at the junction between the bottom row of tiles and the basin. Create a guideline with masking tape before applying the sealant so that a neat silicone bead is achieved along the junction.

BLENDING MOSAIC TILES

SKILL LEVEL Low to medium
TIME FRAME ½ day for an average-size room
SPECIAL TOOLS Adhesive spreader, mini roller, grout spreader
SEE PAGES 160–161

Sheets of mosaic tiles provide the practical properties of all tiles, but with a different look. Small, individual tiles are joined together with a backing, so you can quickly apply a large number at a time. Blend different colored sheets of tiles to create further interest. A mini roller is needed to ensure that the tiles are firmly adhered to the wall.

MAKING A MOSAIC TABLETOP

SKILL LEVEL Low to medium
TIME FRAME ½ to 1 day
SPECIAL TOOLS Tile cutter, grout spreader
SEE PAGES 162–163

Creating a mosaic pattern on the top of an old table is the

perfect way to revamp it. Mosaic tiles offer all types of design options, allowing you to show off your own ideas and preferences to their full potential. Although a circular table has been used in the example shown in these pages, there is no reason why designs cannot be successfully applied to tables of other shapes and sizes. Square or rectangular tables, in fact, are often easier because there is no need to use a compass to mark the circular guidelines when planning the design. You can use old, larger tiles as the raw material—make your own mosaic tiles by cutting them to the required size with a tile cutter.

Always plan your design before you start applying the tiles. As with all tiling projects, you will need to grout to make the finished surface waterproof. The finished design can be further embellished by using a colored grout, instead of a plain white one. Colored grout is readily available in most home centers and offers the opportunity to experiment with your mosaic finish.

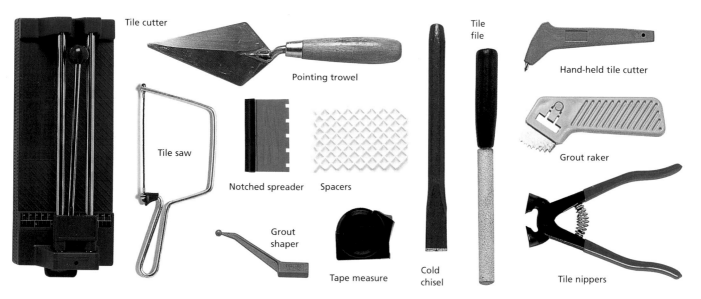

Tile cutter

Pointing trowel

Tile file

Hand-held tile cutter

Tile saw

Notched spreader

Spacers

Grout raker

Grout shaper

Tape measure

Cold chisel

Tile nippers

WALLPAPERING: PREPARATION AND PLANNING

YOU WILL NEED

Bucket of hot water
Scraper or putty knife
Medium-grade sandpaper
Large paintbrush or pasting
brush
Tape measure

MATERIALS

PVA glue

Preparation and planning is an important part of wallpapering. Wallpaper must be hung on a well-prepared, stable surface, or it will not adhere properly. Most mistakes occur when papering over old wallpaper. It is possible to paper over old wallpaper if it is stuck down securely; however, it is usually difficult to know if this is the case until after the new wallpaper has been applied, so success is far from guaranteed. It is better to strip old wallpaper from the walls. Although you can use an electric steam stripper, traditional soaking methods, as shown below, are just as quick if there are only one or two layers of paper on the wall. Once the old paper has been removed, you will need to measure up the room for the new wallcovering and decide where to start wallpapering.

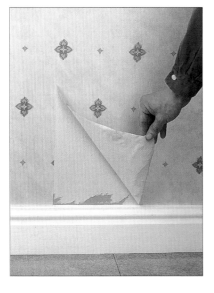

1 The top layer of some types of wallpaper can be easily removed when dry. Try pulling away this layer by lifting from the bottom corners of the lengths and progressing up across the wall surface. You may be surprised at how much paper will come away before any soaking is necessary.

2 Once as much of the top layer has been removed as possible, soak the remaining backing paper on the wall surface with hot water. You can use cold water, but hot water will usually lift the paper more effectively and make it much easier to strip—a scraper or a putty knife are ideal for removing it.

3 Once all the paper has been removed, allow the wall surface to dry out completely. Sand the walls to remove any small remaining scraps of paper and any rough areas on the surface that might otherwise show through the new wallpaper once it has been applied to the wall.

4 Wash down the wall surface, allow it to dry, then apply a coat of PVA solution (5 parts water to 1 of PVA glue). This solution seals and stabilizes the surface, ensuring that the wallpaper will adhere to the wall. Line the walls with lining paper if recommended in the guidelines for your chosen wallpaper.

MEASURING UP AND WHERE TO START

Before you begin wallpapering, you will need to decide how many rolls of wallpaper you require to complete the room. The diagram below illustrates the best way to measure up and calculate your requirements. Wallpaper can be expensive, so it is important to be as accurate as possible. However, it is always better to have one roll too many instead of one roll too few. If you have to buy an extra roll at a later date, you may not get the same batch number as the original rolls, so you may end up with slight color variations. Also, you can always use leftover wallpaper for any future repairs to the wallpaper surface.

When deciding on the best place to start papering in a room, there are few hard-and-fast rules. The most important points to consider are demonstrated in the diagram below.

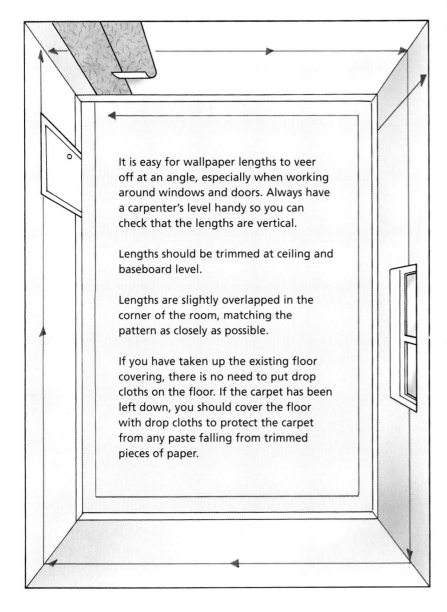

It is easy for wallpaper lengths to veer off at an angle, especially when working around windows and doors. Always have a carpenter's level handy so you can check that the lengths are vertical.

Lengths should be trimmed at ceiling and baseboard level.

Lengths are slightly overlapped in the corner of the room, matching the pattern as closely as possible.

If you have taken up the existing floor covering, there is no need to put drop cloths on the floor. If the carpet has been left down, you should cover the floor with drop cloths to protect the carpet from any paste falling from trimmed pieces of paper.

➤ Measuring up

Measure around the perimeter of your room and multiply the entire distance with the height to which you want the wallpaper to reach. This will give you the wall surface area. Divide into this figure the surface area of one roll of the wallpaper you are going to use. This will give you the number of rolls required.

Wallapers with a large repeat pattern will produce more waste than those with a small repeat pattern. If the paper has a large repeat pattern, add the repeat figure onto that of the room height before you start to work out the surface area. Include the doors and windows in your calculations—treating them as part of the wall surface allows for unavoidable wastage when trimming wallpaper lengths to size.

➤ Where to start

The first length must be hung precisely vertical and in a position where there are no wall obstacles that you will need to trim around. In a relatively square, obstacle-free room, begin close to a corner. Continue wallpapering around the room, butting the edges of lengths together, and finishing in the corner. Slightly overlap one length on top of another at the corner junctions. In rooms with prominent features, such as a fireplace, and where the wallpaper pattern design is large, it is better to start in the middle of the fireplace so that you can centralize the wallpaper pattern and provide a balanced effect in the room.

WALLPAPERING A ROOM

Wallpaper is a very popular form of decoration because it is a simple way to add color and pattern to what would otherwise be plain wall surfaces.

Wallpapering is a straightforward decorative technique, as long as you take time to plan thoroughly (see pp.146–147) and follow a few simple rules when applying wallpaper to the wall. Always read the wallpaper manufacturer's guidelines; these will explain how to apply the paste to the paper and give any special instructions for handling your chosen wallpaper. The manufacturer's guidelines will also recommend whether the walls should be lined first. If in doubt, lining the walls in the same way as wallpaper, but horizontally, is always the best course of action to follow.

PASTING UP

For papers that need pasting, mix up some wallpaper paste according to the weight of paper you are using, following the manufacturer's directions. Apply the paste to lengths of wallpaper cut with paper-hanging scissors, working it from the center of the length outward, ensuring even and complete coverage.

PREPASTED PAPER

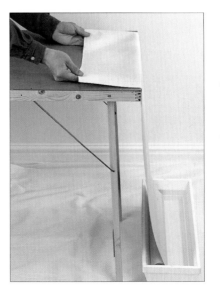

Prepasted paper requires no mixing of paste and simply needs a wallpaper tray filled with cold water. Roll up the cut length and soak it in the water before pulling it up onto the pasting table. The water activates the dried paste that has been impregnated into the back of the wallpaper.

HANGING PAPER

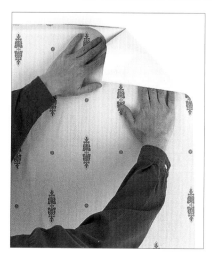

1 Whichever type of paper is being used, the method of applying it to the wall is the same. At your starting point (see pp.146–147), draw a vertical pencil line on the wall. Apply the first length of paper, using this guideline along one edge of the length. Allow an overlap onto the ceiling.

2 Use a paper-hanging brush to smooth the wallpaper into the wall/ceiling junction, ensuring it is firmly adhered in position on the wall. Allow the bristles of the brush to create a crease in the paper all the way along the junction, to provide a guideline for trimming purposes.

3 With the top section of paper in position, work down the length of the wallpaper using the paper-hanging brush to smooth it in position and remove air bubbles from below the paper surface. Work from the center of the length outward to the sides.

4 Once the length has been secured in position at the bottom level, usually next to the baseboard, you can trim the paper. Use a utility knife or paper-hanging scissors to cut along the creased guideline at ceiling level. Trim in the same way at the junction of the wall and baseboard.

5 Continue papering, butting together subsequent lengths as you progress across the wall surface, ensuring that the pattern matches as precisely as possible. Use the paper-hanging brush to smooth along the edges. Remove any excess paste on the wallpaper with a clean damp sponge.

HELPFUL HINTS

When cutting the lengths of wallpaper to size, you should take into account the size of the pattern repeat. Most manufacturers state the size on the label on the roll of wallpaper, but it is always a good idea to measure it yourself to be as precise as possible. When cutting lengths to size, the size of the pattern must be added to the height requirement for a length. This allows for adjustment on the wall to match the pattern. Watch out for "drop pattern" designs, where a pattern drops down from one length to another—these require a further allowance added to the length.

WALLPAPERING PANELS

YOU WILL NEED

Tape measure
Straightedge and pencil
Utility knife
Cutting board
Carpenter's level
Pasting brush
Paper-hanging brush
Sponge

MATERIALS

Wallpaper and border
Paste

As well as being an attractive feature in its own right, a panel may act as a background for items such as paintings or mirrors.

U sing lengths of wallpaper to create panels is an alternative but highly effective way of decorating wall surfaces. The technique is not difficult, but it is essential to plan how to use the particular wallpaper design to achieve a balanced effect. Be sure to measure very accurately. It is also important to choose a border for the panel's frame that will complement the design on the wallpaper panel. Some manufacturers supply borders that are made to match particular papers, but not all are suitable for paneling.

The border has to be mitered at the corners to fit around the panel, and the pattern on the border itself must be suitable for this procedure. Strong geometric border designs are often unsuitable, because cutting through the design at a 45-degree angle for each corner would provide a disjointed finish. Choose instead a border design that has flowing patterns, with areas that can be mitered to give precisely fitted corners for the panel effect, or busy floral designs where any inconsistencies in the pattern match will not be noticed. Unless you are going to create particularly small panels, it will be necessary to join at least two pieces of wallpaper to make up the central panel size. Cut the panels down to size before applying them to the wall so that the patterns can be aligned and the correct length chosen.

1 Cut wallpaper lengths to slightly larger than the panel requirement and place them side by side (dry) on a tabletop or other flat surface. Position a piece of border to provide a guide for the panel size. Use a straightedge and pencil to mark the panel size on top of the paper lengths.

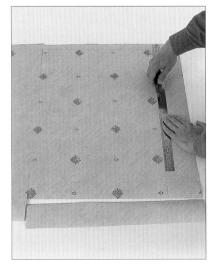

2 Place one of the paper lengths on a cutting board, which will prevent marks or grooves being made on the table or any other surface. Using the straightedge and a utility knife, cut along the pencil guidelines. Repeat the procedure with the other paper lengths.

3 Use a carpenter's level, pencil, and tape measure to mark the position of the bottom edge of the panel on the wall surface. If you are having more than one panel on the wall, measure off similar guidelines for each panel at the required distance on either side of this first panel.

4 Paste up the lengths of wallpaper and apply them to the wall surface, smoothing them into place using a paper-hanging brush. Ensure that the bottom edges of the wallpaper lengths are precisely positioned along the guideline and that you carefully butt together the two lengths along their edges. Leave to dry.

5 Once the panel has dried, apply the first length of border along the top of the wallpaper panel. Use the top edge of the panel as the guide for the top edge of the border. Allow the border length to slightly overlap onto the wall surface at both corners of the panel.

6 Apply the first vertical border length over the top of the horizontal length, matching the pattern at the point where they meet as accurately as possible. Hold a straightedge at 45 degrees across the joint, from corner to corner, and cut through the two pieces of overlapping border with a utility knife.

7 Carefully peel back the two pieces of border and remove the excess paper that has been released by the cut with the utility knife. Discard these off cuts and secure the two border lengths on the wall by smoothing them back into position, making a perfect miter joint.

8 Wipe away any excess paste from the border surface with a clean damp sponge. Repeat the process for the other corners of the panel, mitering each corner in turn to produce the final panel effect.

USING BORDERS AND FRIEZES

YOU WILL NEED

Scissors

Pasting borders
Pasting brush or large paintbrush
Pasting table
Sponge

Applying to a wall
Pencil
Carpenter's level
Paper-hanging brush
Sponge

MATERIALS

Border

Pasting borders
Border adhesive

SEE ALSO

Wallpapering: Preparation and planning pp.146–147

Borders act as excellent chair rails, especially between two different styles of wallpaper.

B orders and friezes are decorative strips of wallpaper that act as stylish accents to a room's color scheme. They can be used over the top of wallpaper or on plain painted walls. They are an excellent way of dividing up a wall surface to add greater interest to what might otherwise be a fairly monotonous open surface.

Borders are often self-adhesive; others can be pasted on the back in the same way as many wallpapers— some are prepasted and simply require soaking in water to activate the paste that is impregnated on the back. When buying a border, make sure that you know which type you have chosen.

Borders can be used on wall surfaces at any level, whether close to the ceiling or creating a clear dividing line at picture- or chair-rail level. Wherever you plan to position the border, make sure that it runs level or it may create an unbalanced effect—you can do this by marking a pencil guideline to follow. Check that there are no kinks or curves in the border as these could detract from the overall effect.

SELF-ADHESIVE BORDERS

Peel the self-adhesive border away from the backing paper and apply it directly to the wall surface. Position the border quickly, because the adhesive usually adheres in seconds and any adjustment becomes difficult after only a short while.

HELPFUL HINTS

● Border adhesive dries quickly, so always position a border on one wall at a time.

● When applying a border over the top of newly hung wallpaper, make sure that the wallpaper has dried out thoroughly.

● Wallpapers often have symmetrical patterns that can be used as an accurate guideline for border positioning.

● Pay attention to border edges—if they are not stuck down properly, the border will quickly lift away from the wall.

● Add a little extra to border lengths to allow trimming for an exact fit.

PASTING BORDERS

1 Cut borders for pasting to the required lengths before applying them to the wall (see *Helpful hints*). Paste the back using border adhesive, ensuring complete and even coverage. Try to keep the adhesive off the pasting table or it may be transferred to the front of subsequent lengths when pasting.

2 To allow easy transportation to the wall surface, fold the border up into a fan once it is pasted. Once removed from the table, clean away any excess adhesive from the table surface using a clean damp sponge. Allow the table to dry before you paste any subsequent lengths.

APPLYING TO A WALL

1 Draw a level guideline around the perimeter of the room. Apply a length of border to one wall surface, allowing the excess to bend around the internal corner onto the adjacent wall. Smooth it in position with a paper-hanging brush, removing air bubbles below the surface.

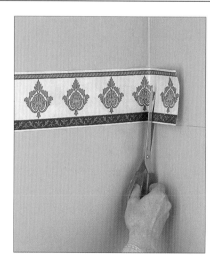

2 Trim back the excess border on the adjacent wall at a position close to the corner junction. Remove the excess, and, once again, use the paper-hanging brush to smooth the remaining border back in place, ensuring that the fold around the corner is adhered firmly in position.

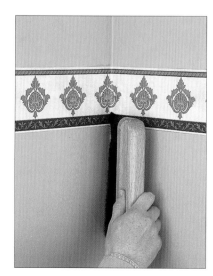

3 Apply the next length of border, overlapping it onto the previous one and matching the pattern on the overlap. Once it is in position, draw a pencil guideline down the crease made by the new length, tight into the corner. Peel the border back and cut the section away, trimming along the pencil guideline.

4 Smooth the border back into position using the paper-hanging brush, revealing a perfect corner joint. Continue applying subsequent lengths, cleaning excess adhesive from the wall and border surfaces with a clean damp sponge.

TILING A WALL

Tile designs are so varied that you can choose a look to suit any scheme.

Tiles are often used in kitchens and bathrooms because they are the most practical form of wall decoration for these areas. Tile surfaces are easily wiped and cleaned, repelling mold and moisture far better than a painted or wallpapered surface.

Tiling is a straightforward task as long as you prepare the surface before you start. Wall surfaces must be smooth and stabilized. Fill any holes in the wall before tiling. To stabilize the walls, apply a coat of PVA solution (one part PVA—white glue— to five parts water). This is essential on newly plastered walls, or tile adhesive applied to the wall will be difficult to spread because the plaster drains the moisture from the adhesive.

The most testing area of tiling is cutting, but as long as you have a good quality tile cutter and measure accurately, there is no reason why you cannot produce a successful finish. Where curved cuts are needed, such as around pipes, it is necessary to use a tile saw. This tool is designed specially for the purpose and makes the job straightforward. Remember that tiling can be a messy job, so it is important to clean tools periodically, and don't allow splashes of adhesive to dry and harden on the tile surface.

1 Before you start, line up the tiles (dry), with spacers, next to a length of furring strip, then mark off the joints on the side of the strip. This strip can now act as a tile gauge. Hold it against the wall surface to decide on the best position for the tiles. Try to avoid having less than half a tile at the edges of the wall.

2 Drill pilot holes in furring strips and position them on the wall to act as guides for the uncut tiles; temporarily screw or nail them to the wall. The horizontal strip is the most important— it ensures that the first row of tiles will be positioned level, with the vertical one helping to keep the tiles in line as you work up the wall.

3 Using a notched spreader, apply tile adhesive to the wall surface, starting at a bottom corner. The teeth of the spreader ensure that the adhesive is spread evenly. Cover an area of no more than 1 sq yd (1 sq m) at a time, otherwise the adhesive will dry out before you have time to apply the tiles.

4 Apply the tiles, using the bottom furring strip as an initial guide. Position tile spacers between the tiles to keep the gap between each tile consistent. Continue adding tiles along the length of the room, and gradually build up the rows on the wall.

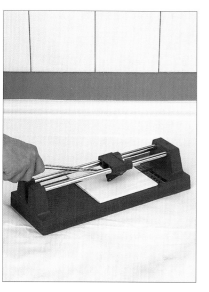

5 Once the main body of tiles has dried (normally about 24 hours), remove the strips; cut and apply any tiles that are necessary to fill the gaps. For each tile, measure and mark it with a wax pencil, score the tile in the tile cutter, and snap it in the tool. Apply adhesive to the back of the tile; position it on the wall.

6 Once all the cut tiles have been positioned, allow the surface to dry for 24 hours. Mix the grout and press it in position between the tiles, using a grout spreader. Work across the tile surface in all directions, forcing the grout into place.

7 Wipe away excess grout from the tile surface with a damp sponge. Use a grout shaper or small dowel to shape each grout joint between the tiles, making a perfect, slightly concave finish. Once the grout has dried, polish the tiles with a clean dry cloth to remove any cloudy grout residue from the surface of the tiles.

USE OF COLOR

It can be very effective to mix together two different colors to achieve an interesting decorative pattern. Combining dark colors with white tiles in a checkerboard design adds interest to the wall surfaces in this contemporary bathroom (see p.21). Similar tiles have also been used on the floor to create an integrated color scheme throughout the room.

USING DIFFERENT PATTERNS AND DESIGNS

YOU WILL NEED
....
Graph paper
Pencil
Furring strips
Carpenter's level
Tape measure
Adhesive spreader
Tile cutter
Wax pencil
Grout spreader
Sponge
Cloth

Diamonds
Torpedo level

MATERIALS
....
Tiles
Tile adhesive
Grout

SEE ALSO
....

Tiling a wall pp.154–155

Using tiles of varying size and pattern can enhance the different areas and features in a room such as this welcoming kitchen.

Although tiles can be used in many simple designs with great effect, it is also possible to experiment with size, color, and the way in which the actual tiles are applied to the wall surface to achieve a more ambitious finished look. There are any number of different patterns that can be made using this approach, and such finishes can cover entire wall surfaces or be incorporated into a larger design. It is always worth laying out tiles dry on a flat surface and experimenting before committing them to a finished design.

PLANNING

When using different colors and sizes of tile, it is sensible to draw a scaled-down picture of your proposed design. This gives you a better guide to what the finish will look like and makes it much easier to estimate the tile requirements and the quantities needed.

HELPFUL HINTS

● When choosing different tiles to use in the same design, take care to ensure that the depth of the tiles is the same. Different manufacturers make tiles with varying thicknesses, and trying to combine them in a design while producing a flush finished surface is very difficult, because adhesive layers will need to be constantly adjusted during application.

● Some tiles have straight, square edges and corners, but other tiles have more undulating or rustic-looking edges, and combining these types can also be difficult. When using handmade tiles, or ones that have that effect, use a strong adhesive that does not require spacers—slightly random spacing can be interesting.

VARYING SIZE

1 Combining large tiles with smaller ones provides an effective finish. Choose the smaller tiles so that a grouping (four in this design) will equal the size of one of the larger tiles. Use a furring strip to act as a guideline for the first tiles (see p.154).

2 Build up the design in rows, alternating groups of four tiles between each of the larger ones. Using different colors for the various sizes will emphasize the effect being created. It can be further enhanced by changing colors within each size category.

DIAMONDS

1 A diamond design involves rotating tiles 45 degrees from a standard position, so that they are aligned and positioned using the corners of tiles to create the level guideline. Use a torpedo level to establish the first positions of the bottom row of tiles.

2 Continue to add tiles, building up the design and varying colors, as you desire. When using tiles with undulating edges— without spacers— stand back from the wall from time to time to make sure that a balanced diamond design is being achieved; adjust the tiles if necessary.

RANDOM

1 Using a number of different colors in a simple standard tile design can be a very effective way of providing a decorative tile finish. Begin in the normal way and add tiles in rows or blocks of four, mixing the colors as required.

2 Continue to build up the design, following no particular sequence of colors, so that a random effect is achieved. A good number of colors to choose for this finish is three to four. Whether these colors complement each other or provide a contrast is a matter of personal choice.

TILING A BACKSPLASH

YOU WILL NEED

Tape measure
Pencil
Carpenter's level
Adhesive spreader
Tile cutter
Grout spreader
Sponge
Cloth
Caulking gun
Masking tape

MATERIALS

Tiles
Tile adhesive
Grout
Silicone sealant

SEE ALSO

Tiling a wall pp.154–155

A backsplash with a geometric pattern offers an interesting finish for a practical area.

The area directly behind and above a basin or sink always requires protection from water overspray. The most effective way of protecting this area is to apply a tiled backsplash, so that any overspray can be wiped away easily. As long as the basin or sink is level against the wall surface, it is usually possible to use its back edge as the support for the first row of tiles in your design.

The backsplash will be much more attractive if you can plan your design so that only full tiles are used, with no cuts or other interruptions. You can use border tiles around the edge of the main body of tiles to frame the finish. Any size of tile can be used for the main body of the design. However, larger tiles reduce the number of grout joints, which will extend the life of the backsplash because grout is the first area of a backsplash to deteriorate— so the fewer grout joints there are, the less upkeep will be required. Because backsplashes are small in size and do not need a great many tiles, this is a good opportunity to spend a little more money on the tiles you choose. This small extravagance can often make a significant difference to the final finish, providing a practical feature that is also decorative.

1 Tile a backsplash from the center outward so that the design is centered. Begin by finding the central point along the back edge of the basin. Position a carpenter's level vertically at the central point and draw a guideline along it with a pencil.

2 When dealing with relatively small areas of tiles, it is easier to apply adhesive directly to the back of the tiles before positioning them on the wall, instead of using the usual technique of applying adhesive to the wall.

3 Apply the first tile to the backsplash area, aligning the vertical edge precisely with the pencil guideline. Press the tile on to the wall surface to create a good bond between the tile and the wall.

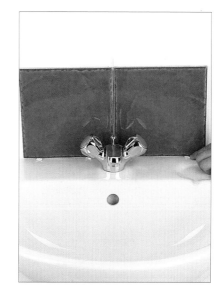

4 Apply the next tile on the other side of the pencil guideline, working toward the opposite edge of the basin. Again, ensure that it is precisely positioned, and use spacers to maintain a consistent gap between tiles and between the bottom layer of tiles and the basin. Continue applying all the main body of tiles.

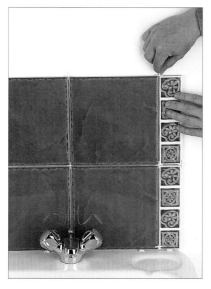

5 In this particular design, a border is being used around the edge of the main body of tiles. Apply the border tiles, being sure to use spacers in the normal way to maintain an even gap between the large tiles and the border sections. Again, apply the adhesive to the back of the tiles.

6 It may be necessary to cut some border tiles to fit precisely around the main tile design edge. In this case, the square design of the border tiles lends itself to being cut into the required sections to make a continuous border pattern. Plan ahead to place cut tiles in the least obvious position.

7 After applying all the tiles, allow the adhesive to dry for 24 hours. Grout the entire backsplash (see p.155). Once the grout has dried, wipe off any residue. Using a caulking gun, seal the junction between the bottom row of tiles and basin with silicone sealant. For a neat finish, first apply strips of masking tape along the junction.

8 Once the sealant has been applied, remove the tape before it dries, revealing a perfectly neat silicone bead along the tile/basin junction. Allow the sealant to dry for 24 hours before you begin using the basin.

BLENDING MOSAIC TILES

Mosaic tiles allow you to produce complex designs to create a highly decorative look.

Scaled-down tiles—sheet mosaics—provide an effective alternative to large or standard-size tiles. Mosaics create a completely different look from conventional tiles, and their size produces a finely detailed surface that is highly decorative but hard-wearing. Mosaic tiles can be applied in large blocks of continuous color, borders can run through them, or two different colors can be blended together to create a merging pattern between the tiles. This is effective when entire walls are covered with tiles or where a more random, colorful finish is desired.

Because the tiles are small, they are attached to sheets of a backing material so that a large number can be applied at one time. Single tiles or strips of tiles can be cut away from the backing for smaller areas of tiles or to create a random effect. Even when the finish is random, careful planning needs to take place to achieve a satisfying finish—it is a good idea to lay out the blocks of tiles on the floor, without adhesive, before applying them to the wall. If tiling a large area, use a tile gauge (see step 1, p.154).

1 Before securing the mosaic sheets to the wall, decide on the way that two joining sheets will be divided. Place them on a flat surface or cutting board, because it will be necessary to cut through some of the backing, allowing one sheet to overlap onto the other.

2 On each row of tiles in the overlapping section, cut through both tile layers with a utility knife. To create random lengths of mosaic tiles, trim away up to five tiles or as few as one tile in some rows, and any number between these two in the other rows.

3 Remove the excess tiles and allow the cut rows to interlock on the flat surface. This gives an initial pattern, which can then be altered by exchanging tiles of each color within the main body of the sheets. Decide where you want single mosaic tiles on the sheets, and mark the position of each one with a wax pencil.

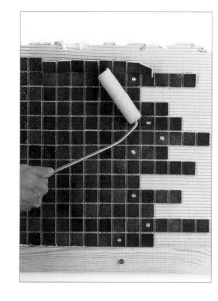

4 Apply the first tile sheet to the wall, using a furring strip to support the first layer of tiles in the usual way. A mini roller is the ideal tool for flattening the tiles in position, helping them to adhere firmly and evenly to the wall.

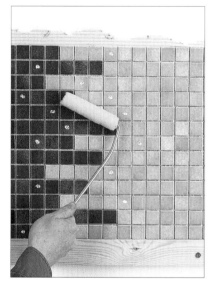

5 Apply the second color of tiles, interlocking them with the first color, as planned. Again use the mini roller to flatten the tiles in position, paying particular attention to the join between the two colors to ensure that the rows of each color are neatly aligned.

6 Before the adhesive dries, use a utility knife to cut out the marked tiles from the design. This procedure is better done at this stage, instead of when the tiles were laid out flat—if cut into numerous different sections at that stage, the mosaic sheets would be far more difficult to handle.

7 Position the single mosaic tiles of the opposite colors in the appropriate cut holes in the design layout. Continue to add sheets of tiles, following this random design until the pattern is complete. Once the adhesive has dried, grout in the usual way (see p.155).

SURFACE COMBINATIONS

Mosaic tiles can be very effective in a small bathroom; their colorful surfaces can lift the whole atmosphere of the room. Combining mosaic tiles with glass blocks provides an unusual contrast of color and finish (see p.101). The reflective qualities of the blocks provide a similar effect to a mirror, making the room feel much larger.

MAKING A MOSAIC TABLETOP

YOU WILL NEED
....

Screwdriver
Abrasive paper
Cloth
Pencil
String
Felt-tip pen or wax pencil
Tape measure
Tile cutter
Adhesive spreader
Tile nippers
Grout spreader

MATERIALS
....

Tiles
Tile adhesive
Tile grout
Polish

Creating a mosaic pattern on a tabletop is a decorative and effective way of adding interest to an old occasional table that is in need of some refurbishment.

Special mosaic tiles can be bought for making mosaics—pick ones of similar depth, because this will make it easier to produce a flat mosaic finish, instead of one with an uneven surface. Alternatively, you can make your own from standard-size tiles—breaking them into irregular pieces or, as shown below, cutting them all to the same size to produce a more uniform pattern. Depending on your artistic skills, mosaic tiles can be used to create intricate patterns such as on the tabletop above. However, simple designs such as the concentric circle pattern shown below also work well.

1 In this example, the table has a better beveled edge if it is turned over. Unscrew the tabletop, and sand the side you wish to tile, removing any rough areas from the surface. Clean it with a damp cloth to remove any dust.

2 Decide how many circles or bands of mosaic tiles you want. Attach some string to a pencil and use it as a compass to draw circular guidelines on the table surface. Simply anchor the string in the center of the table with one finger, while drawing the pencil guideline with the other hand at the required distances.

3 Use a felt-tip pen or wax pencil to mark off the size requirements for the mosaic tiles on the standard-size tiles. The size of the mosaic tiles will depend on your design; in this case, square mosaic tiles of about ⅜ in (1 cm) are ideal. Mark off at the required intervals along adjacent edges of the tile.

4 Position the marked-off tile in the tile cutter and score a line across the tile at each of the marked-off positions along one edge. Apply enough pressure to allow the cutting wheel to break the surface of the tile glaze as it moves across the tile. Rotate the tile and score lines at the marks on the second edge.

5 Once you have scored all the necessary lines across the tile surface, place the tile in the snapping position on the tile cutter, clamping it beneath the rails of the tool. Apply pressure with the handle to break away each strip of tile.

6 Take each tile strip and snap across the shorter dimension, using the scored lines as a guide, to break each strip down into a number of small mosaic tiles. Once you have completed one tile, repeat the process for all the other tiles.

7 Begin applying the tiles on the outer edge of the tabletop. Apply some tile adhesive to the back of each tile, then position it on the table surface. Try to use mosaic tiles that have a glazed edge on the outer circle of tiles, because this edge will be visible on the finished tabletop.

8 Continue to build up the design, adding tiles as required. You may have to use tile nippers to trim a few tiles where the ends of the rows meet. Once the design is finished, allow the adhesive to dry before grouting the mosaic with tile grout. Polish the surface after grouting in order to achieve the best possible finish.

WORKING WITH WOOD DIRECTORY

MAKING A BUILT-IN BOOKCASE

SKILL LEVEL Medium
TIME FRAME 1 day
SPECIAL TOOLS Torpedo level, small crosscut saw, miter saw
SEE PAGES 166–167

Making a built-in bookcase is an ideal way of providing storage space and an opportunity to create an attractive and decorative feature in a room. This type of shelving is best suited for alcoves, and they are often built on either side of a fireplace to make use of what would otherwise be wasted space. To create the built-in look, most of these bookcases are lined, either partially or completely, with MDF (medium-density fiberboard); the edges of the bookcase are finished with a molding. In this type of space there is also the option of making a built-in cabinet at the lower level to provide more storage space. Shelving supports should be attached, so that the shelves can be adjusted once the bookcase is finished.

MAKING BUILT-IN SHELVING

SKILL LEVEL Low to medium
TIME FRAME ½ to 1 day
SPECIAL TOOLS Miter saw or small crosscut saw
SEE PAGES 168–169

Built-in shelving is a simple form of construction, and, as with built-in bookcases (see pp.166–167), it is ideal for fitting into alcoves. However, when making built-in shelving for an alcove, there is no need to line the alcove with MDF (medium-density fiberboard). The shelves are supported by wood strips attached to the wall surface. They are quick to construct and provide an excellent storage system—however, bear in mind that the shelf levels cannot be adjusted once they have been secured in place. The front of the shelves can be covered with lengths of prepared softwood to give them a neat finish. Make sure that this front edge of softwood covers the edge of the MDF shelf itself to give the shelving a professional-looking finish.

ASSEMBLING ADJUSTABLE SHELVING

SKILL LEVEL Low to medium
TIME FRAME ½ day
SPECIAL TOOLS Awl
SEE PAGES 170–171

Manufacturers have developed ready-made shelving systems that are designed in such a way that they can be fitted into almost any area in the home that requires some kind of storage system. Most of these shelving systems are based on tracks, or upright supports, which are attached to the wall; brackets are then fitted into these tracks to support the shelves. Aligning and leveling up the tracks accurately is essential for making sure that the shelves will be level once they are in position. System design and appearance of shelves vary slightly from manufacturer to manufacturer, with wooden shelves being particularly popular. However, in the example on these pages, glass shelving has been used to produce an attractive and different finished effect.

INSTALLING SHELVES WITH HIDDEN SUPPORTS

SKILL LEVEL Low to medium
TIME FRAME 2 hours
SPECIAL TOOLS None
SEE PAGES 172–173

The fastening mechanisms for attaching shelves to the walls can often be prominent and unsightly and may detract from the neat appearance of the shelves—so finding a method for hiding these mechanisms has to be a more attractive option. Some manufacturers design shelving with brackets that are positioned on the back of shelves so that when the shelves are hung on the wall, the brackets are hidden. You can also create your own system for supporting shelves by using a resin inserted into drilled holes in the wall to hold support rods. Once the resin has hardened, the shelves are inserted onto the rods with no visible hanging system. Both these systems are good ways of hiding the fastening mechanisms.

Electric drill

Tape measure

Hammer

Screwdrivers

Workbench

Router

MAKING CORNER SHELVING

SKILL LEVEL Medium
TIME FRAME 3 hours
SPECIAL TOOLS Jigsaw, metal straightedge, router, torpedo level
SEE PAGES 174–175

By making your own corner shelving you can create a storage system that suits both your needs and the available space. The design demonstrated on these pages makes good use of the space and provides an ideal storage system for a small bathroom. Using a router on the shelf edges will require practice, but it provides an extra decorative touch.

UPDATING A CABINET

SKILL LEVEL Low to medium
TIME FRAME 2 hours per door
SPECIAL TOOLS Miter saw
SEE PAGES 176–177

Cabinets and cabinet doors are ideal areas in the home to benefit from an occasional revamp to update their style or to simply provide a different decorative finish. By using aerosol paints and a store-bought fretwork panel as a stencil, it is possible to completely change the appearance of a cabinet. Fitting a molding around the door edges and replacing the handles will complete the transformation. This system may also be used to give drawer fronts a makeover when you want to change the look of your kitchen units.

MAKING A BASIC PICTURE FRAME

SKILL LEVEL Low to medium
TIME FRAME 1 hour
SPECIAL TOOLS Mount cutter, staple gun, tack hammer, awl
SEE PAGES 178–179

Making a picture frame is a relatively straightforward and rewarding task—and it allows you to show off your picture, painting, or print to its full potential. The materials are readily available and the beauty of making your own frame is that it can be adapted to meet your precise needs. Before you start, you should think about the frame design and the mounting board color you want, and always measure the picture you are framing carefully.

GILDING A FRAME

SKILL LEVEL Medium
TIME FRAME 2 hours
SPECIAL TOOLS Artist's paintbrush
SEE PAGES 180–181

Gilding a wooden frame is an excellent way of transforming its appearance. Whether the frame is for a mirror, painting, or picture, the technique remains the same. It involves applying metal leaf to the intricate molding of the frame, using adhesive or size. The quality of the finish depends on your skill at applying the metal to the frame with the help of an artist's paintbrush. You can then give the gilded frame an aged or antiqued appearance by rubbing on some raw umber.

INSTALLING TONGUE AND GROOVE

SKILL LEVEL Medium
TIME FRAME 1 day for an average-size room
SPECIAL TOOLS Nail punch
SEE PAGES 182–183

The secret of good tongue-and-groove paneling is to make a sound framework and attach the paneling to it, making sure that tongue-and-groove lengths are secured precisely vertically with hidden fasteners. This type of paneling is hardwearing and attractive. You can use it up to chair rail level or to cover entire walls. When used up to chair level, a rail should be secured along the top of the paneling to give a neat finish.

INSTALLING WALL PANELS

SKILL LEVEL Low to medium
TIME FRAME 1 day for an average-size room
SPECIAL TOOLS Small crosscut saw, caulking gun, miter saw
SEE PAGES 184–185

Ready-made paneling kits are a quick and effective way of providing a decorative wall finish. These systems, which are assembled much in the same way as a jigsaw puzzle, are designed to be labor-saving while appearing as if they have been made by the old-fashioned traditional method. As with tongue and groove paneling, visible fasteners are eliminated by using bonding adhesive instead of nails.

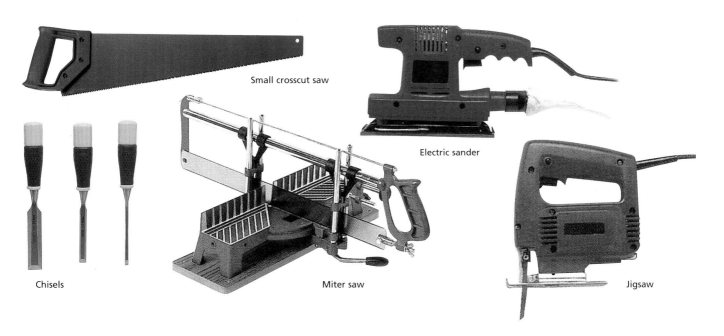

Small crosscut saw

Electric sander

Chisels

Miter saw

Jigsaw

MAKING A BUILT-IN BOOKCASE

YOU WILL NEED

Small crosscut saw
Torpedo level
Electric drill and drill bits, including screwdriver bits
Tape measure
Pencil
Carpenter's level
Miter saw
Hammer

MATERIALS

1 x 1½ in (25 mm x 38 mm) softwood strips
Woodscrews or concrete screws
Wall anchors (if required)
MDF (medium-density fiberboard)
Shelf support standards
Shelf pegs
Casing molding
Nails

Built-in bookcases often form part of the traditional design in period properties.

A built-in bookcase is a good space-saving storage option and can be tailored to play a decorative role in a room scheme. Both simple and more complex designs can be equally effective. Bookcases can be built as freestanding pieces of furniture, but alcoves are ideal areas in which to make built-in bookcases, because they provide the basic foundations on which to build a framework. Building a bookcase in an alcove also makes the best use of available room space—alcoves are often awkward areas in which to place furniture.

In most cases, an alcove will need partial or complete lining with MDF (medium-density fiberboard) to produce the built-in effect. In the example below, the sides of an alcove are lined with MDF to square off the walls and provide a base for shelf support standards (or tracks) and a framework of casing molding. You can make a built-in bookcase with a cabinet at the lower level, turning the structure into an interesting feature in the room.

A built-in bookcase can be painted the same color as the walls, so that it blends into the room's surroundings, or it can be painted a contrasting color to make it stand out.

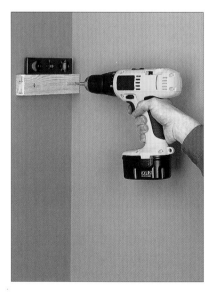

1 Cut pieces of softwood strips to a length equal to the alcove depth less the depth of the casing molding, which will be used to finish the bookcase. Drill a pilot hole on each end of a strip, position it on a side wall of the alcove, using a torpedo level to align it, and drive in the screws (you may need wallplugs, see step 3 p.169).

2 Sometimes concrete screws are used, which are screwed through the strip, directly into the wall behind. You can use a scrap of wood to secure a strip if the wall is not even. Continue securing the strips in place, spacing them every 1 ft (30 cm) on each side of the alcove.

3 Cut a piece of MDF to the height for the bookcase and equal to the depth of the wood strips. Hold the MDF and a shelf support standard, or track, in position against the strips; mark the required position for the track on the MDF with a pencil. You'll need two tracks on each side of the alcove, 2 in (5 cm) form the edge.

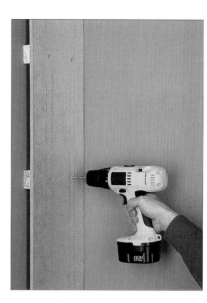

4 Remove the shelf support track, then drill pilot holes through the MDF and into the strips. These holes should be inside the bounds of the guidelines for the shelf support tracks, so that, once the tracks themselves are secured in place, the MDF fasteners will be hidden from view, creating a neat finish.

5 Screw the tracks in place, using a carpenter's level to check that they are precisely vertical. Normal wood screws or those supplied with the tracks will be adequate for fastening purposes— the screws should only extend as far as the wood strip and not into the wall behind.

6 Cut casing molding to fit around the edge of the bookcase and nail it in position, allowing the nails to go into the ends of the softwood strips. If the bookcase requires a top edge of molding, it will be necessary to secure softwood strips and apply MDF to the top of the bookcase in the same way as for the sides.

7 The shelf support tracks normally come supplied with pegs, which are inserted into the tracks to bear the weight of the shelves. Because this design is adjustable, you can change the shelf height whenever your collection of books or other items dictates.

8 Finally, cut MDF shelves to size and position them on the pegs. Once you are happy with the fit, you can paint the bookcase It is easier to paint the shelves separately before placing them in their final position.

MAKING BUILT-IN SHELVING

YOU WILL NEED

Pencil
Tape measure
Carpenter's level
Miter saw
Small crosscut saw
Awl
Electric drill and drill bits, including screwdriver bits
Hammer

MATERIALS

MDF (medium-density fiberboard)
2 x 1 in (5 x 2 cm) softwood strips
Softwood strips for edges of shelves
Woodscrews
Wall anchors (if required)
Nails

Built-in shelving is simple in design, but it provides effective storage while retaining a fresh decorative edge.

Using inexpensive materials, built-in shelving makes an excellent storage system that is simple and relatively quick to construct. As with all shelving mechanisms, it is crucial that the shelves and supports are fastened precisely level—any inaccuracies are accentuated once the shelves are finished. The side and back walls of an alcove provide substantial support for shelves, making them suitable for bearing heavy objects such as large books. In the example below, 2 x 1 in (5 x 2 cm) softwood strips have been used as the supports, but this size can be varied according to the width of the shelves and the weight that they will be required to support.

1 Use a pencil, tape measure, and carpenter's level to mark off the shelf heights you require on the wall. This pencil guideline can be used as the guide for positioning supporting wood strips. Built-in shelving is permanent and you cannot adjust it once secured, so take time to decide on the precise height requirements.

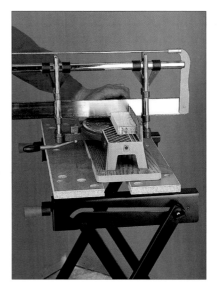

2 Cut strips to size, using a miter saw, as shown here, or a small crosscut saw. It is easier to cut accurately with a miter saw, and this ensures that the joints between sections of strips will be neater. Drill pilot holes about 1 in (2 cm) for the end of each strip.

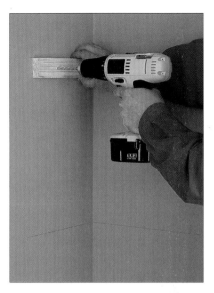

3 Position the short strips on the sides of the alcove, using the pencil guidelines to position them accurately. Use a torpedo level to ensure they are level. Mark the position for wallplugs with an awl, drill the holes, and insert the wallplugs. Drive screws into the strip.

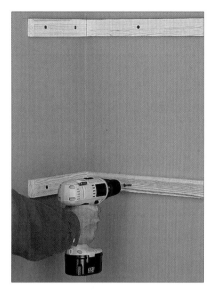

4 Check that the heights of corresponding strips on the opposite side of the alcove are exactly the same. Once the side strips are screwed in place, lengths of strips for the back wall of the alcove can be cut to size and positioned in the same way, again remembering to check the level before fastening them.

5 Measure the size for each shelf individually, being careful to measure the width for the shelf at both the back and front edges of the strips. Alcoves are rarely completely square and careful measuring is required to produce a good fit.

6 Once the shelves are cut from the MDF, you can leave them free fitting. However, for added strength, it is best that you nail or screw them in position by fastening through the top of the shelves, down into the strips below the shelves.

7 To finish off, nail lengths of softwood with dimensions equal to the height of the strips and the thickness of the MDF to the front of each shelf. Punch in the nailheads before painting or varnishing.

HELPFUL HINTS

Where alcoves are not completely square, it is always difficult to cut shelves precisely so that they fit tight up against the wall junctions. Where there is any gap between the shelf and the wall it can be filled with flexible filler or decorator's caulk. For this particular job, these are better than all-purpose filler because they can cope more effectively with any shelf movement once the shelves have been painted and are in use. An all-purpose filler is less tolerant of movement and is more likely to crack along the junctions, spoiling the finished look of the shelves.

ASSEMBLING ADJUSTABLE SHELVING

YOU WILL NEED

Carpenter's level
Pencil
Awl
Electric drill and drill bits,
including screwdriver bits

MATERIALS

Shelves
Tracks
Brackets
Woodscrews
Wall anchors (if required)

Adjustable ready-made shelves are the ideal choice for fitting into a space with a sloping ceiling—the shelf edges can be positioned to follow the angle of the slope.

There are a variety of adjustable shelving systems available that are based on a design of attaching adjustable tracks to the walls, to which brackets are then attached at the desired heights to support shelves. Because they are so easy to adjust, these systems are perfect for fitting shelving into awkward areas, such as a space under a sloping ceiling. They can also be used in more traditional ways to form standard shelving stacks or as single shelves on a wall surface.

As with all shelving systems, you should make sure that the bracket supports are positioned precisely level, otherwise the shelves will slope and look unsightly.

1 Use a spirit level and pencil to draw precise vertical guidelines on the wall. These lines should be the exact length of the tracks you are using. Manufacturers will generally provide guidelines on how far apart the tracks should be positioned for the shelves you are using.

2 Hold a track in position on the first pencil guideline and use an awl to mark the wall surface through the screw holes in the track (you can try using a pencil for this purpose, but generally the screw hole will not be large enough to allow the pencil's head to go through the hole).

3 Remove the track from its position on the wall and drill holes into the wall at the marked-off positions along the line. Make sure that the drill bit size is the same size as that of the wall anchors you are using. Once the holes have been drilled, insert wall anchors as needed.

4 Reposition the track, aligning the screw holes with the anchored holes on the wall surface, and screw the track into place. As you screw the track in position, hold a spirit level to the side of the track to make sure that it is still vertical.

5 Hold the next track on the next pencil guideline and double-check its position by holding a carpenter's level across the top of the two tracks to make sure they are exactly level. Mark, drill, and anchor the required holes before screwing the second track in place.

6 Attach the shelf brackets to the adjustable tracks in the positions required for your desired shelf heights. Designs vary slightly between manufacturers, but, generally, each bracket has two to four protrusions along the back edge that clip into the tracks.

7 Once the shelves are positioned on the brackets, you can secure them in place with setscrews. If using glass shelves, as shown here, adhere protective pads to the top of the brackets, followed by adhesive pads to hold the shelves in place.

8 Sit the shelves in position on the brackets and use a carpenter's level to make sure that the shelf edges align vertically. You can adjust the shelf height by repositioning the shelf brackets.

INSTALLING SHELVES WITH HIDDEN SUPPORTS

YOU WILL NEED

Tape measure
Pencil
Carpenter's level
Electric drill and drill bits,
including screwdriver bits

Resin fixing system
Workbench

MATERIALS

Ready-made shelving system

Bracket system
Woodscrews
Wall anchors

Resin fixing system
Resin
Threaded rod

Shelves hung with hidden supports provide a neat storage solution for a home office in a visible location.

Although shelves have a clear, practical function, there are ways of designing or decorating them so that they can become an attractive part of a room's decorative scheme and layout. One way of improving the appearance of shelving is to try to hide the way in which the shelves are attached to the wall—in many cases the actual hardware detracts from the aesthetics of the system. Two methods are demonstrated here, one using hidden brackets and the other a resin fastening technique on a simple shelf.

BRACKET SYSTEM

1 Many ready-made shelving systems have hidden brackets positioned on their backs, but it is still necessary to transfer this measurement to the wall surface. Use a tape measure to find the distance between the brackets, taking care to measure precisely from the center of one to the center of the other.

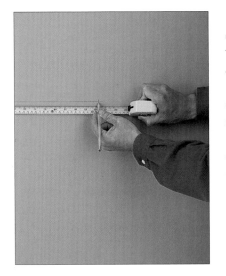

2 Transfer this measurement to the wall surface as accurately as possible. Make two small crosses on the wall surface to mark their positions. Use a carpenter's level to check that the marks are horizontal. If you draw a line, this can be touched in with some paint before the shelving is hung.

3 Drill into the wall at the marked-off points and insert the wall anchors into the drilled holes. Insert screws into the wall anchors far enough into the wall to provide a solid load-bearing fixture, but with the heads of the screws extending out far enough to be housed in the brackets on the back of the shelving system.

4 Hang the shelving system in place, hooking the brackets over the screwheads. The accuracy of the measurement will show here, because anything that is less than perfect will not allow the brackets to hook over the screws and fit snugly in place.

RESIN SYSTEM

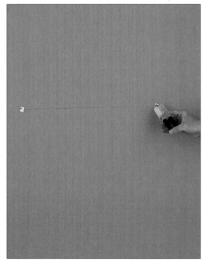

1 For a single wooden shelf, measure and draw a level line on the wall surface that is slightly shorter than the shelf width. At each end of the line, drill a hole large enough to take a threaded rod and far enough in to be two-thirds the depth of the shelf. Inject proprietary resin into the drilled holes.

2 Cut two lengths of threaded rod to one and one-third times the depth of the shelf. Insert each rod into a hole, allowing half of its length to protrude. Use a torpedo level to make sure that the rods protrude horizontally from the wall. Allow the resin to dry, which will secure the rods firmly in place.

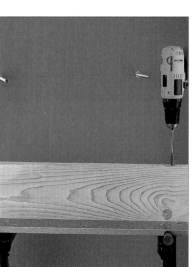

3 Clamp the shelf upright in a workbench, with its back edge on top. Drill two holes in the back edge of the shelf, corresponding to the distance between the rods in the wall. Each hole should be the same diameter as a rod and the depth should be equal to two-thirds the depth of the shelf.

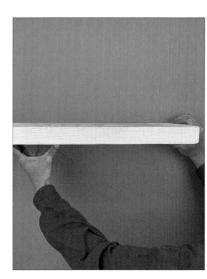

4 To hang the shelf on the wall, position it so that the threaded rods in the wall slide into the drilled holes on the back of the shelf. For a stronger hold, apply resin to the holes in the back of the shelf before hanging it on the wall. The result is a simple shelf with no visible hardware to spoil it.

MAKING CORNER SHELVING

YOU WILL NEED

Push pin
String
Pencil
Metal ruler
Jigsaw or small crosscut saw
Dust mask
Router
Electric drill and drill bits,
including screwdriver bits
Torpedo level

MATERIALS

MDF (medium-density
fiberboard)
Woodscrews
Wall anchors (if required)

*Corner shelving makes a compact storage
system that is ideal where there is limited space.*

an individual design that will enhance
the room's decorative scheme. The
rounded design of this shelving system
can counteract a corner's angularity
and provide a larger surface area than
shelves with straight edges across the
corner, thus creating more space.

The two sides and shelves are cut
from a circle, but you will need to buy
a square of MDF (medium density
fiberboard). To calculate the size
required, measure from the corner
along one wall as far as you want the
deeper, bottom shelf to extend. Double
this measurement and add 2 in (5 cm)
for trimming. This is the measurement
for each side of the square of MDF.

You can use a router, an electric
cutting tool, to make curved edges on
the shelves. Follow the manufacturer's
safety guidelines, and, before routing
the edges of new shelves, practice the
technique on scrap pieces of MDF—it
can take time to get used to a router.

Corners are often underused when
it comes to space management in
the home, however, they are ideal
areas for storage systems. Corner
shelving and cabinets can be bought
ready-made, but there are many
situations where it may be necessary to
build your own shelving system to fit a
particular space, or simply to provide

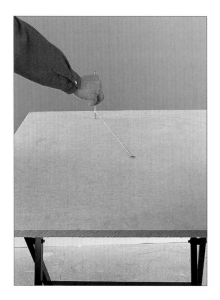

1 Attach a pencil
to one end of
the string, pin the
opposite end to the
piece of MDF, and
draw a circular
guideline on the MDF
surface. The exact
size of the guideline
depends on your
particular shelving
requirements, but, in
the example shown
here, the length of
the string is 16 in (40 cm).

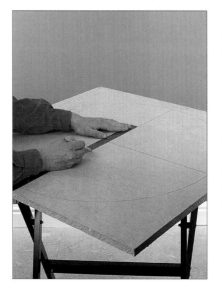

2 Using a metal
ruler, divide the
circle into quarters.
These sections will be
used to create the
sides and shelves in
the shelving system,
so it is important
that they are equal—
otherwise, the
finished shelving
system will not be
balanced on the wall.

3 Cut around the edge of the circular guideline with a jigsaw. A small crosscut saw can be used, but a power tool is more accurate. When cutting MDF, always wear a dust mask to avoid inhaling any of the dust created by the sawing.

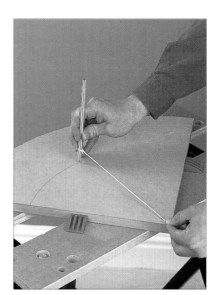

4 Cut the circle into four quarters. On one section use the pencil and a shorter piece of string—the string used here is 10 in (25 cm) long—to draw another pencil guideline. This will be the smaller of the two shelves. Cut around this guideline with the jigsaw.

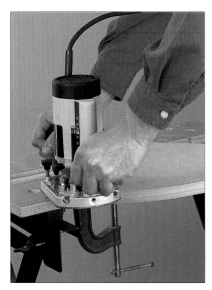

5 Route the curved edge of the three other quarters, using a side cutter blade to give a molded finish. Do not allow the router to extend all the way to the end of each curved edge—these areas must be left square-edged to give a good fit.

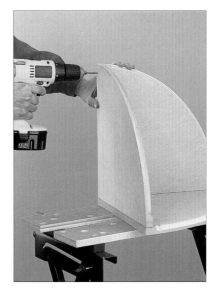

6 Screw the three larger sections of MDF together, drilling pilot holes before adding the screws (see Helpful hints). The screws should go through the first section, with one-third of their length going into the second piece. By fastening from the back of the shelving, the screws will not be visible when the system is complete.

7 Drill more pilot holes for the screws for the smallest of the four sections and secure it in position to provide the second shelf. Hold a torpedo level on top of the smaller shelf to ensure that it is precisely positioned and both the shelves are level.

HELPFUL HINTS

● To achieve neat joints when joining the three larger sections of this system together, you may need to adjust the exact position where the routed edges finish. You may also want to trim the back edge of one of the sections to ensure a tight fit, depending on your initial measurements. Try to keep a flexible approach in terms of fitting this system together.

● Once complete, the shelving system can be painted. After the paint is dry, screw the system into the wall using standard woodscrews and wall anchors.

UPDATING A CABINET

Masking cabinet door fronts to help create individual designs is an effective way of transforming their appearance. Here, doors have been painted with a dark blue base color, then low-tack masking tape has been used to mask off all sides of selected areas. These areas have been painted a paler blue before removing the tape.

When you want a change of style or design, replacing cabinets can be an expensive option, and it can be far more economical to simply revamp the existing cabinet system. The internal sections of cabinets are generally hidden from view, so, from an aesthetic point of view, it is only the cabinet faces that need changing. Simple options include replacing the handles, adding trims or moldings, and a general paint overhaul to transform their look. In the example below, all of these ideas are used on a cabinet door from a basic kitchen unit. A store-bought fretwork panel is used as a stencil to create an intricate painted design on the door, illustrating how a complete change of style can be achieved without replacing the door.

1 Unscrew the cabinet door from the kitchen unit. Take off any hinges and remove the handle. Most handles are secured in position with screws inserted from the inside surface of the door. Lay the door front-side down to gain access to the screwheads.

2 Turn the door right-side up and fill in the old handle holes. Once the filler is dry, sand it down along with the rest of the door face. For a melamine door surface, such as the one shown here, use an all-purpose primer to prepare the sanded surface for painting, following the manufacturer's instructions.

3 Paint the face of the door with a base coat. Latex paint may be used, or you can use an oil-base alternative. The advantage of latex paint is that it dries quickly, allowing you to apply two coats to the door surface on the same day.

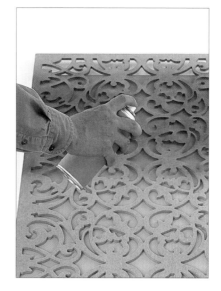

4 Take your chosen fretwork panel and use it as a stencil on the door surface. Place it in position on the door face, making sure that it is aligned precisely with the door edges. Shake the aerosol paint can before applying two light coats of paint across the fretwork and door surface.

5 Carefully remove the fretwork panel, lifting it upward instead of sideways to avoid smudging the paint. The fretwork panel can be reused.

6 Cut lengths of molding the height and width of the cabinet door. Miter the ends so they will join in each corner on the door face. Paint each section with the aerosol. When dry, apply double-sided self-adhesive tape to the back of each molding. Peel away the second strip to secure it to the door.

7 Press each of the the moldings in position on the edge of the door face, ensuring that the mitered ends match precisely for a neat finish. Once applied, there is a short period of time when you can adjust the moldings before the adhesive hardens and secures them permanently.

8 Mark the position of the new door handles on the door face, then drill holes and secure them in place. Reattach the hinges, and screw the door back in position on the kitchen unit.

MAKING A BASIC PICTURE FRAME

YOU WILL NEED

Tape measure
Scissors or craft knife and
metal rule
Pencil
Mount cutter or bevel cutter
Miter saw
Staple gun
Tack hammer
Awl

MATERIALS

Mounting board
Frame molding
Wood glue
Staples
Picture glass
Masking tape
Nails
Backing board
Screw-in eyes
String or cord

A light-colored picture frame sits well against a dramatic wall color such as this, producing a harmonious and coordinated effect.

Pictures, paintings, and prints are an important decorative feature in most homes, covering the walls to a larger or smaller degree, according to personal preference. Most of these are framed in some way or another, and it is well worth knowing how to frame pictures yourself so that you can avoid the added expense of having it done professionally.

In the example shown below, a print has been framed using mounting board and an outer frame of wooden molding. There is plenty of choice with these two items—different qualities and colors of mounting boards are available, as well as numerous types of molding to make the frame. This means you can choose a board that both sets off the picture attractively and complements the rest of the decor in the room. These choices are even more important if you are planning to hang a series or group of pictures on a wall. Because they will make a forceful visual impact on the room decoration, it is vital to consider the frame design and mounting board color before you begin.

1 Measure the exact size of the picture you want to frame, using a tape measure. If the picture has any roughened edges that need to be trimmed or you want to cut down its size, do so before you take the measurements, using scissors or a craft knife alongside a metal rule to make the cuts.

2 Using a sharp pencil, mark out the dimensions of the picture as accurately as possible in the center of a piece of mounting board. Cut out this central square using a mount cutter or bevel cutter, making sure that your cuts are as precise as possible. Lift out the central cutout area.

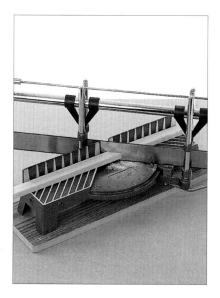

3 Measure the outer edges of the mounting board; these will be the inside dimensions of the frame. Cut four pieces of wooden molding to these dimensions, using a miter saw to miter each end. Make sure you miter the ends in the right direction, with the outside edge extending beyond your measurement.

4 Apply a small amount of wood glue to each mitered end of the pieces of wooden molding and join them together to form the frame. To strengthen the frame, use a staple gun to add two staples at each mitered corner. Make sure they are on the back of the frame, where they will be hidden. Leave the wood glue to dry.

5 Ask a glazier to cut a piece of picture glass to fit your frame. Insert it into the frame, so that it rests precisely on the molding ledge. Insert the mounting board into the back of the frame, ensuring that the fit is tight. Carefully trim the board if it is too tight; if it is too loose, cut a new mounting board to fit the frame.

6 Secure the picture or print in place on the back of the mounting board, using masking tape. This can be slightly tricky, as you must make sure that the picture is precisely positioned so that when viewed from the front it fills the window in the mounting board.

7 Cut a piece of backing board to size, and fit it into the back of the frame, covering over the mounting board and picture. Secure it in position by tacking it in place with a few small nails around the internal edge of the picture frame.

8 Tape over the joint between the frame and the backing board, then fasten a hanging system for the picture. Use an awl to make pilot holes in the back of the frame, screw in the eyes, and attach some string or cord between them. The picture is now ready to be hung.

GILDING A FRAME

YOU WILL NEED

Paintbrushes
Small artist's paintbrush
Cloth

MATERIALS

Latex paint
Dutch metal size
Dutch metal
Raw umber

A gilded frame offers classical elegance and style in any room scheme. It may be used as part of the overall room design or can stand alone as a decorative feature in its own right.

Old wooden frames can often benefit from a revamp of some kind. This may simply involve a new coat of paint, but there are other options available such as the gilding effect shown here.

In bygone years, gilding was always carried out with real gold leaf, but nowadays you can buy substitutes, such as Dutch metal, which is sold in sheets and gives the same effect at a fraction of the cost. It is applied over a coat of Dutch metal size, which bonds the Dutch metal to the surface. For an antiqued effect, the finish can be aged slightly by rubbing some raw umber into the molding on the frame after it has been gilded.

1 To enliven the gilded effect, it is best to apply the Dutch metal over a colored basecoat. Both dark and pale colors work well—in this case a deep red latex paint is applied to the frame. Apply the paint with a small paintbrush, ensuring that the paint gets into all the molded areas of the frame.

2 Once the basecoat paint has dried, apply a coat of size to the area that you are going to gild first. It is a good idea to gild one width or length at a time, so only apply size along one length at a time.

3 Let the size dry so that it is tacky to the touch. This normally becomes apparent when the size loses its initial milky color and becomes transparent. Lay a sheet of Dutch metal on the frame, pulling away the backing paper, if any, once it is in position (not all Dutch metal comes with backing paper).

4 Use a small clean artist's paintbrush to gently brush and push the metal onto the frame surface. The tacky nature of the size makes the metal bond to its surface. The ornate nature of the frame means that some areas will be left without metal in place. These can be filled in later or left alone to give a more worn or aged look.

5 Take the excess from each sheet as it is applied and use it to fill in other areas as required. The level of gap-filling in the molding is a matter of personal preference and depends on how much of the basecoat you want to be visible in the finished frame.

6 Once the entire frame has been gilded, you may find small, loose flakes of Dutch metal attached to the frame. These unfixed areas can simply be brushed away with a clean, dry soft-bristled paintbrush.

7 To finish, dip a cloth in a little raw umber and rub it across the surface of the frame, pushing the color into all the intricate areas in the molding of the frame. This helps to create an aged antique effect.

COORDINATING FRAMES

Pictures create a homely, welcoming atmosphere (see p.107). Although the pictures themselves provide the focal points on the wall, the frames are often used as a design link. A series of similar colored frames with different styles of pictures make a striking feature without detracting from the coordinated feel of the overall decor.

INSTALLING TONGUE AND GROOVE

YOU WILL NEED

Tape measure
Pencil
Carpenter's level
Electric drill and drill bits,
including screwdriver bits
Hammer
Nail punch

MATERIALS

Furring strips
Concrete screws or
woodscrews and wall
anchors
Tongue-and-groove boards
Nails
Bonding adhesive
Molding
Baseboard

A tongue-and-groove effect in pastel colors brings a relaxed, calm atmosphere to a room.

level on a wall surface, but it can also be effective covering the entire wall and even the ceiling. It is a versatile form of paneling that can be used to good effect in any room in the home.

The decorative options for tongue and groove are numerous, with some people preferring to keep the natural wood look, while others opt for stains, paint, or even special paint effects. These decorating decisions can be made according to your personal taste and the surroundings.

Much of the tongue and groove's decorative exterior is left unscathed by the technique in which it is fastened to the wall surface, with all the fasteners invisible to the naked eye. This "toe" nailing method provides the best technique for applying this type of finish. Tongue and groove should be applied over a framework of furring strips, and this is the first step necessary before applying the boards.

T ongue and groove is a traditional form of wall paneling that is making a comeback in modern house design, mainly because it is highly decorative and very durable, able to withstand the knocks and scrapes of everyday living with more success than painted or papered walls. Tongue and groove is mainly used up to chair rail

1 To fit a tongue-and-groove chair rail 3 ft 3 in (1 m) high, you will need to fasten at least three furring strips to the wall. Use a tape measure and pencil to mark the wall surface for a central strip and a top strip. The first strip will be attached at floor level.

2 At the marks, use a carpenter's level to draw horizontal lines across the wall surface. These lines will act as guidelines for positioning the furring strips. Make sure that they are exactly level, so that the finished paneling will be precisely aligned.

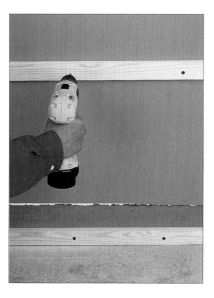

3 Drill pilot holes and attach the furring strips, following the pencil guidelines. Join separate lengths as necessary, depending on the width of your wall and the length of the strips you are using. Use concrete screws, as shown here; or wall anchors and normal screws can be used with equal effect.

4 Cut the boards to exactly the same height, from floor level up to the top edge of the top furring strip. The boards are initially fitted together by hand, interlocking the groove of one board with the tongue of the previous one.

5 Once a board is interlocked, "toe" nail it in place. Nail through the tongue at a 45 degree angle, into the strip below. Use a nail punch to knock the head of the nail in well. Do this on each of the three strips to secure the board in place. As each new board is fastened in place, it covers the previous fasteners.

6 To finish the top edge of the tongue and groove, some type of chair rail is required. In this case, a further length of furring strip has been cut to fit and is attached along the top edge of the top strip and the top edge of the tongue-and-groove boarding.

7 Finally, apply a molding cap to the front edge of this strip for decoration. Use a bonding adhesive to adhere it in place so that the invisible fastening theme is continued. Finish the job by applying baseboard to the base of the paneling.

TILE ALTERNATIVE

Tongue and groove is a good alternative to tiles in a bathroom. Tiles and tongue and groove can also be used together very effectively, as shown here (see p.14), to produce an unusual combination of finishes. You should coat wooden paneling that is likely to get splashed with water with an oil-based finish to provide extra dampproof protection.

INSTALLING WALL PANELS

YOU WILL NEED
....

Tape measure
Small crosscut saw
Caulking gun
Carpenter's level
Miter saw

MATERIALS
....

Paneling system
Bonding adhesive

SEE ALSO
....

Installing tongue and groove
pp.182–183

Paneling may be applied on one level or it can be used to climb alongside a staircase with equally successful results. Matching the finish with other features, such as doors, will link the room layout and panel design very effectively.

Paneling offers a slightly different effect from tongue and groove, but it has equally decorative appeal. Traditionally, it was made by craftsmen over a considerable period of time. Nowadays, there are various proprietary systems that enable the home improvement hobbyist to create the same effect. The paneling is supplied in a kit, which is assembled as you position it on the wall surface. This means that most of the fitting work has been eliminated and the task is little more than a straightforward process of adding factory-made panels to the wall in the correct order. Unlike tongue and groove, you don't need to attach furring strips to the wall.

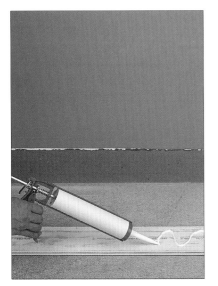

1 In order to use the complete system, it is necessary to take the old baseboard off the wall. The new baseboard sections should be cut to the correct length before they are attached to the wall with bonding adhesive, instead of nails. The panels are designed to slot into this baseboard.

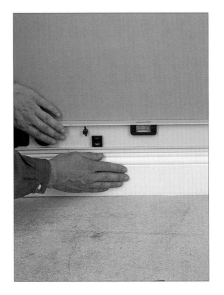

2 Position the new baseboard, pressing it into place on the wall surface. Use a carpenter's level to make sure the top edge is level, because floors are not always completely level. If necessary, make a slight adjustment to the baseboard to ensure that its top edge is level.

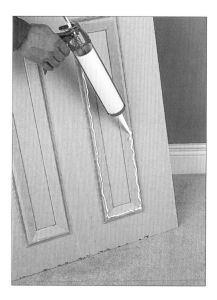

3 To attach the panels to the wall, apply bonding adhesive to them along those sections that will come into immediate contact with the wall surface when it is positioned on the wall.

4 Position the panel on the top edge of the baseboard, pressing it in place so that the adhesive creates a good bond with the wall surface. As long as the baseboard has been positioned level, it follows that the panels will also be correctly positioned.

5 To join panels, most of these paneling systems use joining strips between the panels. Apply adhesive along the back of the strip and position it next to the previously applied panel. The edge of the strip should join with the panel using a tongue-and-groove interlocking system.

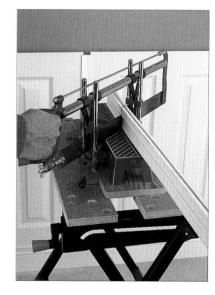

6 Continue to add panels and strips along the wall surface as required, cutting to size the final panels to fit tightly into the room corners. Miter the ends of the chair rail so that it also fits tightly between lengths in the corners of the room.

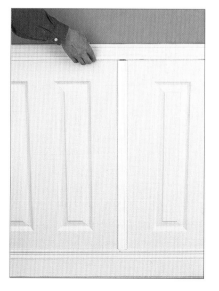

7 Apply adhesive to the back of the rail and position it along the top level of the paneling. Once all the adhesive has dried, check for any small gaps or cracks between panel sections and fill these before decorating. The paneling can now be painted as desired.

HELPFUL HINTS

● To make sure the panels are aesthetically pleasing, take time to decide where to start in a room to avoid cuts going through panels. Beginning at either side of a door will provide a balanced effect.

● Try to have two panels meet at the bottom of a stairway, so that half panels can be used to make the stepped ascent.

● If unsightly cuts are required, plan it so that these areas are positioned in one of the less conspicuous parts of the room or where they will be hidden by furniture.

FLOORING DIRECTORY

FLOORS: MEASURING UP A ROOM

SKILL LEVEL Low
TIME FRAME ½ day for an average-size room
SPECIAL TOOLS None
SEE PAGES 190–191

Measuring up a room before laying any type of flooring is an essential part of a flooring task. You need to do this to make sure that you buy the correct amount of floor covering and any other materials. It is also essential that the floor is properly prepared before starting. This preparation varies according to the type of floor and the covering that is going to be laid. Concrete floors require leveling, whereas wooden floors may need the addition of a plywood or hardboard layer to provide a good base for the new flooring.

There is always a right and a wrong place to start when laying a floor, particularly when working with any type of tiled flooring. These pages give guidelines on where to start tiling a floor, showing you how to find the center of

the room and how to plan your designs from this point. Achieving the correct balance for full tiles and cut tiles in a room is important for the look of the finished design. It is also worth remembering that, although some rooms are relatively square in shape, others have awkward angles or features, such as alcoves, and your calculations—especially for tiling—need to be adjusted to take this into account. A practical thought process is needed to divide the room shape up into square components so that you can work out an order of work in the usual way.

Flooring is expensive to buy, and it can never be emphasized enough that the planning process, if carried out correctly, will eliminate costly mistakes. If you cut a sheet of vinyl too small or begin to tile a floor in the wrong place, the results will be very difficult to rectify. Therefore, it is worth taking the time to check and double-check all your measurements and finalize your planning strategy before you start laying a floor.

LAYING VINYL TILES

SKILL LEVEL Low to medium
TIME FRAME 1 day for an average-size room
SPECIAL TOOLS Chalk line, adhesive spreader, metal straightedge
SEE PAGES 192–193

Vinyl tiles can be laid on a concrete screed as long as it is completely dry, or they can be laid on sound subfloors such as plywood or hardboard. They may also be laid on particleboard. It is vital that the surface is completely flat so that good adhesion is achieved. Traditionally, tiles are laid with all the joints aligned across the floor surface, but a brick bond pattern can also be used.

Whichever pattern you choose to use, careful planning is essential to make sure that you start tiling in the correct place in the room (see pp.190–191). A chalk line is the best tool to use for finding the center of the room, and you can plan all the measurements from this point. Vinyl tiles can usually be cut successfully with a utility

knife but, because blades become blunt quickly, you should make sure that you have a large enough supply on hand to finish the job. It is also essential to have a metal straightedge and a cutting board for making the cuts as accurately as possible—edges that are not straight will be noticeable on the finished floor. Wipe away any excess adhesive from the tile surfaces as you proceed, so it does not harden and spoil the surface.

LAYING SHEET VINYL

SKILL LEVEL High
TIME FRAME 1 day for an average-size room
SPECIAL TOOLS None
SEE PAGES 194–195

Although vinyl tiles and sheet vinyl are constructed from the same material, this is where the similarity ends. The techniques needed to lay the two types of floor covering are very different. As with vinyl tiles, the subfloor should be a concrete screed, plywood, or hardboard, but whereas tiles are used one at a time to

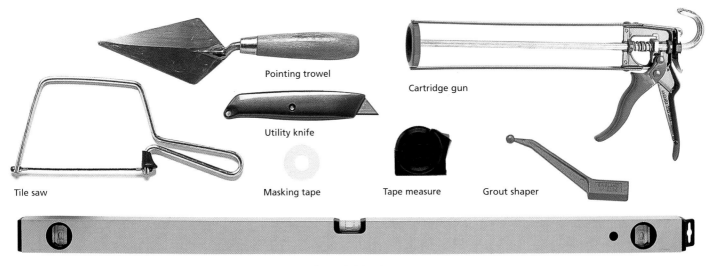

Pointing trowel

Cartridge gun

Utility knife

Tile saw

Masking tape

Tape measure

Grout shaper

Carpenter's level

cover the floor, with sheet vinyl the whole floor is covered with one piece of vinyl sheeting, except where the floor is so large that you need to join one or more sheets. This means that the sheet must be accurately trimmed to get a good fit.

It is a good idea to make a template of the floor you are going to cover, because this will make the fitting process easier. Although professional floor layers are unlikely to use this technique, it is by far the best option for the home improvement enthusiast. Take your time to make an accurate template, and take care when transferring it to the vinyl. Make sure that a balanced effect will be achieved once the vinyl is fitted, particularly with vinyls that have any type of directional pattern. Sheet vinyl can be stuck down around the edges with adhesive, but this is not usually essential except where two pieces are being joined.

If you do need to join two pieces of sheet vinyl, the join will look neater if you place two factory-cut edges next to each other. If you use edges that you have cut yourself with a utility knife, it is likely that the cut edges won't match and there may be gaps.

LAYING FOAM-BACKED CARPET

SKILL LEVEL Low to medium
TIME FRAME ½ day for an average-size room
SPECIAL TOOLS Brick chisel
SEE PAGES 196–197

Foam-backed carpet is much easier to lay than hessian-backed alternatives. However, traditionalists would say that there is a large difference in the quality of the two finishes. Although this is true to a certain extent, in recent years foam-backed carpets have increased in quality while still remaining a cheaper option to hessian-backed carpets. In addition, with foam-backed carpets there is no need to lay underlay, which saves on the cost. However, foam-backed carpets must be laid on sound floor surfaces, because they are usually relatively thin, so even slight imperfections in the flooring underneath the carpet will show up and increase the wear in these uneven areas.

You should use double-sided adhesive tape to secure the carpet around the perimeter of the room. In larger rooms where joins are required, you can apply double-sided tape underneath

any joining seams. You must trim the carpet to roughly the right size before it is laid in the room, then you should cut it more exactly to the precise dimensions of the room. A utility knife is the ideal tool for cutting the foam-backed carpet to the correct size.

LAYING JUTE-BACKED CARPET

SKILL LEVEL Medium
TIME FRAME ½ to 1 day for an average-size room
SPECIAL TOOLS Knee kicker, brick chisel
SEE PAGES 198–199

Jute-backed carpet requires more time and effort to lay than foam-backed equivalents, because it is necessary to install gripper strips around the room and to lay underlay before you can lay the jute-backed carpet. Another drawback is that jute-backed carpets are more difficult to lay. However, the result of all this extra effort is a more cushioned effect than that achieved with foam-backed carpet. Remember that the quality of the finish underfoot will depend on the quality of the carpet and the depth of the underlay. The best effect

will be achieved if good-quality materials are used.

Once the preparation has been done and the carpet has been put down, it is necessary to use a knee kicker to put the carpet under slight tension as it is fitted over and behind the gripper strips secured to the floor around the perimeter of the room. Because you are able to stretch the carpet slightly, the cuts around the edge of the room will be neatened to a certain degree during the fitting process.

At entrances to the room, you'll need something to differentiate between the floor covering in one room and that in the next room. If the same carpet continues into the next room, this shouldn't be a problem, otherwise it will be necessary to secure a threshold strip, so that a neat join can be made between the different types of floor coverings. Choose the threshold strips carefully to make sure that you have the right one, and pick a finish that suits the room decoration. For example, metal threshold strips such as those finished in a chrome effect are ideal in some room situations, while hardwood threshold strips are more appropriate for others.

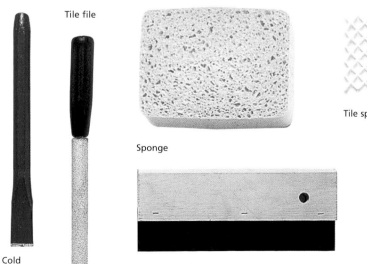

Tile file

Sponge

Cold chisel

Grout spreader

Tile spacers

Small notched adhesive spreader

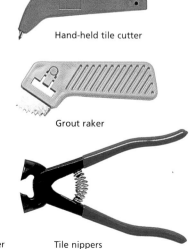

Hand-held tile cutter

Grout raker

Tile nippers

LAYING CORK TILES

SKILL LEVEL Low to medium
TIME FRAME 1 day for an average-size room
SPECIAL TOOLS Adhesive spreader, rolling pin
SEE PAGES 200–201

Planning the layout is essential when laying cork tiles. You'll have to find the center of the room and work back from this point to find the appropriate starting position (see pp.190–191). Instead of using traditional brown cork tiles, a colored variety has been used, giving the opportunity to introduce more of a pattern to the floor covering. The tiles are cut with a utility knife, using a cutting board and a metal straightedge for precision. A good tip is to roll an ordinary household rolling pin over the tiles to improve the adhesion between the tiles and the subfloor and to ensure that the tiles are laid completely flat. The type of cork tile illustrated on these pages does not require sealing once laid, but some types of cork tile will need a few coats of varnish or sealer once the tiles have been laid and the adhesive has dried.

LAYING CERAMIC TILES

SKILL LEVEL Medium
TIME FRAME 1 to 1½ days for an average-size room
SPECIAL TOOLS Adhesive spreader, tile cutter
SEE PAGES 202–203

Ceramic tiles are heavier than vinyl or cork tiles, and they require a slightly different technique when it comes to laying them. They can be laid on a concrete screed subfloor, or they can be laid on wooden floors as long as plywood has been laid to make sure that the surface is flat and that there is no flexibility or movement in the floor surface.

Planning for the positioning of ceramic tiles is similar to vinyl and cork tiles; however, because a different adhesive is required, it is a good idea to nail a temporary wooden strip into the floor along the starting line for the design, because this provides a solid support for positioning the first row of tiles. You will need to use spacers to maintain an even distance between the individual tiles. You should make any tile cuts with a tile cutter that is robust enough to deal with the thickness and strength of ceramic floor tiles.

Ceramic tiles will also need grouting after they are laid, because most of them are laid with gaps between the joints, unlike soft tiles, such as vinyl and cork, which tend to be butted tightly together at each joint. The neatness and general appearance of the surface depends on the quality of the grouting. This final stage is crucial to the overall finish of the tiles.

LAYING A NATURAL SLATE FLOOR

SKILL LEVEL Medium to high
TIME FRAME 1 to 1½ days for an average-size room
SPECIAL TOOLS Adhesive spreader, tile cutter
SEE PAGES 204–205

Laying natural slate floors involves many of the processes described for laying ceramic tiles, but a few refinements are necessary to deal with slight variations in the tile makeup and structure.

Your first job may be sealing the slate tiles to make sure that no dirt or excess adhesive becomes ingrained in the tile surfaces during the installation process. Slate tiles may not have the uniform shape or depth of ceramic tiles, in which case it will be necessary to vary the thickness of the adhesive layer in order to make the floor as level as possible. These tiles have a more handmade appearance that lends itself to spacing the tiles by eye instead of using tile spacers when laying them.

Slate tiles are particularly hard and it will be necessary to rent an electrically operated tile saw to cut them. These machines make cleaner, more accurate cuts than hand-operated tools, improving the tile finish, and they make it less likely that tiles will be broken when they are being cut.

LAYING A LAMINATE WOODSTRIP FLOOR

SKILL LEVEL Low to medium
TIME FRAME ½ to 1 day for an average-size room
SPECIAL TOOLS Jemmy bar
SEE PAGES 206–207

Floor sander

Electric drill

Knee kicker

Protective gloves

Paintbrushes

Laminate wood floors are attractive, hardwearing, and generally maintenance-free surfaces that look similar to natural floorboards that have been given a more polished appearance. These floors are mainly supplied in kit form and are often laid "floating," with no physical mechanisms joining the laminate floor to the subfloor below. A special underlay is generally laid on the subfloor before the laminate floor is put down.

You can join together sections of laminate boards with clips or, as in this case, glue together boards with tongue-and-groove edges. You'll have to cut the lengths of flooring to make them fit in the room, and use a jemmy bar to join sections at the end of rows as you progress across the floor surface.

Spacers are necessary to maintain a gap around the edge of the room between the floor and walls. Once the floor is laid, this gap acts as an expansion area, so that any slight floor movement will be tolerated without distorting the laminate woodstrip flooring. This gap is usually covered over with molding attached directly to the baseboard or base of the wall.

PAINTING A FLOOR

SKILL LEVEL Low
TIME FRAME 1 day for an average-size room
SPECIAL TOOLS Flooring chisel
SEE PAGES 208–209

Painting floors is a simple and straightforward way of adding a decorative finish to bare floor areas, and one that can be achieved quickly. The best painted floor effects are generally created by painting floorboards, although other surfaces, such as concrete, particleboard, and, in some cases, hardboard can be painted. There are many different options when it comes to painting floors, and you should consider all of them in terms of the style and atmosphere you would like to convey.

In the example shown on these pages, a pattern has been painted on floorboards to create an alternate color effect across the floor surface. Fake joints between the floorboards have been created with a flooring chisel, which add to the overall effect and provide lines of division between the different paint colors. Remember that floors receive a great deal of wear and tear, and bear this in mind when choosing between using standard floor paint (which will last longer) or other types of paint, such as latex paint, which will wear more quickly—however, this type of distressed, aging appearance may be the look that you want.

FINISHING WOOD FLOORING

SKILL LEVEL Low
TIME FRAME 2 days, sanding on the first day and finishing on the second
SPECIAL TOOLS Floor sander, edging sander, corner sander
SEE PAGES 210–211

Instead of painting your floorboards, you can maintain the natural grain effect of the wood by sanding the floor back and staining or varnishing it. Sanding a floor involves renting a floor sander, edging sander, and corner sander. It is a messy job, so be sure to mask or cover up areas as necessary.

Once the floor has been sanded, you can finish it with the desired natural wood finish. You can use traditional colors, but manufacturers now produce any number of colors that can give a greater impact to a floor finish. For example, pale blues and greens provide an effective alternative when applied to light-colored floorboards— these colors can make it easier to plan your color scheme and integrate floor and wall surfaces more convincingly.

Whichever finish you choose, remember that floors receive a lot of wear and tear. No matter how good the quality of the materials you use for your new floor, it will still be necessary to apply some type of maintenance coat to the floor from time to time. This does not need to involve all areas of the floor, simply those that get the most use and are most likely to show signs of wear. When applying these maintenance coats, make sure that the floor has been cleaned thoroughly so you get the best adhesion possible between the new coat and the floor surface. This simple process also maintains the look of the floor without causing too much disruption to the household, because there is no need to remove all the furniture from the room, eliminating the turmoil such events usually produce.

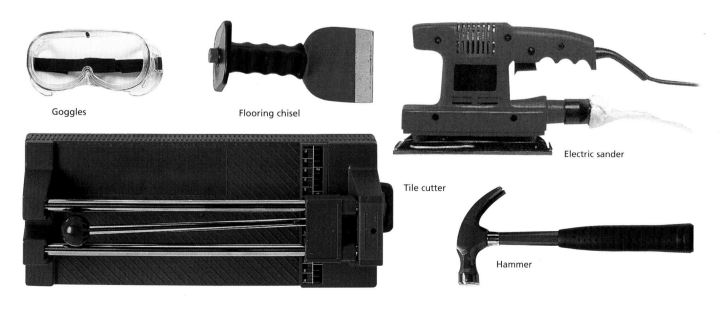

Goggles

Flooring chisel

Electric sander

Tile cutter

Hammer

FLOORS: MEASURING UP A ROOM

YOU WILL NEED

Filling concrete floors
Trowel and bucket
Sand/cement mortar mix

Laying plywood
Plywood and nails
Hammer and crosscut saw

Laying hardboard
Hardboard and nails or staples
Hammer or stapler
Utility knife

Measuring up a room for new flooring is a straightforward process and simply needs accurate measurements of the floor dimensions to calculate the surface area. From these measurements, you can estimate the quantity of material you need and purchase the floor covering.

Good preparation is essential for all flooring to produce a stable subfloor underneath the new floor covering.

The type of subfloor required depends on the flooring you are planning to use—whether it is vinyl, hard tiles, or carpet (see pp.192–207). Whichever flooring you use, be sure to prepare it correctly, following the manufacturer's guidelines where necessary. The better the preparation, the easier it will be to lay your chosen floor covering, and the longer the new floor will last after it has been laid.

FILLING CONCRETE FLOORS

On a concrete floor, any holes or cracks must be filled prior to laying the floor covering. A mixture of 5 parts sand to 1 part cement mortar mix is ideal for this. Press the mixture firmly into any holes or cracks and smooth it before it dries.

LAYING PLYWOOD

Plywood must be laid over floorboards when a sound surface is required for hard tiles. It also acts as a good base for soft tiles such as those made of cork or carpet. Nail the plywood down, making sure that it forms a rigid base and taking care to stagger the joints between sheets. Cut sheets with a saw to fit at the end of rows.

LAYING HARDBOARD

Hardboard subfloors are used as a base for vinyl or carpet. They can either be stapled or nailed to existing floorboards. Stagger edges between sheets and make sure that the hardboard is laid smooth side up. Cut sheets to size with a utility knife to fit at the ends of rows.

HELPFUL HINTS

● You'll need to cut hardboard or plywood to fit a room layout. Cut plywood with a crosscut saw, but use a utility knife to cut hardboard. Draw a pencil guideline on the hardboard and score it with the knife, then snap the board along the guideline.

● When securing either of these types of board with nails or staples, make sure that the fasteners penetrate securely into the floorboards, but are not so long that they can extend below the floor level and damage any cables or pipes underneath.

WHERE TO START TILING A FLOOR

1 To find the center of the room, measure the central point of each wall and hammer in a small nail. Attach a chalk line between two of the nails on opposite walls. Lift the line and let go to allow the line to snap onto the floor, leaving a chalk line **A.** Repeat on the opposite wall to make line **B.** Where they cross is the center of the room. Place a tile (dry) in an angle created by the intersection of **A** and **B.**

2 Measure back or position tiles to where the last full tile can be placed before a cut tile will be needed.

3 At this point draw a line parallel with chalk line **A.** Measure or place tiles along this line until you reach a point in the corner where the last full tile can be placed before a cut tile will be required.

4 Start applying adhesive and tiling from position **3** or **4.** Build up rows of full tiles; fill in with cut tiles at the room edges.

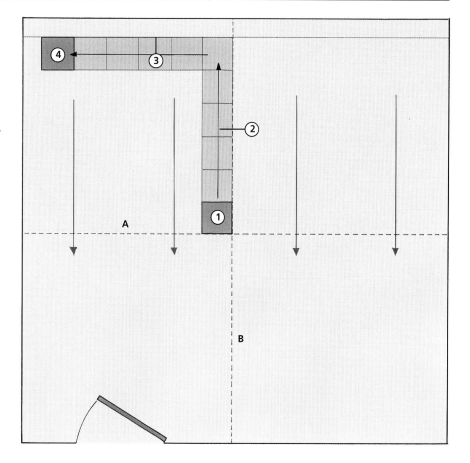

TILING AN AWKWARD-SHAPED ROOM

1 For an awkward-shaped room, the chalk lines are attached and snapped in different positions. In this example, the chalk line is first attached centered on the two short walls. For the correct position on the two opposite long walls, transfer the short wall measurements to the longer walls and measure out to the central point of these lengths to give the anchoring points for the chalk lines.

2 and **3** Measure or position tiles as a guide and draw a further guideline parallel with chalk line **A,** as above.

4 Start from position **3** or position **4,** as before, and build up tiles in rows, taking care to work toward the door and not get trapped in a corner.

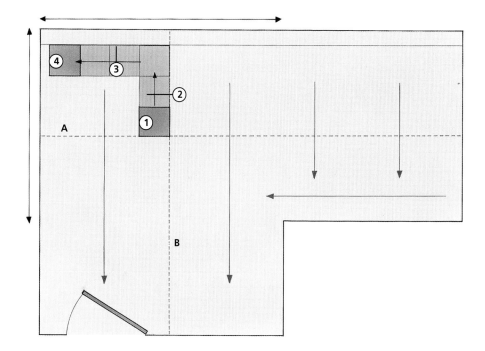

LAYING VINYL TILES

YOU WILL NEED

Chalk line
Tape measure
Pencil
Notched spreader
Cutting board
Utility knife
Straightedge

MATERIALS

Vinyl tiles
Flooring adhesive

SEE ALSO

Floors: Measuring up a
room pp.190–191

The marble effect of vinyl tiles gives an elegant and luxurious feel to this bathroom, but without the characteristic "cold to the touch" feel of genuine marble floor tiles.

Vinyl tiles provide an attractive, durable floor finish that is easily cleaned, making them ideal for the kitchen or bathroom. They are becoming increasingly popular, with innovative manufacturers producing tiles in a wide range of patterns and colors. Vinyl tiles can be laid in a traditional fashion so that the joints are aligned. Alternatively, a staggered tile pattern can be more effective, as shown in the example below. Apply these tiles on top of either plywood or hardboard subfloors for the best results. Check the manufacturer's guidelines to see if the floor surface requires sealing before applying the tiles and for any other suggestions.

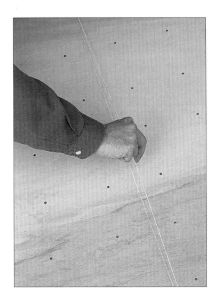

1 Find the center of the room by attaching and snapping a chalk line between the opposite walls. Work back from this central guideline to determine the best starting position for laying the tiles (see the diagram on p.191).

2 Because of the staggered design, attaining position 3 on the diagram requires a slightly different technique than for a joint-aligned design. It is often best to lay out the tiles dry—without adhesive—from the room's center guideline to establish the best starting point.

3 When you have the effect you want to achieve, simply draw a pencil guideline along the edge of the last row of full-size tiles closest to the wall to act as your starting point for applying the tiles. (You will fill the edges with cut tiles at a later stage.)

4 Remove all the tiles from their dry layout position and use a notched spreader to apply adhesive to the floor surface. Begin by working along the edge of the guideline, so that the first row of tiles can be applied, spreading enough adhesive for three to four tiles in the row at a time.

5 Apply the first tile, using the pencil guideline to ensure that it is accurately positioned. Take extra time here, because the position of this first tile will set the position for all the other tiles on the floor. Continue to apply tiles in rows until all the full-size tiles are in place.

6 Fill in around the edge of the room with cut tiles. To measure each edge tile, place one tile on the closest full-size tile. Place another tile on top, but butted against the baseboard. Use the edge of this top tile to draw a guideline on the middle tile.

7 Place the tile with the pencil guideline onto a cutting board. Using a straightedge as a support, score along the line with a utility knife. Bend the tile along this scored guideline, then simply snap it. Add adhesive to the back of the tile and position it. Continue in the same way around the rest of the room.

HELPFUL HINTS

When laying vinyl tiles on floor areas that are likely to come into contact with water, such as in kitchens and bathrooms, it is sensible to seal around the floor edges once the tiles are laid. This will protect the area from water seepage, which could otherwise lead to moisture penetration into the baseboard or below tile level. This can lead to unsightly bubbling or warping of the tiles, and damage to the floor surface itself. Silicone sealants are ideal for this job and you can apply it with a caulking gun along the tile/baseboard junction. To ensure a neat finish, run lengths of low-tack masking tape along the baseboard and the floor before applying the silicone sealant. Once the sealant has hardened carefully remove the masking tape.

LAYING SHEET VINYL

YOU WILL NEED

Newspaper or lining paper
Packing tape or masking tape
Pencil
Scissors
Utility knife

MATERIALS

Sheet vinyl
Floor adhesive

Good quality vinyl makes a comfortable, cushioned flooring that is easy to clean.

S heet vinyl is a similar form of floor covering to vinyl tiles and has the same feel underfoot. However, because you are using one large sheet (possibly more in large rooms) that involves cutting to fit very precisely, laying this type of floor covering is not something that should be undertaken lightly. The work must be planned carefully, and the process is further complicated if the vinyl has a pattern that requires aligning with the walls in the room. In this case, it is vital to make sure that you achieve a balanced effect. In the example below, for instance, it is important that the tile effect is aligned with the walls so that the tile joints follow the wall direction.

1 Making a template of your floor is the best technique for cutting and fitting vinyl. Old newspaper or lining paper can be used for the template. Position it roughly on the floor and tape the paper edges to join the sheets.

2 Crease the rough template around the edges of the room and draw a pencil guideline along each crease. Cut very accurately along these guidelines with scissors, giving you a precise template for your vinyl sheet sizes.

3 Tape the template on top of your vinyl, then cut around the edge of the template, leaving a 2 to 3 in (5 to 7.5 cm) excess. It may be easier to lay out the vinyl in a larger room, so it can be laid out flat. Protect the floor below the vinyl from the cutting blade of the utility knife, if this is necessary.

4 Remove the template and position the sheet of vinyl where it is to be laid, fitting it roughly in place and allowing the excess vinyl to extend up the wall slightly. Crease the vinyl into the junction of the baseboard and floor, then cut precisely along this guideline to fit the vinyl snugly against the baseboard.

5 With obstacles such as sink pedestals, make a number of cuts in the excess vinyl areas at right angles to the pedestal profile. This will allow you to mold the vinyl edge around the pedestal to give you the required cutting line.

6 Crease the small cut areas of vinyl tightly into the junction at the bottom of the pedestal and use a utility knife to trim each section in turn. Once you have cut around the pedestal, continue cutting the straight baseboard edge.

7 Where you need to join two sheets, try to ensure that you are matching two factory edges instead of cut ones, because you will get greater accuracy with the factory edges. (Make sure you match up any patterns.) Join the vinyl with a strip of adhesive laid under the edges of the vinyl; alternatively, use double-sided tape.

HELPFUL HINTS

● It is not essential to glue down vinyl, especially heavyweight types, but you can use adhesive around the edge of the room to hold the vinyl securely in place. In the same way that adhesive is used to join two sheets (see step 7), apply a band around the perimeter of the room. Once you fit the vinyl, lift it back from the room edges, apply adhesive, and press the vinyl down.

● Another area where adhesive will be required is stairways—the vinyl needs to be held firmly in position to avoid the possibility of it slipping out of place.

LAYING FOAM-BACKED CARPET

YOU WILL NEED

Utility knife
Carpet tool or bolster chisel

MATERIALS

Double-sided carpet tape
Foam-backed carpet

Foam-backed carpets are an excellent choice for bedrooms, where it is likely that you will want to walk about barefoot and will appreciate comfort.

The benefits of wall-to-wall carpet include a comfortable floor with a soft texture underfoot and also improved soundproofing—qualities useful in most areas of the home. Carpeting generally sets the style of a room. Most carpets have either a foam or a jute backing. Foam-backed carpet, normally thought of as the cheaper alternative to jute-backed carpet (see pp.198–199), has the advantage that it is much easier to lay and requires less floor preparation beforehand. Jute-backed carpet is usually better-quality carpeting.

There is a wide range of foam-backed carpets available and these vary considerably in quality. The amount of money you want to spend will determine the quality and type of carpet you can lay.

Because these carpets have a cushion-foam backing, there is no need to put down underlay before fitting them. In years gone by, people often put down newspaper as a form of underlay but modern carpet design makes this procedure unnecessary.

If you have wooden floorboards (which may be uneven), it is advisable to cover them with hardboard before laying the carpet, because this will prolong the life of the carpet. For techniques to prepare the floor, see pp.190–191.

1 Place double-sided tape around the perimeter of the room, but do not remove the backing paper on the top side of the tape yet. The tape will hold the carpet in position after it has been laid.

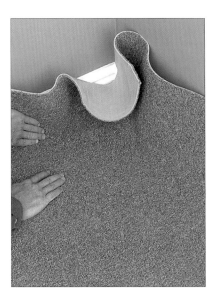

2 Unroll and roughly fit the foam-backed carpet, allowing an excess to extend up the walls. Push the carpet into position across and around the entire floor surface. Check that the whole floor area is covered before you proceed to the next stage.

3 Smooth the carpet flat and trim it back to within 1 to 2 in (2.5 to 5 cm) of the baseboard/floor junction, using a utility knife. Now lift the carpet back along one wall, remove the backing paper from the top side of the double-sided tape, then firmly press the carpet in place.

4 As you work your way around the perimeter of the room, smooth and stretch the carpet into all the wall/baseboard junctions and corners. Press down firmly so that the carpet adheres properly to the double-sided tape.

5 Give the edge of the carpet a final trim to ensure that its edge fits precisely in the baseboard/ floor junction. Trim the edges with a utility knife, taking care not to cut into the surface of the painted baseboard and damage it.

6 Neaten around the edges of the carpet to ensure there are no loose ends or ill-fitting areas. Then give the carpet a neat finish by using a carpet tool or bolster chisel to crease the carpet edge into the junction.

7 You many need to join sections of carpet, especially if it is being laid in a large room. Try to join them along the factory edges to acheive a neat seam. Apply double-sided tape to the floor below the edges, then remove the top backing paper and firmly press the carpet along the edges to secure the seam in place.

HELPFUL HINTS

Once the carpet has been laid, check completely around the baseboard junction. Carpet edges often fray if the cuts made when fitting are not completely clean. It is worthwhile going along each side of the carpet with a utility knife, trimming any areas where a thread has come loose, or dealing with any other imperfections that spoil the neat looking finish. This doesn't apply just to foam-backed carpets; you should apply the same technique to laying jute-backed carpet. At the same time, you should also check that all the edges are adhered securely to the floor.

LAYING JUTE-BACKED CARPET

YOU WILL NEED
....
Hammer
Utility knife
Knee kicker (rented)
Carpet tool or bolster chisel

MATERIALS
....
Gripper strips
Underlay
Jute-backed carpet

Using the same carpet throughout a number of rooms in the house helps to link color themes and provide continuity of style.

Usually better quality than foam-backed alternatives, jute-backed carpet is also more hardwearing, and these differences can often be seen in the price. Even if you choose a relatively inexpensive jute-backed carpet, you will still need underlay and gripper strips, which add to the cost. Once laid, however, this type of carpet will provide years of good service. Because underlay is used, it can be laid on most subfloors, including floorboards, particleboard, plywood, hardboard, and concrete screeds.

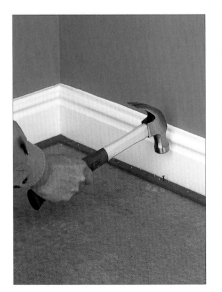

1 Nail gripper strips along each wall of the room and across the door opening. Leave a ¼ in (5 mm) gap between the strips and baseboard. You should take care not to damage the baseboard with the hammer—it is easy to scuff the surface of the baseboard.

2 Roll out lengths of underlay across the floor, butting them together where necessary. Do not allow the underlay to extend over the top of the gripper strips— use a utility knife to trim it back flush with the inside edge of the strips.

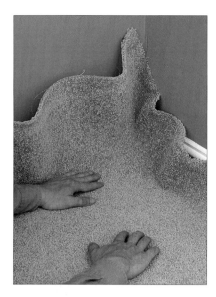

3 Lay out the carpet across the room surface, allowing the excess to extend up the walls. Using a utility knife, trim large excess amounts so that the carpet does not extend up the wall higher than the baseboard.

4 Trim the carpet back into the floor/baseboard junction, using a utility knife. Jute-backed carpet can be fairly rigid and inflexible, so make sure that it is pushed tightly into the junction before you begin to trim it.

5 A knee kicker, which stretches the carpet, is required to lay jute-backed carpet effectively. You should adjust the teeth on the knee kicker according to the depth of pile of your carpet. Turn a dial on top of the tool to extend or reduce the protruding distance of the teeth.

6 Work from the central areas of the carpet out toward each wall, gradually pushing and stretching the carpet toward the gripper strips and baseboard. Do not overstretch the carpet—simply allow it to fit evenly and lie flat on the floor.

7 Using either a carpet tool or bolster chisel at the baseboard/floor junction, push the edge of the carpet over and beyond the gripper strips to secure it in place. The teeth on the strips grab hold of the jute backing and grip the carpet in position.

DESIGN INFLUENCE

Carpeting is an important color factor in a room. Wall-to-wall carpets cover a large surface area, so they can be a major influence on the overall look. Take the carpet color into consideration at an early stage and coordinate it with the rest of the room design (see p.99). If you have a strong carpet color, for example, it may be best to have pale walls.

LAYING CORK TILES

YOU WILL NEED

Chalk line
Tape measure
Pencil
Notched spreader
Rolling pin
Utility knife
Straightedge
Cutting board
Cloth

MATERIALS

Floor adhesive
Cork tiles

SEE ALSO

Floors: Measuring up a
room pp.190–191

The attractive natural appearance of cork tiles make them an ideal choice for a stylish flooring. These tiles are also comfortable to walk on with bare feet and are easy to maintain.

Cork tiles are an easily cleaned and hardwearing floor surface that is suitable for most rooms and hallways. The tiles are laid in a similar manner to vinyl tiles (see pp.192–193) and require a sound subfloor—hardboard or plywood are both suitable choices. Cork tiles should not be laid directly onto floorboards.

The tiles are available in a range of styles; some have a sealed finish, while others require sealing once they have been laid. The most traditional tiles are the natural cork color, but some tile manufacturers offer a range of colors, giving you more options for the patterns and designs that you can create on your floor.

1 Find the center of the room by attaching and snapping a chalk line between opposite walls; plan your tile layout from this point. Use the diagram on p.191 as a guide to finding the right starting position. It is a good idea to start by laying out the design dry—without adhesive—to help plan your layout.

2 Make a pencil guideline along the back edge of the tiles closest to the wall (see step 3, p.193) before removing the tiles. Starting in a corner, apply adhesive to the floor, using a notched spreader. Spread enough adhesive for several tiles at a time. (Make sure you can lay the tiles without standing on the adhesive.)

3 Position the first tile in the corner, setting it down onto the adhesive layer. Take extra care when positioning this first tile so that it sits precisely along the pencil guidelines— this tile will be the one that ensures that the rest of the design is balanced.

4 Build up the design in rows, aligning subsequent tiles accurately to ensure all joints are precise and butted together tightly. Run a rolling pin over the tile surface to make sure that the tiles are adhered securely to the floor with no lifting edges.

5 To fill in gaps around the edge, position the tile that requires cutting on top of the nearest full tile to that edge. Place another tile on top, but with its edge butted up against the baseboard. Use the top tile as a guide to draw a pencil cutting line along the surface of the middle tile.

6 Using a utility knife and a straightedge, cut along this line. When cutting through tiles, place them on a cutting board so that you do not damage the floor below. Apply adhesive to the back of the tile before positioning it.

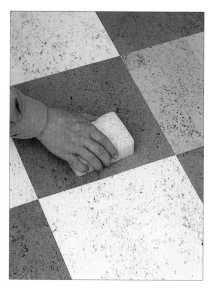

7 Finally, clean the floor surface with a damp cloth to remove any excess adhesive. Depending on the tiles you have used, the floor may be ready for use, or a sealant coat may be needed. Follow the manufacturer's guidelines for cleaning and sealing.

HELPFUL HINTS

● Most manufacturers advise that cork tiles be left in the room in which they are to be laid for 24 hours to acclimatize them to the room temperature.

● With untreated cork tiles, apply a coat of sealant before they are laid. This protects the surface so there is no danger of them becoming dirty while being laid. However careful you are, some adhesive gets onto the tiles, and, if they are not sealed, the adhesive can become ingrained in the cork and stain it. Apply further coats of sealant once the floor is laid.

LAYING CERAMIC TILES

YOU WILL NEED

Chalk line
Tape measure
Pencil
Long wooden straightedge
Hammer
Notched spreader
Carpenter's level
Wax pencil
Tile cutter
Grout spreader
Sponge
Grout shaper or small
wooden dowel

MATERIALS

Nails
Tiles
Tile adhesive
Grout

SEE ALSO

Floors: Measuring up a
room pp.190–191

Ceramic floor tiles are hardwearing and easy to clean, making them ideal for kitchens.

Ceramic floor tiles are among the most durable of surfaces. They are available in a huge range of sizes, shapes, and colors; some are plain, others are hand-painted. The quality differs considerably and it is essential to use tiles that are intended to be used on floors. You should also take into account the thickness of the tiles, and whether they might affect a door opening into the room.

Ceramic floor tiles do not require treatment once they have been laid, other than grouting. It is important that ceramic floor tiles are laid on a firm base—concrete screeds are ideal, as is plywood, which gives an even cover to floorboards. Some manufacturers may recommend using a flexible sheet sandwiched between adhesive layers before tile application (this is not always necessary); it is important to read the manufacturer's guidelines and follow any specific instructions when laying the tiles.

Take time to plan your strategy for application—mistakes are not easily rectified once the floor is finished. A good quality tile cutter is necessary because many floor tiles are thick and difficult to cut. In some cases, it may be necessary to rent a tile-cutting saw (see pp.204–205).

1 Find the starting position for tiling by referring to the diagrams on p.191. Nail a temporary wooden straightedge in position here. You are now ready to start laying the first row of floor tiles, butting them up against the straightedge.

2 Apply adhesive across the floor surface, working in manageable-sized areas, about 1 yd (1 m) long and just wider than the tiles. Use a coarse-tooth notched spreader— this provides an even coverage of adhesive with relatively deep channels, which will help to provide good adhesion between the tiles and the floor.

3 Position the first tile, pressing it in position snugly against the temporary straightedge and using a slight twisting motion to ensure good adhesion. Be careful not to exaggerate any movement, because this can upset the consistent level of the adhesive.

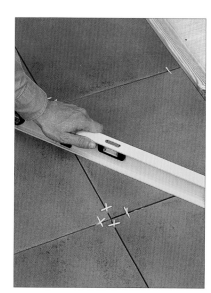

4 Continue to apply tiles and position spacers between them to ensure the correct gap is maintained between all the tiles across the floor. Hold a carpenter's level across groups of tiles from time to time to make sure that they are all sitting level.

5 Once all the full tiles have been applied, allow the adhesive to dry before returning to cut tiles to fit around the perimeter of the room. One by one, carefully measure the size of cuts required, using a tape measure, and transfer this measurement to a full tile, drawing a guideline with a wax pencil.

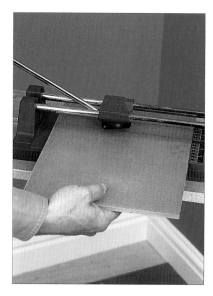

6 Position the tile in the tile cutter and score along the pencil line with the cutting wheel. Make one run with the wheel; apply enough pressure to scratch through the glazed surface of the tile and leave a clear scored line. Move the tile under the rails of the cutter and bring the cutting arm down to snap the tile along the line.

7 Apply adhesive to the back of the tile and position it. Continue with the other cut tiles. Once the adhesive has dried, mix up floor grout and apply it to all the gaps across the floor. Wipe away any excess grout from the tiles with a damp clean sponge before it can dry. Finish off with a grout shaper (see Helpful hints).

HELPFUL HINTS

● A new ceramic tile floor is set off to perfection by the grouting in the joints between tiles. Once you have applied the grout, remove any excess with a damp clean sponge, then use a grout shaper to ensure that all the joints are smooth.

● If you do not have a grout shaper, a similar effect may be achieved by using the end of a cylindrical piece of wooden dowel—running the dowel along the grout joints makes a slightly concave finish of an even depth and gives the grout a neat, uniform finish across the tiled surface.

LAYING A NATURAL SLATE FLOOR

YOU WILL NEED

Paintbrush
Protective gloves
Notched spreader
Long wooden straightedge
Spacers (optional)
Chalk line
Pencil
Tape measure
Carpenter's level
Tile-cutting saw (rented)
Safety goggles
Grout spreader
Sponge
Grout shaper or small
wooden dowel

MATERIALS

Slate tiles
Proprietary sealer
Tile adhesive
Grout

SEE ALSO

Floors: Measuring up a
room pp.190–191

The dusty tones of slate tiles have a natural elegance that helps to set off the other features in the room.

Laying tiles that have a natural look or composition, such as slate tiles, requires a different technique than laying standard ceramic tiles. Although their sizes are generally consistent, slate tiles often vary slightly in depth. The tile surface is usually untreated when supplied, so it is necessary to add a finish to the tiles so that they can be cleaned once laid.

Slate tiles must be laid on a sound subfloor—a concrete screed is the ideal surface, but plywood is also acceptable as long as there is no give in the floor surface and it provides a completely rigid base. Obtain the starting position for tiling by referring to the diagrams on p.191, and adjust the tile position as required to produce balanced cuts around the edge of the room. Be careful when handling slate tiles, because they are easily chipped and damaged. Their strength and hard-wearing properties only come into effect once they are adhered to the floor and the grouting is complete.

1 Before you begin to lay the tiles, seal their surfaces with a coat of proprietary sealer. In this way, they will be protected and any smears of adhesive can be wiped away easily as you lay the floor, before they have a chance of adhering to the tile surfaces. You should wear protective gloves while using the sealer.

2 Find the center of the room and lay the first row of tiles (see p.191), butting them up against a wooden straightedge and applying tile adhesive to the floor as shown in steps 1 and 2 on p.202. Using spacers is optional, because the slight variations in gaps between tiles add to the natural look of this floor.

3 After every few tiles have been laid, hold a carpenter's level across their surface to check that they are level. The tile surfaces themselves are often slightly undulating, so you may have to make some judgments by eye when carrying out this process.

4 Because of slight variations in tile thickness, from time to time it may be necessary to either reduce or increase the amount of adhesive underneath a tile to make it level with the surrounding floor. Remove any such tiles before the adhesive dries and adjust the levels accordingly.

5 Once all full tiles have been laid and are dry, you can deal with cuts around the edge of the room. Measure the tiles as shown on p.203, and use a tile cutting machine to cut tiles to size. These machines may be rented from rental centers and are usually required for slate tiles, which are harder than normal ceramic tiles.

6 Grout the floor in the normal way, making sure that the grout is firmly pressed into every joint. Wipe away the excess grout with a damp sponge before using a grout shaper or wooden dowel to shape the joints and give them a neat finish.

7 Once the grout has dried, you can apply another coat of proprietary floor sealer to finish the floor. Once dry, the slate surface is ready for everyday use. A fresh coat of sealer from time to time will keep it in good condition.

HELPFUL HINTS

There can be considerable variation in color between slate tiles. When buying your tiles, it is important to make sure that they are all from the same batch. Even within the same batch of tiles, the color may vary from one box to another. Therefore, it can be well worth mixing the tiles from different boxes before you start to tile. In this way, any small differences in color will be diluted across the entire floor surface, reducing the risk of clear divisions, or lines, between tiles of one specific color and those of a slightly different shade.

LAYING A LAMINATE WOODSTRIP FLOOR

YOU WILL NEED

Tape measure
Wood wedges
Hammer
Wood block
Sponge
Small crosscut saw
Jemmy bar
Pencil
Nail punch

MATERIALS

Sheet underlay
Laminate woodstrip flooring
PVA glue
Molding
Nails

Woodstrip flooring has a wonderful polished appearance and comes in a variety of widths and designs.

Laminate woodstrip flooring has become an increasingly popular option for home owners. It is an easy floor to lay, although there can be subtle variations in laying technique, depending on the type of floor you purchase, so it is important to strictly follow any instructions stipulated by the manufacturer of your flooring system. Most of these floors are laid "floating," where there are no fastenings between the laminate floor and the subfloor below. This allows the floor to expand and contract slightly to deal with changes in atmospheric conditions.

Woodstrip floors can be laid on the majority of subfloors. If laying it on concrete, the screed must be completely dry—it can take several months before a new screed is dry enough for laying this type of flooring. Otherwise, woodstrip floors can be laid on floorboards, plywood, particleboard, or hardboard, as long as the surface is fastened securely. In the example below, the floor has been fitted with the baseboard left in place. Alternatively, you can remove the baseboard before laying the flooring, then replace it afterward, eliminating the need for a molding (see step 7).

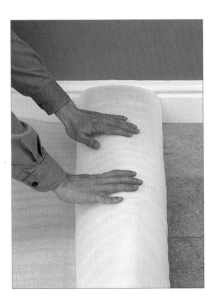

1 Most laminate floors must be laid on sheet underlay, which is sandwiched between the boards and the subfloor. Simply roll out lengths of the underlay across the floor surface, butting together their edges. Generally, the underlay does not require adhering down with any adhesive or tape.

2 Beginning along one edge of the room, position a length of woodstrip flooring close to the baseboard. Use wedges, supplied with the flooring, to maintain a consistent gap between boards and baseboard. This gap will allow the floor to expand with atmospheric changes without buckling the boards.

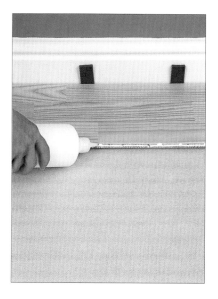

3 These floors interlock with a tongue-and-groove joint. Use PVA glue along the top of the tongue of the board, taking care not to allow the glue to get onto the surface of the board.

4 Position the next length of floor and use a hammer and scrap wood block to force the groove of the board onto the tongue of the previous one. Never use the hammer directly on a board because it will damage the tongue. Join subsequent boards in a staggered position as shown.

5 Inevitably, some PVA glue will be squeezed out of the joint between the boards. Wipe this away immediately with a damp sponge; once it dries it will be difficult to remove from the floor surface.

6 When you reach the end of a row of boards, you will have to cut a board to size before you can position it. To join the tongue-and-groove ends of the boards at the end of the row, you should use a specially designed jimmy bar to knock the ends in position.

7 Once the floor is laid, remove the wedges from around the edge of the room and cover the resulting gap with a length of molding. Secure this to the baseboard, instead of the floor surface, nailing it in position. Punch in nailheads as required.

HELPFUL HINTS

Laminate woodstrip floors have several advantages over the similar effect created by stripped floorboards, particularly in their soundproofing possibilities. While you may not think of a wooden floor as ideal for soundproofing, the advantage with a woodstrip floor is that, because it is floating, you can lay acoustic underlay underneath it to reduce any sound penetration to floors below. It would be more work-intensive to achieve the same effect with normal floorboards, because they would have to be taken up to lay soundproofing in the floor space below.

PAINTING A FLOOR

YOU WILL NEED

Hammer
Nail punch
Flooring chisel
Floor sander
Cloth or sponge
Paintbrush
Small artist's paintbrush

Caulking joints
Caulking gun

MATERIALS

Primer
Proprietary floor paint (two colors) or latex paint (two colors) and floor-grade varnish

Caulking joints
Decorator's caulk

Adding a decorative border to a painted floor is a simple way to enhance its effect and create a very individual finish.

Painting floors is a good way to give these surfaces an attractive decorative finish at a relatively low cost. Although concrete floors can be painted, the best effects are usually achieved on wooden floorboards. The floorboards must be free of any other finishes such as stain, varnish, and wax. If necessary, you can use a rented floor sander to remove any such layers (see pp.210–211).

Proprietary floor paints can be used on floorboards, but ordinary latex paint is just as effective, as long as you protect it with a floor-grade varnish. The example below shows how you can use more than one color to paint a pattern on the floorboards.

1 Make sure that any protruding nailheads are knocked into the floorboard surface, using a hammer and nail punch. You should also secure any loose boards as required (see step 1 on p.210).

2 You can increase the floorboard effect by simulating extra joints along the longer board length. Use a hammer and flooring chisel to cut an indentation across the widths of these boards at random intervals—these fake joints will be further enhanced when paint is applied.

3 Give the floor a final sanding to remove any rough areas before painting. This is especially important if the floor has not been sanded with a floor sander. A handheld electrical sander is ideal for this, but be sure to keep it in line with the grain of the wood. Wipe away the dust with a damp cloth after you have finished sanding.

4 Seal the entire floor surface with a good-quality primer to provide a sound base for further paint application. Work the primer well into the wood surface, and make sure that it has dried completely before you add the next coats.

5 Using your first color, paint alternate floorboards, taking care to be precise with the board joints and the fake joints that you made with the chisel. Use a large brush and, if necessary, a small paintbrush for any detail work.

6 Add the second color to the remainder of the floorboards, paying attention to joints between the boards. Because of the primer coat, one coat of each color may be enough, depending on how opaque you want the finish to be. If you are using latex paint, after the paint dries, brush on three coats of floor-grade varnish.

CAULKING JOINTS

In the example above, the joints between the boards are left relatively open, but you can create a completely sealed surface by applying some decorator's caulk along the floorboard joints. Smooth it with a sponge or a damp cloth before it dries.

CHILD'S ROOM

A painted floor is ideal for a child's bedroom, where you can create a finish that is not easily damaged (see p.93). You can have fun making different patterns and designs to appeal to children. Maintenance is a simple matter of a new coat of paint from time to time, and this offers the option of changing designs at a relatively low cost as the child grows.

FINISHING WOOD FLOORING

YOU WILL NEED

Hammer
Nail punch
Dust mask
Goggles
Ear protectors
Floor sander (rented)
Edging sander (rented)
Corner sander (rented)
Broom
Cloths
Mineral spirits
Paintbrush

MATERIALS

Nails
Wax or stain and varnish

Stripped and stained floorboards produce a very natural look that blends in well with furniture made of a similar material.

The alternative finish to painting floorboards is to revive their natural look by sanding, then staining and varnishing or waxing them. You will almost certainly need to use a floor sander. These can be rented on a daily rate, and it is usually possible to rent an edging sander and a corner sander in the same package.

Floor sanding is a messy task, and it is advisable to mask around doors to prevent dust traveling throughout the house. Also, open windows in the room where you are working and wear a dust mask, goggles, and ear plugs. Different sanders generally work on similar principles, but always check the manufacturer's guidelines.

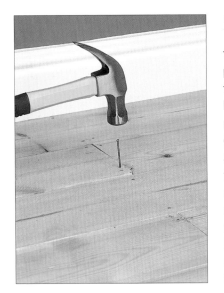

1 Before sanding, make sure that there are no nails protruding from the floor surface, using a hammer and nail punch to sink them (see step 1 on p.208), and that all the floorboards are secured. Add extra nails as required, but take care they are not long enough to hit any pipes or cables below the floorboards.

2 Use the sander, first across the floor at a 45 degree angle to the direction of the boards, then at the opposite 45 degree angle. Finish by sanding along the floorboards with the grain; reduce the coarseness of the abrasive paper you are using as you progress.

3 The large floor sander is unable to reach right up to the edges of the floor surface, so it is necessary to finish around the perimeter of the room with a specially designed edging sander. Hold on tightly to the handles because it can be difficult to control.

4 Just as the large floor sander cannot reach the edges of the floor, the edging sander is unable to get right into the corners. For this, use a corner sander that has a specially designed head to allow access right into the apex of the corner.

5 Once sanding is complete, it is necessary to remove all the dust from the floor surface. The worst can be removed by simply sweeping it up with a broom, then use a cloth dampened with mineral spirits to pick up the rest of the dust and residue.

6 If you are waxing the floor, the wax can now be applied. If you are staining the floor, as shown here, be sure to stain the boards one at a time. Maintain a wet edge at all times, and only allow the brush to flow in the direction of the wood grain.

7 Once the stain has dried, you can varnish the floor to give it a tough protective coating. Water-base varnishes are particularly effective, and their quick drying time will allow you to apply more than one coat in a day.

STAIN COLORS

Most floorboards are made from softwoods, which are pale in color. However, you can use colored stains to change this appearance and make them darker to give the illusion that the floorboards are made from hardwood. This gives more flexibility when deciding on color themes for the room, increasing your options for blending floor color and room decoration (see p.29).

SOFT FURNISHINGS DIRECTORY

USING SEWING MATERIALS

SEE PAGES 214–215

A guide to the tools for soft furnishing projects, including multipurpose tools and those specific for particular jobs.

MEASURING FOR CURTAINS

SKILL LEVEL Low
TIME FRAME about 30 minutes
SPECIAL TOOLS None
SEE PAGES 216–217

Measuring is essential for making sure you have enough material for the job.

MAKING UNLINED CURTAINS

SKILL LEVEL Low to medium
TIME FRAME ½ day
SPECIAL TOOLS None
SEE PAGES 218–219

Unlined curtains are relatively quick and easy to make. This form of lightweight curtain is ideal in most rooms, as long you do not want to achieve a complete light blackout.

MAKING A LOOSE LINING FOR CURTAINS

SKILL LEVEL Medium
TIME FRAME ½ to 1 day
SPECIAL TOOLS None
SEE PAGES 220–221

With a loose curtain lining, it is possible to wash the lining and curtain separately. You can also transfer linings that were hung with old curtains to be used with new curtains.

MAKING LINED CURTAINS

SKILL LEVEL Medium
TIME FRAME ½ to 1 day
SPECIAL TOOLS None
SEE PAGES 222–223

When a curtain fabric is not machine washable, there is no advantage in making a loose lining. Attached linings make curtains hang better. They are made using methods similar to those for loose linings.

MAKING A FRENCH PLEAT HEADING

SKILL LEVEL Medium
TIME FRAME ½ day
SPECIAL TOOLS None
SEE PAGE 224

Most curtain headings are finished with pencil pleats. However, you can achieve a more ornate finish for your curtains by making your own French pleat heading.

MAKING TIEBACKS

SKILL LEVEL Low to medium
TIME FRAME ½ day
SPECIAL TOOLS None
SEE PAGE 225

Tiebacks make an attractive decorative accessory for curtains, drawing them away from window recesses.

HANGING CURTAINS

SKILL LEVEL Low to medium
TIME FRAME 2 hours
SPECIAL TOOLS None
SEE PAGES 226–227

Curtains are often hung on curtain tracks or poles. They require careful measuring when positioning them.

MAKING A ROLLER SHADE

SKILL LEVEL Low to medium
TIME FRAME ½ day
SPECIAL TOOLS None
SEE PAGES 228–229

Shades are often supplied in kit form. You can position one close to a window or outside a window recess.

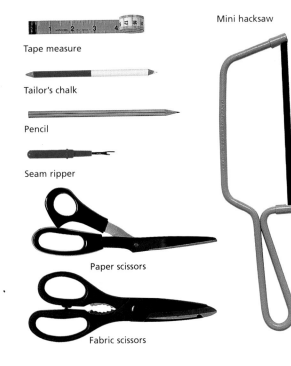

Tape measure

Tailor's chalk

Pencil

Seam ripper

Paper scissors

Fabric scissors

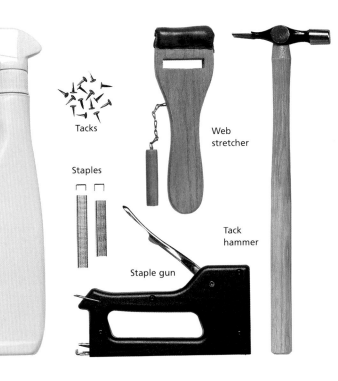

Mini hacksaw

Stiffener spray

Tacks

Staples

Web stretcher

Tack hammer

Staple gun

MAKING A ROMAN SHADE

SKILL LEVEL Medium
TIME FRAME ½ day
SPECIAL TOOLS None
SEE PAGES 230–231

Roman shades are a more complicated variation on simple shades. They have wooden dowels sewn into the fabric to create a drawing mechanism, with pleats of fabric on show when the shade is raised.

MAKING A SQUARE CUSHION

SKILL LEVEL Low to medium
TIME FRAME 2 hours
SPECIAL TOOLS None
SEE PAGES 232–233

Cushions are one of the most common soft furnishing accessories and can add a splash of color to a room. A simple square cushion with a zipper fastening is an inexpensive, effective design, and it takes only a couple of hours at the most to make.

MAKING AN OPEN-BACK PILLOW

SKILL LEVEL Low to medium
TIME FRAME 2 hours
SPECIAL TOOLS None
SEE PAGE 234

An alternative way of making a cushion cover, without the need for a zipper, is to create a back-opening cushion. You can use one of many fastening mechanisms, including hook-and-loop tape, hooks and eyes, ties, and buttons, or you can create an overlap vent.

MAKING DECORATIVE PIPING

SKILL LEVEL Low to medium
TIME FRAME 2 hours
SPECIAL TOOLS None
SEE PAGE 235

Cushions may be given further decorative appeal by attaching piping around the edges. It is relatively simple to make your own piping, and it can be attached to new cushion covers or added to old ones as part of a makeover.

MAKING A CUSTOM-FITTED CUSHION

SKILL LEVEL Medium
TIME FRAME 2 hours
SPECIAL TOOLS Curved needle, thimble
SEE PAGES 236–237

Invariably, the fitted cushion in a comfortable chair will need replacing or re-covering before any other part of the chair. Making a new cushion is a straightforward procedure, as long as you carefully measure and make a pattern for a new cushion before you start.

COVERING A DROP-IN SEAT

SKILL LEVEL Low to medium
TIME FRAME 2 hours
SPECIAL TOOLS Tack hammer, block of wood (or web stretcher, if you have one), staple gun
SEE PAGES 238–239

Whether you are replacing the worn covering on a drop-in seat or just changing the style, this is an excellent way of smartening up this type of dining room chair and giving it a new lease on life.

COVERING AN UPRIGHT CHAIR

SKILL LEVEL Medium to high
TIME FRAME ½ day
SPECIAL TOOLS None
SEE PAGES 240–241

Making a simple loose cover that fits over a standard upright chair is a quick and easy way of changing its appearance to create a piece of furniture that fits in with a new decoration scheme.

MAKING A LOOSE COUCH COVER

SKILL LEVEL High
TIME FRAME 1 to 2 days
SPECIAL TOOLS None
SEE PAGES 242–245

A loose cover is a great way of giving a completely new look to an old couch, as well as providing a cover that is easy to clean.

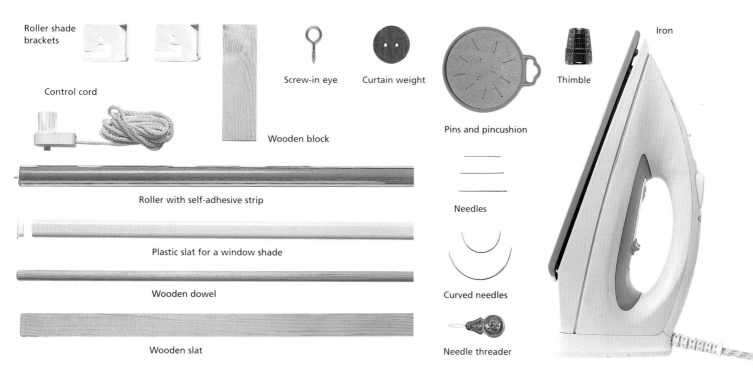

Roller shade brackets

Control cord

Screw-in eye

Curtain weight

Pins and pincushion

Thimble

Iron

Wooden block

Roller with self-adhesive strip

Plastic slat for a window shade

Wooden dowel

Wooden slat

Needles

Curved needles

Needle threader

USING SEWING MATERIALS

As with all home improvement projects, it is important to have some understanding of the way in which soft furnishing tools and materials are used to achieve the desired result. Illustrated on these pages are the main features on a sewing machine, a selection of important materials required for the soft furnishing projects in this book, and a brief explanation of their uses.

SEWING MACHINE

A sewing machine is the most expensive piece of equipment you will need to buy. It is important, therefore, to take plenty of time when making your choice, so that you will understand the machine's various features and the way they work. Although, in principle, sewing machines are the same, there are subtle differences between models, relating to how different stitches are selected and even simple tasks such as how to thread the needle. It is important to read the instruction manual supplied with the machine; if you are buying a secondhand one, you should make sure that the manual is included. The most important features to look for on any sewing machine are the functions for straight stitch, reverse stitch, and zigzag stitch. It is also necessary to have a normal presser foot, a zigzag foot, a zipper foot, and some spare bobbins. The illustration below shows the main features on a typical sewing machine.

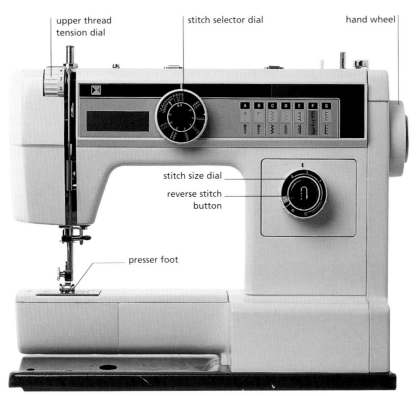

upper thread tension dial

stitch selector dial

hand wheel

stitch size dial

reverse stitch button

presser foot

CURTAINS AND SHADES

Very little special equipment is necessary for making curtains and shades: a tape measure, scissors, needles, pins, and tailor's chalk plus such items as curtain heading tape, hooks, hook-and-loop tape, buckram, and thread.

◀ PIN HOOKS
These are inserted into the top of the fabric through the fabric, buckram, and heading tape, so that they are not seen from the front of the curtain. They are then hung on the rings or gliders of the pole or track to hang up the curtain.

◀ PLASTIC CURTAIN HOOKS
A cheap and lightweight alternative to metal hooks, these are used on heading tapes with pockets (pencil pleat).

◀ ZINC CURTAIN HOOKS
Metal curtain hooks are stronger than plastic ones and are used on heading tapes with pockets. Where curtains are likely to jump out of gliders, you can slightly squeeze the hooks with a pair of pliers to hold them in place more effectively.

◀ BRASS CURTAIN RINGS
These rings are sewn onto tiebacks so that they can be held in place by a hook on the wall.

◀ AUSTRIAN RINGS
Best sewn on by hand, these small plastic rings are used on blinds for threading cord through. They act as a guide for the cord when the blinds are pulled up.

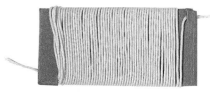

▲ BLIND CORD
Different weights and thicknesses of cord are available to match to the size of blind. A cord can be held neatly wrapped around a "tidy" (see above) if it is not held by a cleat on the wall.

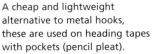

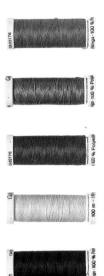

◄ **SEWING THREAD**
Choose a color closest to the color of the fabric it will be used on—a shade darker is better than a shade lighter if an exact match cannot be made, because lighter shades will show up more. Check the composition of the fabric and choose the type of thread accordingly—if the fabric is a synthetic mix, then use a synthetic thread. Only use 100 percent cotton thread on 100 percent cotton fabric; otherwise, you run the risk of the cotton thread shrinking at a different rate to the fabric. A fine silk thread can be used on silk fabrics, and heavyweight threads may be necessary for hand-sewing or heavy-duty upholstery. Some heavyweight threads can be used on sewing machines, but the tension may have to be changed. Read the manual for such adjustments.

▲ **BUCKRAM**
This is used as a stiffener, and it may be sewn or ironed onto fabric to create firm curtain headings or fabric tiebacks. Buckram is supplied in different depths on a roll and is easily cut to any size or shape.

▲ **PENCIL PLEAT HEADING TAPE**
This curtain heading tape is sewn to the top of the curtain; then, when the cords are pulled taut, pencil-size pleats are formed. These pleats are the same depth as the depth of the heading tape being used. The tape is available in different depths. By sewing one of the smaller heading tapes 1 to 2 in (2.5 to 5 cm) down from the top of the curtain, a softer gather is created above the pleat when the cords are pulled up.

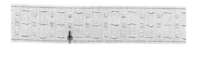

▲ **LOOSE-LINING HEADING TAPE**
This type of heading tape enables a loose lining to be gathered up and attached to the curtains, using the same hooks as the curtains are hung on. The curtain and lining can then be hung together.

▲ **HOOK-AND-LOOP TAPE**
The two sides of this tape fasten together by the hooks on one length catching onto the loops on the other one. It is available as a sew-on or self-adhesive tape.

SEATING AND CUSHIONS

Various types of materials can be used for seating and cushions, including wadding, webbing, foam, or other cushion fillings. When re-covering a drop-in seat, you may need to replace the stuffing and the webbing, as well as the cover.

▶ **CHIP FOAM**
Foam is supplied in different densities. Chip foam tends to be one of the firmer alternatives. Where only a shallow depth of foam is required on a seat, a firmer foam will give a more comfortable seat.

▶ **POLYESTER WADDING**
Wadding is placed between the foam and the fabric to soften the feel of drop-in seats. The extra layer also prevents the foam rubbing the back of the fabric, thereby increasing the life of the fabric. This layer is particularly important when velvet or equivalent fabrics are used, because, without the wadding, the foam will catch the back of the fabric and pull the velvet through the weave.

▶ **CUSHION FILLING**
Fillings for cushions can be bought in different sizes and densities, or as ready-made pads. When choosing your filling, you'll need to decide whether you want your finished cushion to have a relatively firm, padded feel or be slightly less dense for a softer feel. Fillings may be made from various materials such as feather or a polyester fiber construction.

▶ **BROWN PAPER**
An ideal material for making patterns is brown paper. Tape together sheets of paper when large scale work is required.

▲ **ZIPPER**
Zippers are supplied in standard sizes for shorter lengths. Longer lengths can be bought from a roll.

▲ **PIPING CORD**
Different thicknesses of piping cord are available to cover with your own fabric. Always buy more than you need to allow for seams. Check that the cord is preshrunk so that when it is washed it will not shrink at a different rate from the cover.

▲ **WEBBING**
Woven webbing is an inexpensive way of forming a base for a seat. Rubber webbing is also available, but this is fitted in a slightly different way.

MEASURING FOR CURTAINS

To calculate the amount of fabric required for your curtains, you will need to know the width of your curtain fabric and the size of any pattern repeat (this is the depth of one complete design that is repeated along the length of the fabric). This pattern repeat size is important. If you choose a fabric with a design that needs to be matched across the width of the curtain, you'll have to add the drop requirement (the depth of the pattern) to each length of fabric you'll need to make your curtains. This allows you to adjust the position of the fabric to match the pattern.

Measure the windows (see opposite) and check the measurements carefully to avoid costly mistakes. Decide what length you want the curtains to be (their overall drop) and how full they should look once gathered. After you buy the fabric, double-check that you have the correct amount before making the curtains; once you start cutting, you will not be able to change it.

HELPFUL HINTS

Several of the projects in this section will require you to handsew in some areas, such as when finishing a curtain or pillow, using a slipstitch. This allows for the stitches to be hidden inside the folds of fabric. Insert the needle from underneath through one fold of fabric, then push it through the top of the fold on the other side, directly opposite where it emerged from the first fold. Insert the needle back underneath through the first fold, about ⅛ in (4 mm) away from the first stitch. Pull the thread to bring the two pieces of fabric together, and continue in this way.

MEASUREMENTS

1 Rail width The rail width is necessary to help decide how many widths of fabric each curtain needs. Ideally, each curtain should be at least the width of the whole rail. This is referred to as double fullness—in other words, when both curtains are hung and gathered, the total width of fabric is double the rail width. For example, if the rail width is 81 in (206 cm) wide and the fabric is 54 in (137 cm) wide, then each curtain needs one-and-a-half widths of fabric to give double fullness.

2 Recess width A curtain rail should extend at least 6 in (15 cm) beyond each side of the window recess to allow the curtain to be pulled back from the window and let in maximum light. If putting up a curtain pole, it is the bracket that should be 6 in (15 cm) past the recess. For a curtain track, the end of the track itself should be 6 in (15 cm) past the recess. The distance for bracket fasteners can vary, according to the weight and fullness of the curtains. For heavier, fuller curtains, the brackets should be farther away from the recess. Lightweight, unlined curtains will take up less room when drawn than heavier, weight-lined curtains. In the diagram on the opposite page, the solid part of line **2** shows recess width, whereas the dotted continuation of this line denotes the variable distance at which the curtain pole bracket or track bracket can be fastened.

3 Recess drop Sometimes the recess drop measurement will be the finished length of your curtains when you want the curtain next to the window. Avoid this where possible, because the amount of light let into the room is greatly reduced when the fabric cannot be pulled back fully away from the glass. When hanging curtains inside the recess next to the window, you can screw or fasten the curtain tracks into the window frame itself if it is wooden. Because you should not insert screws into nonwooden frames, such as those found with UPVC windows, you will need to use a different type of fastener. You can attach a

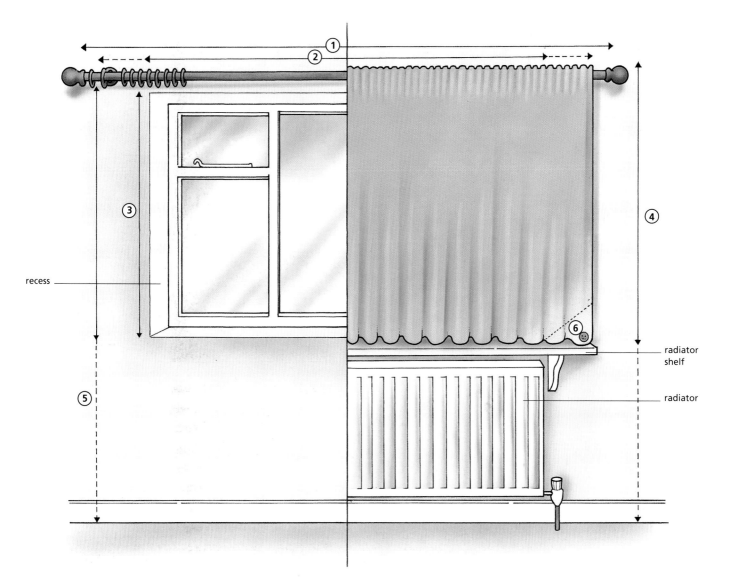

track to brackets that are fastened into the wall at the top of the recess. Install curtain poles, without finials, using special recess brackets. This window measurement will also be needed if you are hanging a window shade inside a recess.

4 Overall curtain drop The length, or overall drop, of the curtain depends on whether you want the top of the curtain to cover the track or pole. When using a pole, it can become more of a feature if you hang the curtain below it. If a radiator is underneath the window, then the bottom hem should end between it and the window sill. A radiator shelf gives a very definite line for measuring. If there are no obstructions, a floor-length curtain provides a luxurious effect. Current fashion uses even more fabric in the length, with the excess draped sumptuously on the floor.

5 Hook-to-hem drop For an accurate hook-to-hem measurement, simply measure from where the hook will be on the curtain ring on a pole, or on the glider on a rail, down to where you wish the curtain to end. To use this measurement, put a hook in the heading tape in the position you want to use it and measure the amount of fabric above it. Add that measurement to the hook-to-hem measurement to give you the overall length (see 4).

6 Position of curtain weights For curtain weights inside an unlined hem, see step 6, p.219. To be most effective on lined curtains, weights are not positioned directly in the curtain corner. Instead, where the curtain fabric folds back behind the curtain at the edge, position the weight at the bottom on the seam where the fabric meets the lining.

MAKING UNLINED CURTAINS

In a bright, sunny room where you want to keep the light and airy feel during the day, but need some privacy at night, unlined curtains will create a simple, uncluttered effect.

Unlined curtains are the easiest and least expensive form of window drapes and are an ideal way to practice making curtains before attempting lined ones. If the curtains are made from washable fabric, they are ideal for bathrooms and kitchens, where they will be exposed to steam from baths or cooking. Where curtains will be hanging inside an alcove, unlined ones are a better choice—they use less fabric than lined curtains and you can draw them back further to let in the most light. Calculate the amount of fabric needed, using the measurements on pp.216–217; allow an extra 6 in (15 cm) on the overall drop for the hem and seam allowances.

1 Cut out the fabric. If cutting a loosely woven fabric, cut along a pulled thread. To do this, make a small cut through the selvage and pull out a single thread, then cut along the channel left by the thread. Join any widths, using a medium-length straight stitch. Trim the edges with pinking shears and press the seam open.

2 Turn under a ½ to ¾ in (1.25 to 2 cm) hem to the wrong side on the side edges and press. Then fold again to form a 1 in (2.5 cm) double hem. Press and pin in place, with the pins across the hem.

3 For sewing hems, use a standard presser foot with a needle that is heavy enough for the fabric; a standard-point 100 (16) needle is ideal for most types. Choose a medium-length straight stitch and sew along the full length of both side hems.

4 On the wrong side of the fabric, mark 1 in (2.5 cm) down from the top of the fabric, using tailor's chalk. Fold the top down to the mark and pin. Place the top of the heading tape ¼ in (5 mm) down from the folded edge and pin. Sew along both edges of the tape, tucking in the corner of the fabric to make a mitered corner.

5 Lay the curtain right side up. Measure from the top and mark the overall curtain drop with a pin. Mark the folds for the hem. The second fold should be about 3½ in (9 cm) from the overall drop mark and there should be about 2 in (5 cm) left for the first fold of the hem.

6 Weights are used on bottom hems or joining seams to make the curtains hang properly. Sew the weights into the bottom hem, just below the pin line for the first fold of the hem. The stitching will be hidden when the curtains are viewed from the front. The curtains are now ready to be hemmed at the bottom.

7 Turn up the hem following the marking pins (see step 5). Secure the two sides first so that the hems line up and line up the center seams of any joined widths of fabric. Hold the side hems and pull to create a little tension, which will make the remainder of the hem easier to fold and pin.

8 If your sewing machine has a backstitch feature, use this to sew the hems on patterned fabrics, or sew them by hand. On plain fabrics, a neater finish can be achieved by hand sewing. Slipstitch (see p.216) along the side of the hem, then along the sides of the top of the curtain to finish.

MAKING A LOOSE LINING FOR CURTAINS

Lining curtains increases the overall life of the fabric. Even if the curtains are not in direct sunlight, over time the light will make them fade and will cause general deterioration of the curtain fabric. Generally, lining curtains will improve the way they hang. In addition, it provides an extra layer of fabric at the window, which in turn improves insulation.

Detachable loose linings are simple to make and fit. They are attached to the back of the curtain with hooks, so it is easy to remove them. They are also transferable—if you change the color theme of the room and want new curtain fabric, you can simply use the old lining with the new curtains.

Some lining fabrics have a "black out" property, which makes them useful for rooms where the early morning sunlight streams in. They are often used in children's bedrooms where the sunlight can cause sleep problems. To calculate the amount of lining fabric needed, see pp.216–217.

A detachable loose lining will ensure that the curtains hang well—it also means they can be washed or replaced very easily.

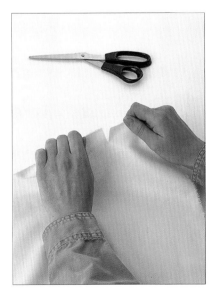

1 Cut the lining, allowing for the hems, so that the finished size of the lining will be slightly smaller than the size of the ungathered curtain. Cotton linings can be ripped along the weave: Cut into it at right angles to the selvage, firmly grip each side of the cut, and rip directly along the weave. Press the edge flat after ripping.

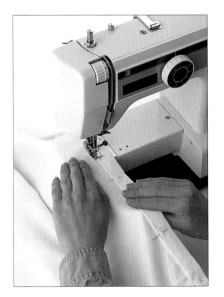

2 Turn and pin the side hem (see step 2, p.218). Because there is no pattern to follow on the lining, measure and mark with tailor's chalk or pins before pinning in place to ensure a straight hem. Sew along the hem, using a standard presser foot on the sewing machine and a straight stitch.

3 Slip the heading tape over the raw top edge of the lining fabric so the raw edge is against the inside of the heading tape's fold. Pin, if desired. Fold the ends of the tape under before sewing. Sew across the cords at the tape ends where the two curtains will meet when they are hanging in place.

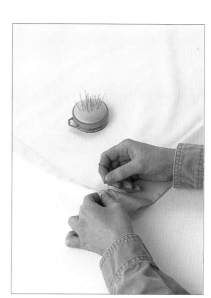

4 Measure the hook to hem length of the curtain to which the lining is to be fitted. The lining needs to be 1 in (2.5 cm) shorter, so that it does not hang below the curtain. Allow a 2 in (5 cm) hem with a 1¾ in (4.5 cm) fold inside the hem.

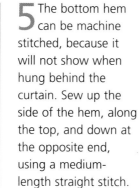

5 The bottom hem can be machine stitched, because it will not show when hung behind the curtain. Sew up the side of the hem, along the top, and down at the opposite end, using a medium-length straight stitch.

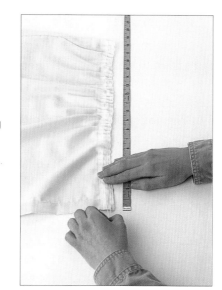

6 Iron the lining. Pull the cords in the loose lining heading tape at the end that was not sewn across in step 3. Make the lining width 2 in (5 cm) less than the curtain width, so that the lining will sit behind the curtain without being seen. Tie a knot in the lining cords to secure them.

7 The lining uses the same hooks as the curtains. Put each hook through the hole in the lining tape, then into the curtain tape. Once all the hooks are in place, you can hang the curtain and lining together on the same gliders or curtain rings.

PRACTICAL LININGS

Loose-lined curtains are practical in kitchens, where the curtains will probably need more frequent washing than in other parts of the house. The curtains and the linings can be washed separately without having to worry about any difference in fabric shrinkage. In this traditional country kitchen (see p.10), floor-length lined curtains provide effective heat insulation.

MAKING LINED CURTAINS

YOU WILL NEED

Tape measure
Fabric scissors
Pins
Iron
Tailor's chalk
Sewing machine
Needle

MATERIALS

Curtain fabric
Curtain lining fabric
Thread
Weights
Heading tape

SEE ALSO

Using sewing materials
pp.214–215
Measuring for curtains
pp.216–217

Lining reduces the amount of light coming into a room, which can be useful in a bedroom that gets the early morning sunlight. Curtains usually hang better if the linings are attached.

If your curtain fabric is not machine-washable, there is little advantage in having a loose lining. In these cases it is just as easy to attach the lining to the curtains when making them.

The lining and the curtain fabric are simply stitched together at the side seams. The lining is cut narrower than the curtain fabric, so that the side seams are hidden at the back of the finished curtain. Both curtain fabric and lining are sewn to the heading tape at the same time. You can then pin and stitch double hems on both the curtain fabric and the lining fabric. Calculate the amount of fabric required following the instructions on pp.216–217.

1 Cut the lining fabric 4 in (10 cm) narrower and 1 in (2.5 cm) shorter than the curtain fabric. With the right sides together, pin the side seams, ensuring that the top corners meet squarely. Sew the side seam from the very top, but stop about 12 in (30 cm) from the bottom to allow for hemming.

2 Repeat for the opposite side of the curtain, then iron the side seams and turn right side out. Holding the top of the curtain, fold the side seams where the lining and curtain fabric are sewn. Holding the side seams together, fold the curtain in half so that the top corners of the side seams face each other and meet.

3 The curtain fabric and lining will have a fold at the center of the curtain where the lining fold is about 2 in (5 cm) shorter than the curtain fold. Mark both the curtain fold and the lining fold with tailor's chalk.

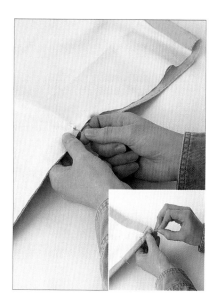

4 Open out the curtain and pin together the two marks (this is the center of the curtain). Measure and mark 1 in (2.5 cm) down from the top on the lining. Turn down the fabric and lining to the marks and pin, keeping the center marks in line. At the top two corners, diagonally fold in ½ in of fabric.

5 Sew on the heading tape (see step 4, p.219). Mark the overall length and the hem length on the right side of the fabric (see step 5, p.219) and sew in the weights (see step 6, p.219). Turn in the bottom hem edges to make a mitered corner. The top corner of the hem should meet the seam.

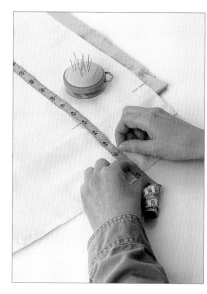

6 Measure the length of the lining, and mark it at the bottom so that it will be 1 in (2.5 cm) shorter than the curtain. Mark 2 in (5 cm) for the first fold of the hem and 2½ in (6 cm) for the second fold (see step 2, p.218). Sew the lining's hem as shown in step 5 on p.221.

7 Slipstitch the corners of the curtain where they are pinned and sew the hem as shown in step 8 on p.219. Where the corners of curtain and lining meet, pin them squarely in place; slipstitch down the seam and continue about 1 in (2.5 cm) around the corner at the bottom to secure them.

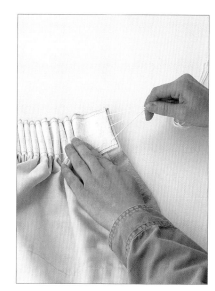

8 Make a note of half the curtain rod length. Pull the heading tape cords from the open end, pulling the pleats as tight as they will go (to make straighter pleats). Measure the cord and knot it at the half rod length point. Let out the gathers so that they are even all along the curtain to the knot. The curtains are ready for hanging.

MAKING A FRENCH PLEAT HEADING

YOU WILL NEED

Measuring tape
Fabric scissors
Tailor's chalk and pins
Iron

MATERIALS

Fabric
Buckram
Thread

SEE ALSO

Using sewing materials
pp.214–215

There are various types of headings that can be used on curtains. While pencil pleat heading is one of the easiest to use, French pleats create more of an impact, especially on plain fabrics. You can buy French pleat (also known as triple pleat) heading tape. However, the advantage of making your own is that you can make neater pleats. Instead of using heading tape, a strip of buckram—a 4 in (10 cm) width is ideal—is attached to the fabric before the pleats are made from the buckram and the fabric.

When calculating the amount of curtain fabric, allow a minimum of double fullness (see pp.216–217), because each pleat uses 5 in (12.5 cm) of fabric. The gap between each pleat should be about 5 in (12.5 cm). Each curtain should finish with a pleat on the outside edge and have a gap with no pleats on the inside edge to allow the curtains to close properly.

1 Make the curtains up to the point where it is necessary to attach the heading tape (see steps 1 to 3, pp.218–219). Do not turn down the top. Line up the top edge of the curtain on the wrong side with the edge of the buckram. Using a zig-zag stitch, sew along the very top to join the buckram and the fabric.

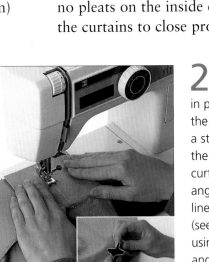

2 Fold the buckram and fabric over; pin in place. Sew above the zigzag line, using a straight stitch. On the right side of the curtain, mark at right angles to the top the lines for the pleats (see *Helpful hints*), using tailor's chalk. Pin and sew along the lines, using a straight stitch. Fold in to make a pleat (see inset).

3 Fold each pleat in place down the depth of the buckram. Sew across the bottom of each pleat just below the buckram; take care— the needle must go through 6 layers of fabric (or 12 if the curtain is lined). Alternatively, handsew the pleats in place. Use pin hooks at the back of the pleats to hang the curtains.

HELPFUL HINTS

To mark pleats, start from the outside edge of the curtain and mark the first line 5 in (12.5 cm) in. Leave a gap and mark the next pleat. The gaps between the pleats must be even across the width, so they should be adjusted accordingly. Continue marking the lines along the length of the curtain. Pin the lines of each pleat so that they match on the back and front, keeping the fabric square at the top. The gap at the meeting edges of the curtains needs to be half the size of the others, so that the pleats are evenly spaced when the curtains are drawn.

MAKING TIEBACKS

YOU WILL NEED

Tailor's chalk
Fabric scissors
Pins
Sewing machine
Iron
Needles

MATERIALS

10-cm- (4-in-) wide buckram
Fabric
Thread
Brass rings

Tiebacks provide a simple, neat finish for curtains. As well as being decorative, they are a good way of holding the curtains away from the window to allow in the light. Measure around the curtain where you want to position the tieback. Cut the buckram to this length, then cut one long edge into a curve. Use this as a template.

Tiebacks can be made from the curtain fabric or from a plain fabric that complements both the curtains and the room's color scheme.

1 Using the buckram template, mark and cut out two pieces of fabric, adding a seam allowance of ½ in (1.25 cm) for the bottom and the sides and 1½ in (4 cm) for the top. Pin and sew the curved edges right sides together, starting and finishing ⅜ in (1 cm) from the end.

2 Insert the buckram so that all of the seam is at the back of the buckram. Fold the top of the front piece of fabric over the top of the buckram and tuck in the excess fabric to give a neat edge. Pin in place. Tuck the sides in, making sure that all the fabric goes in behind the buckram. Pin in place.

3 Using the slipstitch (see p.216), finish the tieback by hand, making sure that the needle does not go through the buckram.

4 Handstitch one ring onto each end of the tieback, using doubled thread. You can then hang the rings on a hook positioned on the wall at the chosen level for the tieback.

HANGING CURTAINS

Curtains are usually hung on either poles or tracks. Although both perform a similar function, there is a slight variation in how the systems are installed. Curtain poles come in many different forms and are made from all types of materials such as iron or various kinds of wood. In most cases, the poles are held in place on the wall by specially designed brackets. For most windows, two brackets are enough, but for large windows or when the curtains are heavy, three or more brackets may be required.

Tracks are generally made from plastic and are more lightweight. They use a number of small brackets to hold them in place on the wall, and differ from poles in that the curtain may be drawn all the way along a track without interruption. (With poles, the brackets will interrupt the curtain flow, so they must be positioned in the right place so that the curtains can be drawn unhindered.)

The initial part of the fitting procedure is the same for both types of hardware. You will need a level guideline on the wall surface to ensure the correct height for either the track or pole. After this step, the steps will vary slightly for each mechanism. For example, you will have to install pole brackets farther away from the recess, but still on the pencil guideline. This will enable you to pull the curtains farther way from the window recess when they are open.

In most cases, the fastening mechanisms shown here are all that are required to secure the tracks or poles in position. However, if the curtains are very heavy or the wall is not particularly stable, you may need to strengthen the fasteners. You can do this easily by injecting some resin into the holes drilled for the brackets, inserting the fasteners, and allowing the resin to dry before installing the tracks or poles (see pp.172–173).

DRAWING GUIDELINES

1 When positioning a curtain rail outside a recess, a suitable height above the top edge of the recess is about 2–3 in (5–7.5 cm). Use a tape measure to mark off this measurement directly above one corner of the recess.

2 Use a carpenter's level aligned with this mark to draw a pencil guideline all the way along the top of the recess. Allow the pencil guideline to extend farther than the recess sides, because the curtain rail track or pole will be longer than the width of the recess (see pp.216–217).

FITTING A TRACK

1 For a track, measure the required distance past the end of the recess at both ends, and mark it off at equal distances along the pencil line to give positions for brackets. These distances will vary according to the length of the line, but brackets should be positioned about every 10 in (25 cm).

2 At each point, drill a hole and fit the bracket. Screw it securely in place, making sure that it is the right way up. The screws and plugs needed for fastening are normally supplied with the track.

3 The track itself is simply clipped onto the front of the brackets. You may need to tighten the adjustable screws on the brackets once the track is in place. You can then position the end pieces at each end of the track, so that once the curtains are hung they cannot slip off at the ends.

FITTING A POLE

1 Pole brackets are fitted farther away from the recess but still on the pencil guideline. First screw a metal-threaded plate onto the wall, then screw the base of the bracket onto the thread of the metal plate until the back face of the bracket is flush against the wall surface.

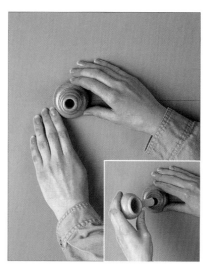

2 Make sure the bracket is secure on the plate, but do not overtighten it. Slip the second part of the bracket into the first piece to act as a loop through which the pole is threaded. Once this loop is in position, secure it by inserting a screw through the top of the first part of the bracket into the loop neck.

3 Once the other bracket has been fitted, thread the pole through the loops. Position the curtain rings so that one is on the outer side of each bracket. This holds the end of each curtain in place when they are drawn. Position a finial on each end of the pole for decoration and to keep the end of the curtain from falling off.

MAKING A ROLLER SHADE

YOU WILL NEED

Tape measure
Mini hacksaw
Fabric scissors
Medium-grade sandpaper
Sewing machine
Adhesive putty (such as Blu Tack)

MATERIALS

Roller shade kit
Fabric
Fabric stiffener spray
Thread

A roller shade can be fitted inside a recess close to the window, as shown here, or outside the recess, so that it covers both the window and the recess.

The simplest type of shade, a roller shade can be bought ready-made or made to measure, but you can make your own, using a kit and the fabric of your choice. To calculate the amount of fabric requir ed, measure the recess width and drop (see pp.216–217) and add an extra 10 percent for shrinkage, which may occur when spraying with fabric stiffener, plus 12 in (30 cm) to the length for fitting the shade around the roller and the wooden slat.

1 Fit the shade brackets; follow the manufacturer's instructions. It is not likely that the roller in a shade kit will exactly fit your window, so measure the width between the brackets and cut the roller of the shade to fit, using a mini hacksaw.

2 Cut the fabric for the shade to a workable size (allow the extra 10 percent for shrinkage and the extra 12 in/30 cm for the length). In a well-ventilated place, spray the fabric with the stiffener, following the manufacturer's instructions. Leave the fabric to dry.

3 When the fabric is dry and stiffened, measure the exact size required and mark it with tailor's chalk, making sure that the marks are square. Cut the shade to size, taking care not to fold or bend it—although stiffened, the fabric will not be rigid. If you need to move the shade, roll it up.

4 Measure around the circumference of the wooden slat. Use the measurement to pin a hem on the wrong side of the fabric to fit the slat. Before sewing the hem, insert the slat into it to check its fit and the length. Mark where the slat needs cutting, if needed, then cut with the hacksaw. Sand off any rough edges.

5 Sew the hem using a straight stitch (with the slat removed). Use the same color thread as the fabric because the stitching will show at front along the bottom. Take care not to fold or bend the stiffened fabric while stitching the hem.

6 Peel the backing paper off the sticky strip on the roller. Making sure the fabric is square to the roller, attach the fabric to the sticky strip. Rub across the fabric to make sure it sticks. Roll the fabric onto the roller—hold the roller still with some adhesive putty, such as Blu Tack, while you are doing this.

7 Insert the slat into the bottom hem and attach the end caps. Hang the shade on its brackets. Once in place, you should gently raise and lower the shade several times to check that it is running square.

ROLLER SHADE KITS

● Some roller shade kits are supplied with a wooden roller instead of a metal one. If using a wooden roller, you can still attach the shade fabric with a self-adhesive strip, but you can make it more secure by adding a few staples, using a staple gun.

● When making shades, always use metal or wooden rollers instead of cardboard ones, which are also available. Cardboard rollers are not as strong, and they tend to sag after time, especially if the shade is hanging in a kitchen or bathroom, where there is a lot of condensation, which can make the cardboard damp.

MAKING A ROMAN SHADE

YOU WILL NEED

Tape measure
Tailor's chalk
Pins
Sewing machine
Needle
Saw
Abrasive paper

MATERIALS

Fabric
Thread
Hook-and-loop tape such as Velcro tape (a piece the width of the blind)
Wooden dowels
Wooden slat
Austrian rings
Blind cord
Screw-in eyes

A Roman shade is a sophisticated version of a roller shade. It lies flat against the window but has deep, horizontal pleats when the shade is raised. It is attached to a mounting board secured above the window. A hanging system of cords threaded through rings on the back of the shade create the pleats, which are formed by wooden dowels sewn into tubes on the back of the shade. The size of the pleats varies according to the number of dowels used—the more pieces, the smaller the pleats.

A Roman shade uses more fabric than a roller shade because the tubes for the dowel and the side hems are sewn in. Calculate the fabric required by measuring the total area to be covered by the shade and adding a hem allowance at top, bottom, and sides, plus an allowance for tubes, multiplied by the number required. If you need to join fabric widths, use a zig-zag stitch along each edge, then join them with a straight stitch; press the seams open.

A Roman shade can add a simple elegance in any room, complementing the walls, furnishings, and floor coverings.

1 Measure and mark the side hems; then pin and sew them (see steps 2 and 3, pp.218–219). Turn down the top as for heading tape on curtains (see step 4, p.219). Pin the loop side of the Velcro tape onto the back of the shade at the top where you have turned it down, then sew all the edges of the tape.

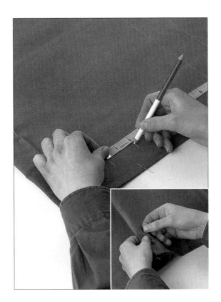

2 Measure and mark with a pin where you want each dowel. Measure the circumference of a dowel to calculate the tube's size. For each tube, mark half the dowel's circumference plus a little extra on each side of each pin. Pinch together the marked lines and pin them, with the tubes on the wrong side of the fabric.

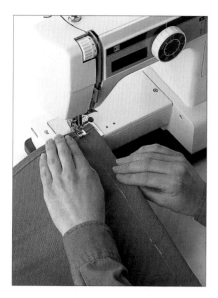

3 Sew along the lines, using a straight stitch to form the tubes for the dowels. At the back of the shade, sew a hem at the bottom of the shade large enough for the wooden slat to be inserted.

4 Handsew rings onto each of the tubes at equal distances from each edge. Wider shades may need extra rows of rings in the middle. If uncertain about the number required, add an extra row of rings and extra cord. If the dowels show any sign of bowing after fitting, additional rings and cords can be added at that point.

5 Thread the cord through the rings, securing it with a knot on the bottom ring. Allow enough cord to go across to the side where the controls will be operated. Cut the dowels and the wooden slat for the hem to the required length—just shorter than the finished width of the shade. Sand any rough ends and insert them.

6 Screw the eyes into the bottom of the mounting board secured over the window, placing them the same distance in from the edge as the rings on the shade. Secure the hook side of the Velcro tape onto the board; peel off the backing as you go. If the shade is very heavy, staple the Velcro tape for extra security.

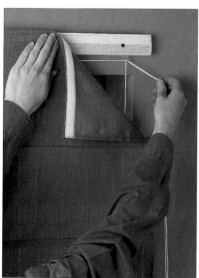

7 Secure the Velcro tape at the top of the shade onto the tape on the mounting board. Thread the cords of the shade through the eyes under the board. Thread the cord across the top to the side of the shade where the control cord will be operated. Wind the cords around a cleat on the wall to secure them in place.

DECORATIVE TOUCH

A Roman shade allows plenty of light to flood through the bedroom window of a converted school during the day (see p.15), and it makes an attractive focal point at night when the shade is lowered. Before fitting a Roman shade, always make sure that the window is large enough to accommodate the bulk of fabric created by the pleats when the shade is pulled up in the daytime.

MAKING A SQUARE CUSHION

YOU WILL NEED

Tape measure
Tailor's chalk
Fabric scissors
Pins
Sewing machine

MATERIALS

Fabric
Zip fastener (the width of
the cushion size)
Thread
Cushion pad or other filling

Cushions made from fabrics with unusual, interesting textures, in bold colors and designs, create a strong focal point in any room.

Making your own cushions is one of the simplest ways to add a stylish—and colorful—finishing touch to a room. You can make them in an enormous variety of shapes and sizes (a simple square is one of the easiest), and they can be made from almost any fabric. If you want your cushion to be hardwearing, choose your fabric accordingly. The cushion filling may be feathers, kapok (fibers from a type of tree), synthetic fibers, polystyrene beads, or foam. Ready-made cushion pads come in many sizes and shapes, covered with fabric such as ticking or calico. For each cushion, you will need two squares of fabric 1¼ in (3 cm) larger than the desired cushion size.

1 Measure and mark on the fabric the squares for the back and the front of the cushion, adding ¾ in (2 cm) to the width for seams, and 1¼ in (3 cm) to the length for seams and the zipper. (If making several cushions from patterned fabric, mark out panels so that the pattern matches on each one.) Cut out the two pieces.

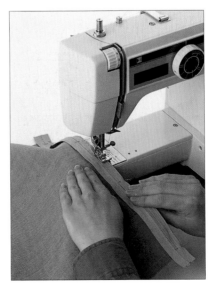

2 Place one piece of fabric right side up and pin the zipper along one length, with the teeth of the zipper fastener facing the fabric. Using a zigzag stitch, sew the zipper and fabric together. This keeps threads from fraying and stops loose threads from getting caught in the zipper once the cushion is in use.

3 Turn the fabric over; mark along the zipper length a line ⅛ in (3 mm) deeper than the depth of the zipper. Fold the zipper back to this mark; pin it in place. This forms a fold of fabric that will hide the zipper. Check that the fold of fabric is pinned flat against the zipper on the right side before sewing.

4 Using a zipper foot, sew a line beside the teeth of the zipper. Repeat steps 2 and 3, sewing the zipper to the other piece of fabric on the other side of the zipper. For zippers with attached slides, stop with the needle through fabric and zipper; lift the foot, move the slide past the needle, lower the foot, and continue.

5 If using a zipper from a roll, add the slide before pinning the edges of the fabric together at the seams, making sure that the top corners are square and that the folds of fabric that cover the zipper are in place right up to the zipper's teeth.

6 Sew the seams together, using a straight stitch and a standard foot. Once the seams are sewn, sew around the seam edges, using a zigzag stitch, to prevent fraying (changing the foot on your sewing machine, if necessary).

7 Turn the fabric right side out. Insert a cushion pad and close the zipper. If the cover fabric is not washable, you may wish to spray it with a fabric protector, which will help to keep it clean.

STRONG INFLUENCE

Cushions can have a big impact on the decorative scheme. A single, well-chosen cushion made from a textured fabric can add considerable warmth to a cool, minimalist interior. Alternatively, cushions can soften the angular lines of a piece of furniture. These eye-catching ikat cushions bring a touch of ethnic style to a small modern living room (see p.29).

MAKING AN OPEN-BACK PILLOW

Pillow cover openings do not necessarily have to be along one of the cover edges. A simple Velcro tape fastening can be positioned across the middle of the back of the pillow. This is a particularly good type of fastening if your sewing machine does not have a zipper foot. If you want to make a pillow with a center-back opening, you will need slightly more fabric than for a side opening, because the back of the pillow is made out of two pieces of fabric instead of the one piece shown in the square pillow on pp.232–233.

ALTERNATIVE FASTENERS

- There are a variety of fasteners to use when making a cushion. Make the pillow in the same way but, instead of Velcro tape, attach hooks and eyes, snaps (these can be bought on tape or individually), ribbons, or buttons and button holes.

- An overlap vent may be used where no fasteners are required. To make this, add at least an extra 1 in (2.5 cm) to the length of each of the back panels when cutting out. Tack the overlap in place before sewing up the side seams. When this is done, cut the tack stitches so that the cushion can be turned right side out.

1 Measure and mark on the fabric the size of the front of the pillow, plus a seam allowance of ⅜ in (1 cm) on each edge. Measure and mark two back panels the same width as the front one, but half the length plus twice the width of the tape and ¾ in (2 cm) for the overlap and hem.

2 On each back panel, on the fastening edge, mark the hem allowance on the wrong side of the fabric. Pin the hems and sew in place, using a straight stitch. Place the two panels side by side with these hems overlapping and check that their total length is the same as that of the front panel.

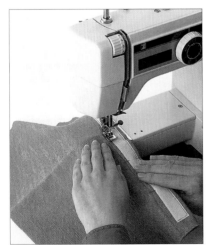

3 Cut the Velcro tape slightly shorter than the width of the pillow. On one back panel, sew the Velcro tape along the hem on the wrong side. On the second panel, sew the other side of the Velcro tape on the hem on the right side of the fabric.

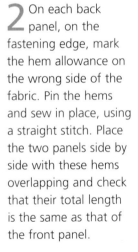

4 Fasten the Velcro tape. With right sides together, pin the front and back pillow pieces together. Sew the seams using a straight stitch. Sew with a zigzag stitch around the edges to prevent fraying. Open the Velcro fastening and turn the cover right side out.

MAKING DECORATIVE PIPING

YOU WILL NEED

Iron
Tailor's chalk
Tape measure
Fabric scissors
Pins
Sewing machine

MATERIALS

Fabric
Thread
Piping cord (choose the width that suits the size of cushion you are making)

A piped edging highlights the shape of a pillow, giving it an elegant finish. When piping needs to bend around corners, it should be made from fabric cut on the bias. To mark bias strips, measure from the corner the same distance up the fabric as across, then draw a diagonal line to join the two points. This is the bias line. Using tailor's chalk, mark strips of identical width (enough to cover the piping cord plus a seam allowance) parallel to the bias line.

Piping can be made from the same fabric as the pillow or from a contrasting color.

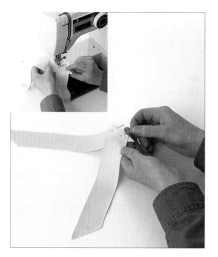

1 Cut out the strips. To join strips, pin two together, right sides facing and matching the seam lines, so they form a V shape; sew together. Continue sewing strips together until the fabric strip is long enough to fit all the way around the pillow, with an allowance for seams.

2 Fold the bias strip around the piping cord so the two edges meet. Sew alongside the cord to secure it in place, using a zipper foot or piping foot (either will work).

3 To sew the piping onto the unfinished pillow, attach it to one side first. Place the piping on the right side of the fabric so that the edges line up; sew along the line that was made in step 2. Start at the back of the pillow so the seam where the two ends meet will be hidden.

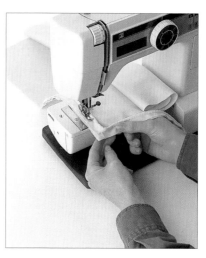

4 At the corners, snip the seam allowance. To join the piping, trim the cord, then cut and fold under excess fabric; sew across. Place the second piece of fabric with the first piece, rights side together. Sew the same line, finishing as in steps 6 and 7 on p.233.

MAKING A CUSTOM-FITTED CUSHION

YOU WILL NEED

Brown paper
Pencil
Paper scissors
Fabric scissors
Tape measure
Tailor's chalk
Pins
Sewing machine
Curved needle
Thimble

MATERIALS

Foam (to a depth of your choice)
Stuffing
Fabric
Thread

A custom-fitted cushion with a foam filling can transform a sagging old chair into a firm new one.

A deep window sill can be made into a window seat by adding a custom-fitted cushion, or a storage chest can be turned into an ottoman by making a cushion for the top. No matter how you use the cushion, the principles of measuring and making are the same. Choose a fabric that is strong enough to be stretched taut over a firm foam filling suitable for upholstery (the foam filling must comply with fire retardant regulations).

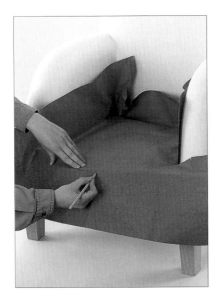

1 Place the sheet of paper on the chair. With a pencil, mark the edges that the cushion will extend to. Where the paper will not lie flat around corners, cut into the paper from its edge. Cut out a template along the pencil line and use it to cut the foam and stuffing. Alternatively, if the chair has a cushion, use it as the template.

2 Make a second paper template by drawing around the first one and adding a seam allowance of ⅜ in (1 cm). Place this template on the fabric and draw around it with tailor's chalk. Repeat for a second panel. Mark the centers and corners of the template and fabric (see *Helpful hints*), then cut out the two panels.

3 Measure around the sewing line from point to point on the second template. Then use these measurements to mark out the side panels on the fabric. The depth will depend on the foam used. Add seam allowances of ⅜ in (1 cm) around each side panel. Use a complete length for the front panel (see *Helpful hints*).

4 With right sides together, pin the panels to make one continuous band. Sew the panels together, starting ⅜ in (1 cm) in from the edge each time (see *Helpful hints*). When the band has been sewn, fold the front panel in half, matching up the seams. Mark the center fold with tailor's chalk. Repeat on the back panel.

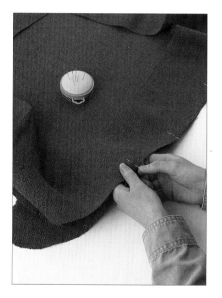

5 Pin the right side of the band to the right side of the top cushion panel, lining up the corners and centers and pinning to the corresponding mark. Pin in between as required. Sew a seam fully around. Repeat on the bottom panel, but do not sew across the back panel. Sew the sewn seams with a zigzag stitch (see *Helpful hints*).

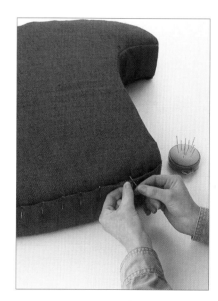

6 Turn the fabric right side out through the open seam. Cover the foam with the stuffing and insert it into the cover, fitting it neatly into the corners. Pin the open seam together, maintaining the ⅜ in (1 cm) seam allowance. Follow the weave or any pattern where possible.

7 Using a curved needle, slipstitch (see *Helpful hints*, p.216) along the pinned seam. The curved needle will allow the stitch to be made into and out of the fabric in one move where there is no access to the back of the fabric. On heavier fabrics, you may need a thimble.

HELPFUL HINTS

● Mark the centers and corners of the template and fabric, making sure that the centers line up with any pattern on the fabric. If the fabric has a pattern, line the center of the front panel on the same pattern as the center of the top cushion.

● When making the band for the side panels, start each seam ⅜ in (1 cm) in from the edge. This makes it easier to sew on the top panel at the corners.

● Sewing a zigzag stitch around all the seams prevents the fabric from fraying.

COVERING A DROP-IN SEAT

A new drop-in seat covering can transform an old dining chair, and it makes an excellent first project for practicing your upholstery skills.

Re-covering a drop-in seat does not require a lot of fabric, so it is easy to change seat covers as part of general redecoration. If the chair is moved between rooms, you can even make a second frame to fit your chairs so that you can have drop-in seats to match the decor in both the kitchen and the dining room.

Calculate the amount of fabric required by measuring the width of the seat plus the drop on each side and 1 in (2.5 cm) on each side for turning in. Repeat for the depth of the seat. The base of the seat is covered with platform cloth to give a neat finish that conceals the webbing and stuffing of the seat. Foam comes in different densities—choose a firm one for drop-in seats. When securing the webbing to the frame, it is a good idea to hammer three tacks in a row with a small gap between each one; then, when the webbing is folded back to make a neat finish, hammer two more tacks into the gaps between the first ones.

1 Drop-in seats will usually pop out easily (if not, give the seat a sharp tap on the base). Remove the fabric. If the webbing is worn out, remove everything from the seat frame—cover, stuffing, and webbing. Work out how many lengths of webbing will be needed on the frame, allowing for a small gap between each length.

2 Mark on the frame the center of each piece of webbing. Secure the end of the roll of webbing to the frame on one of the marks with tacks. At the opposite side of the frame, wrap the webbing around a block of wood to give some tension and secure this end. Cut the webbing, leaving excess to fold over.

3 Secure all the webbing lengths in one direction across the frame, then secure lengths the other way, weaving them in and out of the first lengths. Fold over the excess webbing at the ends of the lengths and secure each with two tacks, hammering them in between the three tacks under the fold. This gives a neat and secure finish.

4 Using the frame as a template, cut a piece of foam. Place the foam over the webbing. Cut a piece of stuffing large enough to go over and down the sides of the foam, but without covering the frame.

5 Cut the new covering fabric to fit over the foam, down the side of the foam and frame, and tuck 1 in (2.5 cm) under the frame at the front and back and widest point of the width. Draw a line 1 in (2.5 cm) in on the bottom back of the frame. Staple the fabric in place along the line, working from the center out.

6 Pull the fabric at the center front and staple it. Work out from the center, maintaining the same tension from back to front while pulling slightly sideways, stapling each side of the center in turn until 1 in (2.5 cm) from the corner. Secure the sides in the same way, keeping the weave or pattern straight from front to back.

7 At the corners, pull the fabric toward the center and secure with a staple sideways to the corner. Fold and staple the excess fabric as flat as possible. The number of folds will vary according to the thickness of the fabric. Once the fabric is secure, cut off any excess at the corners without cutting too close to the staples.

8 Cut some black platform cloth the size of the frame. Fold in the edges of the cloth and staple it to the underside of the frame. The staples do not need to be as close together as on the top, because there is no tension on the platform cloth—its purpose is solely to provide a neat finish.

COVERING AN UPRIGHT CHAIR

YOU WILL NEED

Tape measure
Paper
Tailor's chalk
Fabric scissors
Pins
Sewing machine
Iron

MATERIALS

Fabric
Thread

SEE ALSO

Using sewing materials,
pp.214–215

You can transform a new or old desk chair or dining-room chair with a loose cover. Making this cover is straightforward—there are no arms or cushions to worry about. A loose cover is extremely practical, because it can be easily slipped off for washing or cleaning.

This loose cover is made from four panels—back and seat back, seat, skirt, and two panels in the skirt. The back and seat back of the chair is one panel of fabric, folded over the top of the chair back. The amount of fabric necessary is calculated by measuring all the dimensions of the chair and drawing a cutting plan (see p.243). The fabric for the pleats at the front corners of the skirt are included, but not the skirt panels (see step 5).

1 Measure the height and width of the back and seat back, the depth and width of the seat, and the height and length of the skirt; include 12 in (32 cm) for each of the two pleats. Make a cutting plan, with ⅜-in (1-cm) seam allowances. If the skirt cannot be cut from one width of the fabric, allow extra for joining the pieces. Cut out the panels.

2 Place the panel for the back and seat back on the chair, wrong side out, and pin at the sides. Allow a seam allowance where the seat back will join the seat panel, and a hem allowance where the back panel touches the floor. Fold down each top corner (see inset) and mark a line across the top. This will give a boxed corner when sewn.

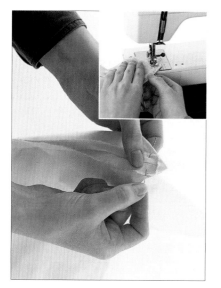

3 Remove the back panel from the chair, sew the side seams that have been pinned, and press them open. Fold the top corner so that the center of the fold and the side seam are in line. Pin in place along the sewing line, making sure that the seam is pinned open. Turn over and sew along the sewing line marked in step 2.

4 Mark the center of the fabric for the skirt. Measuring from the center, mark where the corner will be. To make a corner pleat, measure and mark four equal distances of 1½ in (4 cm). Fold at each mark so that the two outside marks meet on the right side of the fabric. Pin the pleat. Repeat for the second front corner.

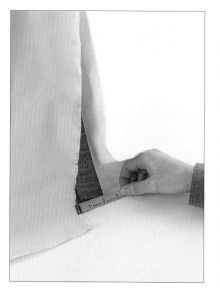

5 Pin the skirt to the seat panel; sew together, allowing for seams at the ends. Place the cover on the chair. Measure for a panel to be inserted on each side where the skirt meets the back panel. If the chair legs are at an angle, these two panels will need to be wider at floor level. Cut out the panels, pin to the skirt, right sides together, and sew.

6 Put the back and seat sections of the cover onto the chair, wrong side out, to make sure that they fit. Where the back and seat join, pin the two sections together. Remove them from the chair and sew them together.

7 Put the cover right side out on the chair. Pin where the skirt meets the back. Pin at floor level where you want to turn up the hem. Remove the cover from the chair, turn up, pin, and sew the hems. Sew ties (see *Helpful Hints*) down the side seams of the skirt and the back panel so they can be held together.

HELPFUL HINTS

● The ties for securing the loose chair cover can be cotton tapes, or you can make ties from the fabric that you are using to make the cover. To make the ties, sew little tubes of the cover fabric, with the fabric inside out, then turn them right side out, turn the ends under, and sew them using the slipstitch (see p.216).

● You can use hooks and eyes or hook-and-loop tape to fasten the cover. If using hook-and-loop tape, you will need to allow slightly more fabric for the hems to give an overlap that will cover the tape.

MAKING A LOOSE COUCH COVER

YOU WILL NEED

Pencil
Graph paper
Tape measure
Fabric scissors
Pins
Tailor's chalk
Sewing machine

MATERIALS

Fabric
Thread
Hook-and-loop tape

SEE ALSO

Using sewing materials,
pp.214–215

A loose cover can give a whole new lease on life to a comfortable but well-worn couch.

To calculate the length of fabric required, you'll need to draw the dimensions of each fabric panel to scale on paper to make a cutting plan (see opposite). The fabric panels for the cover are fitted on the couch and pinned with the wrong sides facing out before marking on the sewing lines. Use the seams on the existing couch cover as a guide to where the sewing lines on the loose cover will need to be marked.

MAKING A LOOSE COVER

1 Cut out all the pieces of fabric roughly. Make a mark on the wrong side of each piece if the weave is similar on front and back. Measure the width of the back of the couch with a tape measure. Find the center point and mark it with a pin at the top of the couch.

2 Take the panel of fabric for the back of the couch and measure and mark its center point. Pin the center of the fabric to the center of the back of the couch with the wrong side out. Pin the fabric in place on the back of the couch.

continued on page 244

MEASUREMENTS

Measuring for a new cover must be done very accurately. Measure all the dimensions of your couch as shown in the two illustrations below. These measurements form the dimensions of the fabric panels required to make the cover. Add seam allowances of 1½ in (4 cm) to each panel's measurements. The panels can be laid out on a cutting plan (see below). If the fabric has a large pattern, allow extra fabric for matching the design.

1 Height of back panel

2 Width of back panel

3 Height of outside arm panel

4 Width of outside arm panel

5 Height of seat back to where it joins back panel plus a tuck-in (at least the depth of cushion)

6 Width of seat back to where it joins back panel

7 Depth of seat and distance from floor plus tuck-in

8 Width of seat to where it joins outside arm panel

9 Height and top of inside arm panel to where it joins outside arm panel

10 Depth, from back to front, of inside arm panel to where it joins outside arm panel

11 Height of skirt

12 Length of skirt

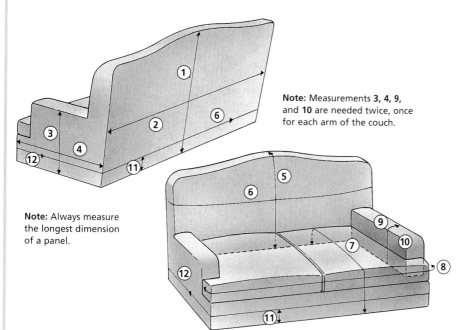

Note: Measurements **3**, **4**, **9**, and **10** are needed twice, once for each arm of the couch.

Note: Always measure the longest dimension of a panel.

CUTTING PLAN

Before cutting the fabric, draw the dimensions of each fabric panel you have measured, including the seam allowances, to scale on graph paper to make a cutting plan. Where a panel is wider than the width of the fabric, you'll need to add equal-size pieces on either side of the panel or make the panel out of two pieces of fabric by joining them along the center line of the couch.

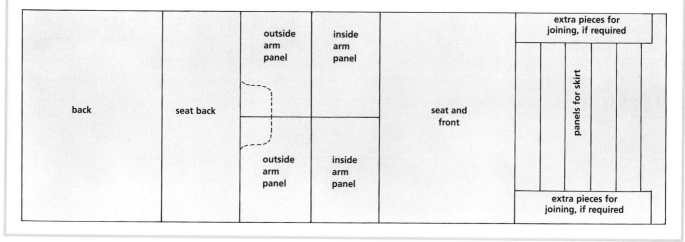

MAKING A LOOSE COUCH COVER

3 Remove the cushions. Mark the center of the seat back panel and line it up with the center of the back panel already pinned to the couch. Pin the two panels together. Holding the excess fabric, mark the sewing line with tailor's chalk on the panels.

4 At any points where the couch is not square, there will be some excess fabric when the panels are pinned together. Cut away this excess fabric, leaving a seam allowance of at least ⅜ in (1 cm).

5 Join the inside and outside arm panels in the same way as the back panels. Mark the sewing line on the seat back and inside arm panels where they meet the seat base. Pin and sew where the seat back and the inside arm panels meet.

6 Replace the cushions and fit the seat panel, wrong side out, allowing for the tuck-in at the back and side of the cushions. Pin and sew the seat panel tucks to the seat back and inside arm where the sewing lines were marked.

7 Sew the outside edges of the front of the seat panel to the side of the outside arm panel. Do this on each side of the couch. Turn the cover right side out and fit it on the couch, making sure that it is tucked in at the back and sides of the cushions so that it stays in place.

8 Fold and pin the hems ½ in (1.25 cm) and 1 in (2.5 cm) on the back panel and outside arm panels so that they cannot be seen from the front of the couch. The hems should be wide enough so that you can sew the Velcro tape onto them.

9 Pin the Velcro tape in place on the right side of the hem on the outside arm panel, and on the inside of the hem on the back panel. Match up and fasten the two sides of Velcro tape while it is pinned in place to guarantee the best fit for the cover.

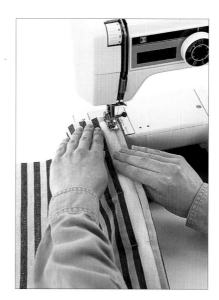

10 Remove the cover and sew the Velcro tape in place. Take care because the needle will now be sewing through the Velcro tape and three layers of fabric.

11 With the cover back on the couch, check the position for the skirt to make sure that it will be in proportion to the overall size of the couch. The skirt should have a seam allowance of ⅜ in (1 cm) at the top and a hem allowance at the bottom.

12 Join enough skirt panels together to add up to three times the distance around the couch plus end hems at each of the back openings. Pin pleats in place as shown, with each 1 in (2.5 cm) pleat using 3 in (7.5 cm) of fabric.

13 On the right side of the cover, mark a line with tailor's chalk or pins ⅜ in (1 cm) down from where the skirt will join. Place the skirt right side down on the cover with the top of the skirt on the marked line (and the rest of the skirt above the line). Sew on the skirt, leaving a ⅜ in (1 cm) allowance.

14 Turn the skirt back down the right way and press the bulky skirt seam. Turn up, pin, and sew the hem on the skirt. When the cover is complete, turn it inside out. Using the sewing machine, zigzag along all the seams to keep them from fraying and to give a neat finish.

GLOSSARY

A

ADOBE A type of sun-dried (not kiln-baked) brick traditionally used for house-building in Mexico.

ALKYD PAINT A solvent-base paint that dries with a hard, shiny finish. It is suitable for painting interior and exterior wood and metal. This type of paint needs a longer drying time and is harder to clean off paint equipment.

B

BALUSTER A post (one of a set) used to support a handrail along an open staircase.

BALUSTRADE The complete barrier installed along open staircases and landings. It consists of the balusters, newels, and handrail.

BASEBOARD A wood molding used horizontally along the walls at the junction where they meet the floor.

BROCADE A heavy silk fabric with a raised pattern that is often highlighted with gold or silver thread.

BUCKRAM Thick, stiffened jute material used for lining fabrics.

BUTT To fit together two pieces of material side by side or edge to edge.

C

CALICO A white or unbleached cotton fabric.

CASING The molding that frames a door or window opening.

CHAIR RAIL A decorative molding, also called a dado rail, installed on walls about waist height, originally to prevent furniture from marring the walls.

CHINTZ A printed cotton fabric, usually glazed.

CORNICE A decorative molding secured at the junction between the walls and ceiling, often used to hide cracks.

COVING A prefabricated concave molding, often used as a cornice.

CRAQUELURE The fine network of cracks, or crazing, that can occur over time in the surface of paints or varnishes.

CURTAIN DROP The length of a curtain from the hanging system to the bottom edge.

D

DHURRIE An Indian flat-weave rug, often with a geometric pattern.

DISTEMPER A primitive, opaque paint made from whiting or chalk dissolved in water and bound with animal glue.

DOWEL A cylindrical, wooden length of wood; it is available in various sizes.

E

EGGSHELL PAINT A paint that dries with a matte finish and is used for interiors.

F

FANLIGHT A window above a door, usually semi-circular in shape, and with glazing bars radiating out like a fan.

FINIAL A carved or molded ornament, often found on the ends of a curtain pole.

FRETWORK Pierced geometrical ornament of intersecting straight, repeated, vertical, and horizontal lines.

FURRING STRIP A thin length of wood; a number of them are mounted in parallel lines across a wall or ceiling, forming a framework to which paneling can be attached.

G

GRAIN The direction of the fibers in a piece of wood.

GROUT A water-resistant paste used for filling joints between tiles to seal the surface.

H

HALF ROUND A type of molding that has a half round profile. It is often used for shelf edging and as decoration.

HARDWOOD Wood that comes from broad-leaf—usually deciduous—trees such as ash, beech, or oak. This type of wood is typically hard; however, balsa is classified as a hardwood but is a soft, lightweight material.

HEADING TAPE A ready-made strip that is sewn to the top of a curtain and attached to the hanging system. It is used to gather the curtain.

K

KELIM A woven woollen rug with a geometric design from the Middle East or Central Asia.

KEY To roughen a surface, often by sanding, to provide a better grip for a material such as paint or adhesive.

L

LATEX PAINT Used on interior walls and ceilings, a water-base paint with a matte or sheen finish. It dries quickly and is easy to clean off paint and equipment.

LIMEWASH A traditional paint consisting of water, slaked lime, and pigment used to paint plaster and stone walls.

LINING PAPER Plain paper used on walls under paint or wallpaper.

LINTEL A supporting beam across the top of an opening such as a doorway, a window, or a hearth.

M

MASKING TAPE An adhesive tape used for masking areas when painting.

MASTIC A nonsetting compound that seals a

joint between two surfaces such as a tiled wall and a worktop, bath, or shower tray.

MATTE FINISH Or matt, a nonreflective finish on a material such as paint or quarry tiles.

MDF Medium density fiberboard, a manufactured board made of compressed fine wood fibers.

METAL LEAF Very thin sheets of metal used for gilding woodwork and other surfaces.

MITER A joint between two beveled pieces that forms an angle, often 45 degrees.

MOLDING A narrow, often decorative, strip of wood or other material. It is available in a variety of profiles. Baseboards and chair and picture rails are types of molding.

N

NEWEL POST Part of the balustrade, the wider post at both the top and bottom of a staircase for supporting the handrail.

P

PATINA A surface sheen resulting from years of handling, polish, and dirt.

PATTERN REPEAT The distance of a motif before it begins to be duplicated, or repeated.

PELMET A decorative wood unit used to hide the top edge of curtains or a structure such as the track of a sliding door.

PILE The fabric raised from a backing, often used to classify a carpet.

PVA GLUE Polyvinyl acetate, a white, odorless glue that dries clear. It can be mixed with paint to seal the surface of objects.

PRIMER A liquid substance used to seal a material, such as plaster, wallboard, wood, or metal, before applying an undercoat.

R

RABBET A step-shaped recess in the edge of a workpiece.

RAKU Molded Japanese earthenware, first produced in the 15th century.

S

SATIN FINISH Also referred to as a semigloss finish, the amount of reflectiveness of a painted or other surface, midway between matte and gloss finishes.

SIZE A thin gelatinous solution used to seal a surface prior to hanging wallpaper.

SOFTWOOD Wood from coniferous trees, including cedar and pine. Although typically soft in nature, there are some hard types such as yew.

STAIN A liquid that changes the color of wood but does not protect it. It comes in water-base, oil-base, and solvent-base versions.

STUCCO A fine cement or plaster applied to walls and moldings.

T

TEMPLATE Paper, metal, cardboard, or other sheet material formed in a specific shape or pattern to be used as a guide for transferring the shape to your work.

TERRA COTTA A hard, unglazed earthenware which has been made from a brownish red clay of the same name. Terra cotta can also refer to the color typical of terra cotta earthenware, which can vary from reddish brown to brownish orange.

TERRAZZO A polished finish for floors and walls consisting of marble or stone chips set in mortar.

TIEBACK A length of ribbon or cord or a metal bracket used to hold curtains clear of a window or bedhead.

TOILE DE JOUY A cotton fabric printed with figurative scenes in a single color.

TONGUE AND GROOVE A joint between two pieces of material, such as paneling or floorboards, in which one piece has a projecting edge (tongue) that fits into a slot (groove) on the edge of the other piece.

TOP COAT The last coat of a finish applied to a surface. There may be several coats underneath it.

TRISODIUM PHOSPHATE A strong powder detergent, also known as TSP, for cleaning painted and other types of surfaces.

TROMPE L'OEIL A style of painting or decoration where a picture is created that is a convincing illusion of reality.

U

UMBER A natural earth pigment with a greenish-brown color that is used in painting. Umber can be heated to form a dark-brown version, known as burnt umber.

UNDERCOAT One or more layers of a paint or varnish to cover a primer or hide another color before applying a top coat.

V

VALANCE A short curtain used to hide a curtain pole or secured around the lower edge of a bed to conceal the base and the space below.

VARNISH A liquid applied to wood materials, it hardens to form a protective surface. It may be clear or colored.

VENEER A thin decorative layer of wood; it is applied to a less attractive, and less expensive, base material to make it more attractive.

VERDIGRIS A bluish-green pigment obtained by scraping off the patina from copper that has been exposed to vinegar fumes.

W

WET AND DRY ABRASIVE PAPER A paper with silicon-carbide granules attached to it for smoothing surfaces. It may be used wet.

USEFUL ADDRESSES

The publisher and authors are not responsible for the products sold by these companies; it is not our intention to promote any of these purveyors.

ASSOCIATIONS

THE AMERICAN LIGHTING ASSOCIATION (ALA)
P.O. Box 420288
Dallas, TX 75432–0288
toll free: (800) 274–4484
website: www. americanlightingassoc.com
An association of lighting manufacturers and distributors, it provides the public with quality residential lighting.

AMERICAN SOCIETY OF INTERIOR DESIGNERS (ASID)
608 Massachusetts Ave. N.E.,
Washington, DC 20002–6006
toll free: (800) 775–3480
e-mail: asid@asid.org
website: www. asid.org
A society that promotes professionalism in interior design services and designs for the workplace and home. It provides a referral service to help find the right interior designer. To find an ASID designer on the Internet use the following address: www.interiors.org.

NATIONAL KITCHEN AND BATH ASSOCIATION (NKBA)
687 Willow Grove St.
Hackettstown, NJ 07840
tele: (908) 852–0033
website: www. nkba.org
The NKBA gives advice and planning guidelines for remodeling kitchens and bathrooms; it offers a list of approved kitchen and bathroom design forms.

CABINETS

ARISTOKRAFT
One Aristokraft Sq.
Jasper, IN 47546
tele: (812) 482–2527
tele: (812) 634–2838
website: www.aristokraft.com
Manufacturers of kitchen, bath, and home cabinetry, offering a variety of different styles from oak to cherry.

PRIMEWOOD
2217 N. Ninth St.
Wahpeton, ND 58075
toll free: (800) 642–8780
tele: (701) 642–2727
fax: (701) 642–2431
Manufacturers of wooden and laminate countertops, and wooden cabinets.

COUNTERTOPS

AVONITE, INC.
1945 Highway 304
Belen, NM 87002
toll free: (800) 428–6648
fax: (805) 864–7790
website: www.avonite.com
Produces solid surface, or synthetic stone, in a range of diverse colors and patterns.

NEVAMAR LAMINATE
8339 Telegraph Rd.
Odentom, MD 21113
tele: (410) 551–5000
fax: (410) 551–0357
website: www.nevamar.com
Supplier of decorative surfaces, including laminates, decorative acrylics, and engineered veneer.

NOCERA ART TILE
HCI Box 1374
Milanville, PA 18443
tele: (570) 729–7946
fax: (570) 729–7317
website: www.art-tile.com
Makers of hand-fashioned tiles; can provide custom-made work.

RYNONE MFG. CORP.
P.O. Box 128
N. Thomas Ave.
Sayre, PA 18840
tele: (717) 888–5272
fax: (717) 888–1175
Manufacturers of laminate countertops.

CLOSETS

CLOSET MAID
650 SW 27th Ave.
P.O. Box 4400
Ocala, FL 34478–4400
toll free: (800) 874–0008
fax: (352) 867–8583
website: www.closetmaid.com
Offers wire storage products suitable for any home.

POLIFORM
150 East 58 St.
New York, NY 10155
tele: (212) 421–1220
tele: (212) 421–1290
website: www.poliformusa.com
Italian manufacturer of closet systems, bedrooms, libraries, dining rooms, and kitchens.

FLOORING

CHICKASAW
Hardwood Floor Products of Memphis
Hardwood Flooring
1551 Thomas Street
Memphis, TN 38107
tele: (901) 526-7306
Offers wood planks, strips, and parquets.

DOMCO TARKETT INC.
4103 Parkway Dr.
Florence, AL 35630
toll free: (800) 465–4030
website: www.domco.com
Produces resilient sheet and tile, laminates, and hardwoods.

HISTORIC FLOORS OF OSHKOSH
911 E. Main St.
Winneconne, WI 54986
tele: (920) 582–9977
e-mail: info@historicfloors.com
Produces decorative hardwood standard and custom inlays, including borders, medallions, and parquet flooring. Offers many designs, wood species, and sizes for use in new or existing floors.

MANNINGTON RESILIENT FLOORS
P.O. Box 30
Salem, NJ 08079
toll free: (800) 356-6787
Provides resilient sheet flooring.

RENAISSANCE OLD WORLD DOOR CO.
743 Sanborn Pl.
Salinas, CA 93901–4532
tele: (831) 759–0558
fax: (831) 759-2635
website: www.carving.com
Manufacturer of hand-planed aged flooring.

HARDWARE

GARRETT WADE COMPANY, INC.
161 Avenue of the Americas
New York, NY 10013
toll free (800) 221-2942
Brass furniture hardware. Small fee for catalog.

IMPORTED EUROPEAN HARDWARE
A Division of Woodworker's Emporium
5461 S. Arville
Las Vegas, NV 89118
tele: (702) 871-0722
Furniture, cabinet, and door hardware. Minimum order required. Small fee for catalog.

WOODWORKER'S HARDWARE
P.O. Box 180
Sauk Rapids, MR 56379
toll free (800) 383–0130
Furniture and cabinet hardware and moldings. Minimum order required.

METALWORKING

COUNTRY ACCENTS
P. O. Box 437
Montoursville, PA 17754
(570) 478-4127
Offers decorative tin panels, prefinished and in kits. Small fee for catalog.

PAINTS AND FINISHES

BENJAMIN MOORE & CO.
51 Chestnut Ridge Rd.
Montvale, NJ 07645
tele: (201) 573–9600
fax: (201) 573–6673
e-mail: benjaminmoore@att.net.
website: www.benjaminmoore.com
Manufacturers of premium paint and architectural coatings.

DEAN & BARRY CO.
970 Woodland Ave.
Columbus, OH 43219
toll free: (800) 325–2829
tele: (614) 258-3131
fax: (614) 258–3530
e-mail: dbpaint@deanandbarrypaint.com
website: www.deanandbarrypaint.com
Carries a full range of paint and coating products.

PRATT & LAMBERT PAINTS
toll free: (800) 289–7728
fax: (216) 566–1655
website: www.prattandlambert.co
Makes acrylic paints with splendid color.

GENERAL FINISHES
P.O. Box 510567
New Berlin, WI 53151
toll free: (800) 783–6050
Natural wood finishes.

TILES

DESIGNS IN TILE
P.O. Box 358
Mt. Shasta, CA 96067
tele: (530) 926–2629
fax: (530) 926–6467
e-mail: info@designsintile.com
website: www.designsintile.com
Specialists in custom-made, historic, Victorian, and late 19th-century tiles.

LAUFEN U.S.A. CERAMIC TILES
6531 N. Laufen Dr.
Tulsa, Okla 74117–1802
tele: (918) 428–0608
fax: (918) 428–0695
e-mail: hdonovan@ laufen.com
website: www.laufen.com
Provides ceramic tiles for wall, floors, and countertops, as well as natural stone tiles and slabs.

MEREDITH COLLECTION
PO Box 8854
Canton, OH 44711
tele: (330) 484–1657
fax: (330) 484–9380
e-mail: info@meredithcollection.com
website: www.meredithtile.com
Makes tiles with hand-carved molds and 19th-century presses.

TERRA-GREEN CERAMICS
1650 Progress Dr.
Richmond, IN 47374
tele: (765) 935–4760
fax: (765) 935–3971
website: www.terragreenceramics.com
Produces ceramic tiles for walls, flooring, and countertops.

WALLCOVERINGS

YORK WALLCOVERINGS, BORDERS & FABRICS
750 Linden Ave.
York, PA 17404
tele: (717) 846–4456
fax: (717) 843–8167
e-mail: intl@yorkwall.com
website: www.yorkwall.com
Manufacturers of wallpapers, borders, and fabrics.

WOODWORKING

BRISTOL VALLEY HARDWOODS
4054 Rt. 64
Canadaigua, NY 14424
toll free: (800) 724–0132
Domestic and exotic hardwood lumber, turning blocks, and flooring planks. Small fee for catalog.

CERTAINLY WOOD
13000 Rt. 78
East Aurora, NY 14052-9515
tele: (716) 655-0206
Veneers. Minimum order required.

GARRETT WADE COMPANY, INC.
161 Avenue of the Americas
New York, NY 10013
toll free: (800) 221–2942
Supplier of hand tools, power tools and accessories, inlays, and finishes. Small fee for catalog.

VINTAGE WOOD WORKS
P.O. Box R
Highway 34 South
Quinlan, TX 75474
tele: (903) 356-2158
Turnings and architectural details. Small fee for catalog.

INDEX

Page numbers in *italics* refer to captions and boxes

ACKNOWLEDGMENTS

Photographic credits:

The publisher would like to thank the following for their kind permission to reproduce their pictures in this book.
t=top, b=bottom, c=center, l=left, r=right
Front Jacket: IPC Syndications; 2 Tim Street-Porter; 4-5 Peter Cook/ View; 6bl Ed Reeve/ Living etc/ IPC Syndication;6br Chris Gascoigne/ View; 7bl Richard Glover; 7br Crowson Fabrics; 8–9 IPC Syndications: 10tr and bl Elizabeth Whiting & Associates; 11t Tim Beddow/ The Interior Archive; 11bl Elizabeth Whiting & Associates; 12t Henry Wilson/ The Interior Archive; 12b Elizabeth Whiting & Associates; 13t Camera Press; 13b Gary Hamish/ Arcaid; 14t Simon Upton/ The Interior Archive; 14b Elizabeth Whiting & Associates; 15t Camera Press; 15b Tim Beddow/ The Interior Archive; 16t Lucinda Symons/ Robert Harding Picture Library; 16b Edina van der Wyck/ The Interior Archive; 16-17 Colin Poole; 17t Henry Wilson/ The Interior Archive; 17b Camera Press; 18t Elizabeth Whiting & Associates; 18c IPC Syndications; 18b Andrew Wood/ The Interior Archive; 19t Colin Poole; 19b Chris Gascoigne / View; 20t Henry Wilson/ The Interior Archive; 20b Tim Beddow/ The Interior Archive; 21t Colin Poole; 21b Peter Cook/ View; 22l Tim Clinch; 22r John Miller/ Robert Harding Picture Library; 22–23 Paul Ryan/ International Interiors; 23t Axel Springer/ Camera Press; 23b John Miller/ Robert Harding Picture Library; 24l Camera Press; 2425 Simon Upton/ The Interior Archive; 25r Nedra Westwater/ Robert Harding Picture Library; 25l Henry Wilson/ The Interior Archive; 26t Simon Upton/ The Interior Archive; 26b Clive Corless; 27t Colin Poole; 27b Tim Clinch; 28l Tim Beddow/ The Interior Archive; 28-29 Camera Press; 29tr Colin Poole; 29b Camera Press; 30t Wayne Vincent/ The Interior Archive; 30b Simon Upton/ The Interior Archive; 31t Denis Gilbert/ View; 31bl Tim Beddow/ The Interior Archive; 31cr Camera Press; 32-33 Chris Gascoigne/ View; 37br Paul Ryan/ International Interiors; 38c & bc IPC Syndications; 42bl Camera Press; 43bl Abode; 43br Abode; 44bl Camera Press; 45bl Camera Press; 45br Abode; 46bl Camera Press;47bl Camera Press; 47br Tim Street-Porter/ Abode; 48bl Houses and Interiors; 49bl Abode; 49br Abode; 50tl Paul Ryan/ International Interiors; 50b Elizabeth Whiting & Associates; 51cl Camera Press; 51tr Robert Harding Picture Library; 51bc Amtico Image Library; 51crb Fired Earth; 52r Camera Press; 52bl Robert Harris; 53tl Elizabeth Whiting & Associates; 53bl Paul Ryan/ International Interiors; 53cr & crb Anna French; 54cl Camera Press; 54tr Houses and Interiors; 54br Journal Fur Die Frau; 55cl Elizabeth Whiting & Associates; 55bl Elizabeth Whiting & Associates; 55cr Fired Earth; 55br Camera Press; 56cl Elizabeth Whiting & Associates; 56bc Andrew Wood/ The Interior Archive; 56-57 Camera Press; 57tc Elizabeth Whiting & Associates; 57tr Camera Press; 57bc Peter Cook/ View; 58tr Houses and Interiors; 58–59 Circus Architects 1999; 59tr Camera Press; 59bc Camera Press; 60tl GE Magazines Ltd/ Robert Harding Syndication; 60–61b Camera Press; 60–61t Peter Cook/ View; 61b Chris Gascoigne/ View; 62t Simon Brown/ The Interior Archive; 62b Camera Press; 63t Elizabeth Whiting & Associates; 63b Peter Cook/ View; 64bl The Interior Archive; 64–65 The Interior Archive; 65tr Simon Upton/ The Interior Archive; 66tl Elizabeth Whiting & Associates; 66bl Elizabeth Whiting & Associates; 66–67 Camera Press; 67tr Henry Wilson/ The Interior Archive; 67br Elizabeth Whiting & Associates; 68cl IPC Syndications; 68c Robert Harding Picture Library; 68br Mosaic Workshop; 69tl Elizabeth Whiting & Associates; 69bc Elizabeth Whiting & Associates; 70tr Camera Press; 70bl Elizabeth Whiting & Associates; 71tr, bl, cr Paul Ryan/ International Interiors; 72-73 Richard Glover; 76 Paul Ryan/ International Interiors; 77tr Elizabeth Whiting & Associates; 77cr Elizabeth Whiting & Associates; 78c Tim Street-Porter; 78–79 Robert Harding Picture Library; 79tr Richard Glover; 79cr Paul Ryan/ International Interiors; 80l Camera Press; 80tr Camera Press; 81tr Camargue PLC; 81b Paul Ryan/ International Interiors; 82b Elizabeth Whiting & Associates; 82-83 IPC Syndications; 83c Camera Press; 83b Elizabeth Whiting & Associates; 84c Elizabeth Whiting & Associates; 84li, iii, iv, v Andrew Sydenham; 84lii Cucina Direct; 84lvi HOUSE; 84lvii, viii, ix, x Royal Doulton Plc; 85bl Colin Poole; 85tl Elizabeth Whiting & Associates; 85tr Elizabeth Whiting & Associates; 86 Tim Street-Porter; 87tr Elizabeth Whiting & Associates; 87cl Elizabeth Whiting & Associates; 87br Camera Press; 88c Tim Beddow/ The Interior Archive; 88b Camera Press; 88l Artisan Curtain Rails except (g) Clayton Munroe Ltd; 89tl Tim Street-Porter; 89br Peter Cook/ View;90bl Camera Press; 90-91 Camera Press; 91bl Elizabeth Whiting & Associates; 91tr Simon Upton/ The Interior Archive; 92 Camera Press; 93tl Paul Ryan/ International Interiors; 93tr Paul Ryan/ International Interiors; 93cb Elizabeth Whiting & Associates; 93br Elizabeth Whiting & Associates; 94l a, c, f, g, Christopher Wray Lighting; b HOUSE; d,e, Andrew Sydenham; 94r Elizabeth Whiting & Associates; 95tl Elizabeth Whiting & Associates; 95tr IPC Syndications; 95b Camera Press; 96t IPC Syndications; 96bl Camera Press; 96br Elizabeth Whiting & Associates; 97t IPC Syndications; 97b IPC Syndications; 98bl Paul Ryan/ International Interiors; 98-99t Camera Press; 98-99b Elizabeth Whiting & Associates; 99tr Elizabeth Whiting & Associates; 99cr Henry Wilson/ The Interior Archive; 100 Camera Press; 101tl Paul Ryan/ International Interiors; 101tr IPC Syndications; 102l a, b Sottini; c-g West One Bathrooms; 102c Elizabeth Whiting & Associates; 102br Tim Street-Porter; 103tl Tim Street-Porter; 103bc Richard Glover; 103cr GE Magazines Ltd/ Robert Harding Syndication; 104tr Camera Press; 104b Camera Press; 105t Colin Poole; 105cr Camera Press; 106l a-d, f, h, k, l, n Tim Ridley;106le, g, i, j, m Turnstyle Designs;106bc Elizabeth Whiting & Associates; 107tl Stephen Ward/ The Amtico Co. Ltd; 107bl Elizabeth Whiting & Associates; 107tr Simon Brown/ The Interior Archive; 108 Abode; 108tr Tom Leighton/ Living etc/ IPC Syndication; 109bc Morgan River; 110bc Colin Poole; 111tl Russell Sadur/ Robert Harding Picture Library; 111bc Russell Sadur/ Robert Harding Picture Library; 111tr Elizabeth Whiting & Associates; 112l all Cotswold Company; 112c Elizabeth Whiting & Associates; 112br Steel-Lok; 113t Elizabeth Whiting & Associates; 113br Elizabeth Whiting & Associates.

All photographs in chapter 4 were taken by Tim Ridley, except 114–115 Crowson Fabrics; 130tc Lyn le Grice/ International Interiors;132tc The Stencil Store; 138tc 148tc Crowson Fabrics; 150tc Crowson Fabrics; 152tc Graham & Brown Wallpaper; 154tc Fired Earth; 155br Colin Poole;156tc Steve Sparrow/ Houses and Interiors; 158tc Arcaid; 160tc Mosaic Workshop; 162tc Mosaic Workshop; 166tc Nick Pope/ Rosalind Burdett; 168tc Elizabeth Whiting & Associates; 166-185 Tim Ridley; 170tc Steel- Lok; 172tc IPC Syndications; 177tl Tim Ridley; 176tc Key Communications; 183br Elizabeth Whiting & Associates; 192tc Amtico Image Library; 194tc International Stransky Thompson PR; 196tc Victoria Carpets Ltd; 198tc Victoria Carpets Ltd; 199br Elizabeth Whiting & Associates; 200tc Amorim UK Ltd; 202tc Fired Earth; 204tc Stonell Ltd; 206tc Kahrs Ash Stockholm; 208tc Paul Ryan/ International Interiors; 190-211 Tim Ridley;210tc Ducal of Somerset; 209br Paul Ryan/ International Interiors; 211br Colin Poole; 218t Next Plc; 220tr Fired Earth; 221br Elizabeth Whiting & Associates; 222t Harlequin Fabrics & Wallcoverings Ltd; 225tr Crowson Fabrics; 228t Eclectics; 230tr Eclectics; 231br Tim Beddow/ The Interior Archive; 232t Next Plc; 233br Camera Press; 235tr Andrew Martin/ Halpern Associates; 236t Kährs Birch, Glasgow; 240tc Paul Ryan/ International Interiors; 242tc Elizabeth Whiting & Associates

Illustrations on pages 34–35, 36–37, 41, 74–75, 77, 101 and 109 by Patrick Mulrey; 122–123, 147, 191, 217 and 243 by Chris Forsey; 40, 42–43, 44–45, 46–47 and 48–49 by Hytex. Mood board on page 39 designed by Nicholas Springman.

Publisher's acknowledgments:
We gratefully acknowledge the assistance of the following companies and individuals:
Miles Hardware 57 Glenthorne Ave, Yeovil, Somerset, BA21 4PN (01935 421281); **B.J. White** 4 Vale Road, Pen Mill Trading Estate, Yeovil, Somerset BA21 5HL (01935 382400); **Magnet Limited** Royd Ings Ave, Keighley, West Yorkshire BD21 4BY (0800 9171696); **Hewden Plant Hire** Station Road, Bruton, Somerset BA10 0EH (01749 812267); **Travis Perkins Trading Company Limited** Mill Street, Wincanton, Somerset BA9 9AP (01963 33881); **The Stencil Store** 20–21 Heronsgate Road, Chorleywood, Herts WD3 5BN (01923 285577/88); **The English Stamp Company** Worth Matravers; Dorset BH19 3JP (01929 439117); **Amorim Ltd** Amorim House, Star Road, Partridge Green, Horsham, West Sussex RH13 8RA (01403 710970); **Dovecote Gallery** 16 High Street, Bruton, Somerset BA10 0AA; **B J Haigh-Lumby** 1 High Street, Castle Cary, Somerset BA7 7AN (01963 351259); **Bruton Classic Furniture Co. Limited** Unit 1 Riverside, Station Road Industrial Estate, Bruton, Somerset BA10 0EH (01749 813266); **MGR Exports** Station Road, Bruton, Somerset BA10 0EH (01749 812460); **Polyvine Limited** Vine House, Rockhampton, Berkeley GL13 9DT (01454 261276); **The Fabric Barn** Clock House, Yeovil, Somerset BA22 7NB (01935 851025); **Aristocast Originals** 14A Ongreave House; Dore House, Industrial Estate, Sheffield, S13 9NP (0114 2690900); **Tile Wise Limited** 12–14 Enterprise Mews, Sea King Road, Lynx Trading Estate, Yeovil, Somerset BA20 2NZ (01935 412220); **The Amtico Company Limited** (0800 667766); **Dulux Decorator Centres** Altrincham, Cheshire, WA14 5PG (0161 9683000); **Kahrs (UK) Limited**; Unit 2 West, 68 Bognor Road, Chichester, West Sussex PO19 2NS (01243 778747); **Claire Minter-Kemp** Tom Dickins Fine Art, The Pump Room, Lower Mill Street, Ludlow, Shropshire (01584 879000); Mr S. Weatherhead, London House, 12 High Street, Wincanton, Somerset.

Thanks also go to:
Ann Argent, Tom and Hennie Buckley, Susan Clothier, Bill Dove, John Fives, Steve Green, George Hearn, David House, Richard Lane, June Parham, Michael and Sue Read, Ann Squires.

A special thank you to the following people for all their help in putting the book together: Peter Adams, Antonia Cunningham, Susie Behar, Alison Bolus, Dorothy Frame, Thomas Keenes, Theresa Lane, Maggie McCormick, Katrina Moore, Tim Ridley.

For Marshall Editions
Project Editor Jane Chapman; **Editor** Felicity Jackson; **Design** John Round & Martin Lovelock; **Managing Editor** Antonia Cunningham; **Managing Art Editor** Philip Gilderdale; **Editorial Director** Ellen Dupont; **Art Director** Dave Goodman; **Picture Researcher** Andrea Sadler; **Production Controller** Anna Pauletti; **Editorial Coordinator** Ros Highstead